PLEASANTON

DISCOVERING YOUR
JEWISH ANCESTORS

DISCOVERING YOUR JEWISH ANCESTORS

Barbara Krasner-Khait

Heritage Quest
North Salt Lake
2001

Heritage Quest®, P.O. Box 540670, North Salt Lake, Utah 84054-0670

Library of Congress Catalog Card Number: 2001089335
ISBN (softbound): 0-944931-85-5
ISBN (hardbound): 0-944931-86-3

To my mother, Lillian Perlman Krasner,

to the memory of my late father, Milton Krasner,

and to all the ancestors who preceded me.

You will not be forgotten.

Contents

Foreword

Genealogy is a world unto itself. Many people are becoming apprehensive by the many obstacles they find along the way. Barbara's book is a long awaited addition in the realm of Jewish Genealogy. To many of us, researching our Jewish family's history has been a long, hard road. Often, we felt like trail-blazers.

For those starting their search, this book will give you a step-by-step blueprint to help and guide you. It will enable you to go from the known facts to the soon-to-be-known facts. In your endeavors, you will always be faced with the question, "What do I do next?" In this book you will find many avenues to explore and places to go to answer that question, from finding the European connection to which library or archive has material you need. Included for the first time is an extensive reference to Internet sites that contain material of use to Jewish genealogists.

It is interesting to note that Barbara takes the reader from the basics into those areas that are beyond. This book will be a friend and helpmate for the researcher from early stumbling efforts even into producing a reference book for the future.

On a personal note, as I read through the book, I found that I had made notes for further follow-through for a number of topics. I have used the Internet notes to e-mail archives and found that they responded within 48 hours. A woman with the same surname as my mother's maiden name responded to my e-mail. We have exchanged some information and are now looking for a connection. You never know where information will come from to help you with your search.

Michael Brenner
Past President,
Jewish Genealogical Society, Inc. (New York)
October 2000

Acknowledgments

No researcher can possibly be an expert in every facet of Jewish genealogy. Through the power of JewishGen, the online resource for Jewish genealogy, I reached out to scores of fellow genealogists who have first-hand knowledge of sources and methodologies in areas I do not. I am grateful to those around the world who responded to my queries and requests and provided great depth to the book: Joel Andrews, Judy Baston, Warren Blatt, Shirley Flaum, Phyllis Goldberg, Hilary Henkin, Robert Heyman, Dan Kazez, Roseanne Leeson, Roni Seibel Liebowitz, Jeff Malka, Marcia Meyers, Julius Mueller, Judie Ostroff-Goldstein, Harriet Rudnit, Randy Schoenfeld, Reba Solomon, Harry Stein, Michael Tobias, and Richard Wanderman, Jr.

I acknowledge David B. Levy of the Enoch Pratt Library Humanities Department in Maryland; Yeshaya Metal, Public Service Librarian at YIVO Institute for Jewish Research; and David Kershen of Yeshurun Library in Jerusalem for their help in identifying useful sources for rabbinic genealogy research. I thank the staff of the Center for Jewish History, including Dana Ledger of the Leo Baeck Institute, Rachel Keegan of the American Jewish Historical Society, Rachel Fisher of the Genealogy Institute, and the reading room assistance of YIVO. Also, my thanks go to Dorothy Smith of the American Jewish Archives, Frank Mecklenburg of the Leo Baeck Institute, Marek Web of YIVO, Lyn Slome of the American Jewish Historical Society, Lawrence Tapper of the National Archives of Canada, and Laura O'Hara of the Western Jewish History Center for their advice on donating materials.

This book would not be possible without the help of many subject matter experts—many of whom are pillars in organized Jewish genealogy—who reviewed the manuscript and those who suggested and provided illustrations, including Werner Frank, Judy Salomon of the North Jersey Jewish Genealogical Society, Neil Rosenstein, Gary Mokotoff of Avotaynu, Miriam Weiner of Routes to Roots, Carol Skydell and Susan King of JewishGen, Stan Diamond of the Montreal Jewish Genealogical Society and Jewish Records Indexing – Poland project, Dean Bell of the Spertus Institute, Doris Teichler Zallen of Virginia Tech, Robert Burk of Albert Einstein College of Medicine at Yeshiva University, Robert Desnick of the Mt. Sinai Center for Jewish Genetic Diseases, and Michael Brenner, former president of the world's largest Jewish Genealogical Society—the New York group.

I owe Leland Meitzler at Heritage Quest a debt of gratitude for his enthusiasm for the project.

Finally, I thank Cindy Levine Zey for her tireless efforts in reading all my manuscripts and providing insightful feedback, Barbara Pollack Chamberlain for her constant encouragement, Theodora Nessas for her expert copy editing, my mother, Lillian Perlman Krasner, and sisters, Eileen Leahy, Evelyn Shore, and Andrea Kozel, for their patience and understanding that I had deadlines to meet, and my son, Matthew, for nagging me to complete the manuscript.

About This Book

This book focuses on the Jewish experience, its sources, meaning, and value. It is not a basic primer on genealogy—other readily available books provide that. It is not a book that will show you how to fill out pedigree charts and family group sheets or teach you basic research skills to access vital and government records. It will not tell you how to use the computer or how to organize your research.

Throughout this book you'll find specially designated boxes to help you trace your family tree:

QUICK TIP—Tidbit to help make your research a little easier and more productive

QUICK HIT—Internet addresses for quick database searches and results

DEFINITION—Explanation of some genealogy jargon, Yiddish, or Hebrew words

SEE ALSO—Cross-reference to other parts of the book with more information

ON THE BOOKSHELF—Critical reference works for the Jewish genealogist

FOR MORE INFORMATION—List of resources that can give you more in-depth information

CASE STUDY—Research methodology and networking in action

There is also an extensive bibliography at the end of the book, arranged by chapter.

PART I

Building the Foundation

The Krasner family in Newark, ca. 1912.
Seated in the center are Mordechai Krasner and his wife, Breina Dvorkin Krasner.

I One Family

"I know my grandmother came from Austria, but she spoke Polish."

"I think my grandparents came from a place called Gubernia."

"I know nothing about my family's history. Mama and Papa never spoke about it, and now they're gone."

"All the records were lost in the Holocaust."

These are common laments at seminars on Jewish genealogy, in online discussion groups, and in everyday conversations.

Many American Jews believe they can't trace their heritage because they don't know about availability of records, surname adoption and changes, migration patterns, and more.

These beliefs are misconceptions. I held them once myself. But, now I know that Grandma was from Galicia, a part of the Austro-Hungarian Empire that had formerly been a part of Poland before the three partitions of Poland in the late eighteenth century. I learned that *Gubernia* is the Russian word for "province." And, I discovered it is possible to access and extract important family information from archival records and specific Jewish sources and that records do exist in at least four places in Israel, Germany, and the United States that can shed light on family members who may have perished during the Holocaust.

Unlike other ethnic groups like Irish, German, or Italian, we have faced millennia of migrations and forced movement, with no single place of origin in recent history. Our pursuit of our ancestors is unique. Standard genealogical guides may frustrate us, because they typically refer to parish records, land records, wills, probates—most of which have no bearing on our searches.

I began researching my family's history in earnest at a time when I found my job boring and unchallenging, and I had just given birth to my son. I spent each weekend and many evenings calling up aunts and uncles and my parents' cousins to learn some basic facts—names of brothers, sisters, children, parents, and grandparents. Every call brought in new information. I discovered my great-grandparents, Mordechai and Breina Krasner, came to America. I learned exactly how my father's cousins, Adele and Merle, fit into the picture and received photos of their parents. I learned of Merle's sister, Dotsie, a first cousin to my father but totally unknown to me for thirty years. She had a picture of Breina, for whom I was named. Adele, who had lived with Breina for many years, was an incredible source of information, not only of names and connections, but of slice-of-life stories. She spoke of Saturday night get-togethers and mentioned family upon family who visited, adding more branches to the family tree.

I joined the North Jersey Jewish Genealogical Society and found kindred spirits. I also found a deeper connection to my father. He drove me to the meetings. (Here I was—fully grown, married with children—and he didn't want I should drive alone in the dark.) It meant a lot to me that he stayed with me during the meetings. I would inundate him with questions on the way back to his house about his parents. He had so much knowledge, but I had to drag it out of him. One night I told him that I found out his mother came from Tarnopol, Galicia—a huge discovery I thought, since I had only known she came from Austria. He very matter-of-factly corrected me and said no, she came from Kozlów, near Tarnopol and that he had her citizenship papers. On another occasion, he drove me to the Newark Public Library so I could research early twentieth century New Jersey census records. (He didn't want I should drive alone in downtown Newark.) After a day of poring over census microfilms, I was delighted to tell him his paternal grandparents had lived at 65 Boston Street in Newark.

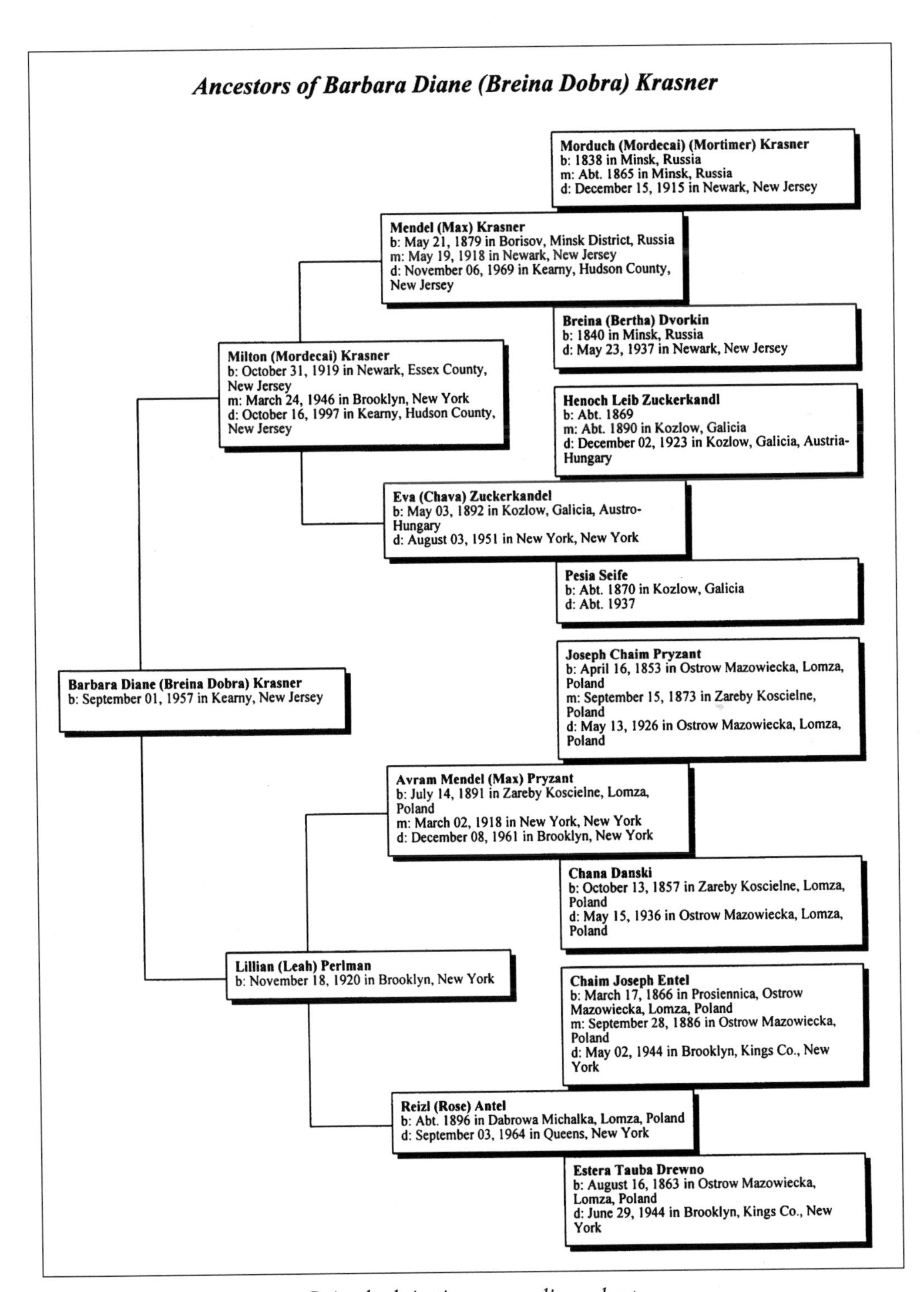
Ancestors of Barbara Diane (Breina Dobra) Krasner
Morduch (Mordecai) (Mortimer) Krasner
b: 1838 in Minsk, Russia
m: Abt. 1865 in Minsk, Russia
d: December 15, 1915 in Newark, New Jersey
Mendel (Max) Krasner
b: May 21, 1879 in Borisov, Minsk District, Russia
m: May 19, 1918 in Newark, New Jersey
d: November 06, 1969 in Kearny, Hudson County, New Jersey
Breina (Bertha) Dvorkin
b: 1840 in Minsk, Russia
d: May 23, 1937 in Newark, New Jersey
Milton (Mordecai) Krasner
b: October 31, 1919 in Newark, Essex County, New Jersey
m: March 24, 1946 in Brooklyn, New York
d: October 16, 1997 in Kearny, Hudson County, New Jersey
Henoch Leib Zuckerkandl
b: Abt. 1869
m: Abt. 1890 in Kozlow, Galicia
d: December 02, 1923 in Kozlow, Galicia, Austria-Hungary
Eva (Chava) Zuckerkandel
b: May 03, 1892 in Kozlow, Galicia, Austro-Hungary
d: August 03, 1951 in New York, New York
Pesia Seife
b: Abt. 1870 in Kozlow, Galicia
d: Abt. 1937
Joseph Chaim Pryzant
b: April 16, 1853 in Ostrow Mazowiecka, Lomza, Poland
m: September 15, 1873 in Zareby Koscielne, Poland
d: May 13, 1926 in Ostrow Mazowiecka, Lomza, Poland
Barbara Diane (Breina Dobra) Krasner
b: September 01, 1957 in Kearny, New Jersey
Avram Mendel (Max) Pryzant
b: July 14, 1891 in Zareby Koscielne, Lomza, Poland
m: March 02, 1918 in New York, New York
d: December 08, 1961 in Brooklyn, New York
Chana Danski
b: October 13, 1857 in Zareby Koscielne, Lomza, Poland
d: May 15, 1936 in Ostrow Mazowiecka, Lomza, Poland
Lillian (Leah) Perlman
b: November 18, 1920 in Brooklyn, New York
Chaim Joseph Entel
b: March 17, 1866 in Prosiennica, Ostrow Mazowiecka, Lomza, Poland
m: September 28, 1886 in Ostrow Mazowiecka, Poland
d: May 02, 1944 in Brooklyn, Kings Co., New York
Reizl (Rose) Antel
b: Abt. 1896 in Dabrowa Michalka, Lomza, Poland
d: September 03, 1964 in Queens, New York
Estera Tauba Drewno
b: August 16, 1863 in Ostrow Mazowiecka, Lomza, Poland
d: June 29, 1944 in Brooklyn, Kings Co., New York

Going back in time: my pedigree chart

(I didn't know they came to America, let alone to Newark—a stone's throw away from my hometown of Kearny.) He replied, "Oh, yeah, I knew that."

But, perhaps the most moving moments were when three of us—my father, my son, and I—representing three generations, visited the graves of my grandparents and great-grandparents. Our family was united, seeking to connect to a greater, broader heritage.

In 1992 at the annual Summer Seminar on Jewish Genealogy in New York City, Gary Mokotoff, then president of the Association of Jewish Genealogical Societies, announced an ambitious new project: the creation of a People Finder, a database to house all the family trees of Jewish genealogists. The project evolved into a massive web-based database called the Family Tree of the Jewish People (more about this in Chapter 13). When you consider the ramifications of such a project, you can understand just how wondrous it is—a way to bring Jews back together, to form a single family tree. Pursuing Jewish genealogy helps you, as an individual researcher, find connections to your past—relatives with whom you've perhaps lost touch and histories of family members no longer with us. As a collective effort, we are piecing together that single tree, inexplicably bound together by common DNA. We are indeed one family.

Since ancient times, patriarchal and tribal genealogy has played a major role in Judaism. Just look at who begat whom in the Bible. The Scriptures, the Talmud, the Mishnah—all speak of genealogy. Look at the tomes written on rabbinic dynasties. Genealogy had a practical purpose—to determine who qualified for temple service based on descent. Later, well after the destruction of the Second Temple, genealogy helped Kohanim and Levites remember their descent even though they were no longer in service. From the twelfth century on in Europe, genealogy took on a social meaning as well, focusing on *yichus* or lineage, particularly important for arranging marriages. Genealogy helps us understand where we fit in. We continue to seek connection to something broader and higher. Finding our ancestors helps us do that.

A Personal Journey

For me, genealogy has been about the thrill of discovery and connection to the past. During my first year of researching my family's history, every bit of data I collected made me say, "Wow, I didn't know that." I learned about the woman for whom I was named. I learned what my grandfather's first job was when he came to America. I learned what my ancestors lives were about, what they feared, what made them happy, what they ate, how they celebrated. I saw the expression of my relatives when I brought them together for the first time after they married and went their separate ways—spanning a chasm of 50 years. I researched names of family who perished in the Holocaust and filled out Pages of Testimony for them so they won't be forgotten. I gathered pictures and stories. And, I was finally able to put my degree in foreign languages to use as I read handwritten records in German, Polish, and Russian. I learned how to read Yiddish and recalled my Hebrew of years long past.

At first my family thought I was nuts for wanting to explore my heritage. After all, they argued, wasn't genealogy just about dead people? But, when I attended my very first summer seminar on Jewish genealogy in 1991, I met people just like me. Genealogy was not a strange hobby or interest—we were hundreds of very smart people from all walks of life with a common goal. The camaraderie was instant. It was the beginning of the connection and my personal journey.

It can do the same for you. The search begins with the genealogist's crash course in Jewish history.

2 A Crash Course in Jewish History

Studying Jewish history in Hebrew school was my passion. I even volunteered to read additional texts for extra credit. I can't say I remember much now. In fact, it wasn't until I attended my first Summer Seminar on Jewish Genealogy more than twenty years later in 1991 that I realized how little I knew. Fellow genealogists tossed about terms I didn't understand. What was a Jew in the Diaspora, and how did I get to be one?

Many Jewish genealogists learn Jewish history as they trace their family trees. Genealogy personalizes historical events and makes them individually relevant.

Having historical context in your back pocket can help put your family's events in perspective. Unlike some other groups, our history spans millennia and the world. The historical background presented here is not intended to be a full history—massive volumes have already been written about that. The idea here is to paint a landscape of events and migrations useful to the genealogist.

The Beginning of the Diaspora

The *Diaspora*, Greek for "scattering," began at the end of the First Temple Period (586 B.C.E.). Some Jews who lived in the Israelite kingdoms were forcibly removed to Mesopotamia while others fled to neighboring countries. Jewish merchants were also anxious to seek opportunities abroad, and as long as the temple

DEFINITION
In Jewish culture, B.C.E. means "Before Common Era" (instead of "Before Christ") and C.E. means "Common Era" (instead of "Anno Domini" or "In the year of our Lord or in the Christian Era").

was standing, Jews were connected to the land of Israel. The destruction of the temple weakened the connection. Jews went to Egypt, North Africa, and Babylonia.

The southern kingdom of Judah—the kingdom of David—was the nursery of the Jewish people and our religion.

The Babylonians deported the population from its homeland in 597-586 B.C.E. The unwilling emigrants retained their linguistic identity. About 40,000 people returned after the fall of Babylon in 538 B.C.E. They made plans to restore the temple in Jerusalem and completed the Second Temple in 515 B.C.E.

When they went into exile, they belonged to the tribes comprising the former kingdom. In exile, they consolidated around Judah. The entire population became known as men of Judah (Yehuda) or Jews, governed by the Law of Moses, the Torah.

In 175 B.C.E. Antiochus IV, a member of the Greek Seleucid dynasty and ruler of Judea, proclaimed an order to combine all nationalities into one people and accept the Greek religion. In 165 B.C.E., religious freedom was granted. The Jewish state then rivaled the size it achieved during the days of David and Solomon.

Palestine became a Roman province in 6 C.E., and Judaism became well entrenched. Though not great in number, there was important Jewish settlement in Egypt.

The Diaspora picked up pace after the Greek conquest, affecting one million Jews in Palestine and approximately 100,000 in Alexandria. Jerusalem fell in 70 C.E., and the Second Temple was destroyed. The High Priesthood came to an end. The synagogue, which, unlike a temple, housed a Torah, and as a house of study, became more than ever the center of local life. It existed in the Diaspora long before it did in Palestine. By the first century C.E., the synagogue was an accepted part—and even a hallmark—of the Jewish community. It was built to face Jerusalem. Just before 100 C.E., schools formed around a spiritual leader, called a rabbi. After the unsuccessful Bar Kokhba revolt in 135 C.E., the center of national life moved north to Galilee. From that time on, Jews were a minority in the land of their fathers.

A new center of Judaism, made up of Jews who had not returned after the Babylonian exile, was flourishing in Mesopotamia when the Roman Empire fell and Palestine fell under Byzantine rule. The community consisted of hundreds of thousands, maybe millions. It became the seat of an intellectual life being permanently influenced by the Jewish people. This center also came to an end by the fifth century C.E.

Jews in Early Europe

Jews were numerous in Greece, particularly as merchants, even before the fall of Jerusalem. There is evidence of Jews in more than 40 places in Italy as well as in France, the Crimea, and elsewhere. In Spain and in Germany, their numbers at the beginning of the fourth century justified special mention in the period's legislation.

Charlemagne, crowned Holy Roman Emperor in 800 C.E., recognized the important contribution the Jews could make to his empire's economy. He encouraged immigration, and many Jewish communities were established during the Carolingian period, including those in northeast France and Germany. England was the last major western European country to receive Jewish settlement.

Intolerance began to appear in the period following the Crusades. By the beginning of the thirteenth century, the tranquility of a former generation began to pass, and Jews throughout Europe, particularly in Spain, were threatened. Edward I of England issued a decree ordering all Jews—about 16,000 people—to leave the country in 1290. In France in 1306, Jews were arrested and condemned to exile. Charles VI signed an order in 1394 that banished the Jews. Some went to the south, including Italy. The majority went across the Pyrenees and Rhine. Individual towns within Germany expelled the Jews. Even the Black Death in 1348 was blamed on the Jews, which precipitated the massacre and extermination of 60 communities. German Jews, too, then moved eastward.

Within the Community

The role of the Jew changed as economies changed. In Imperial Rome, Jews comprised the backbone merchant class. In French and German legal documents, the terms "Jew" and "merchant" were used interchangeably.

However, the debut of the merchant guilds forced Jews into other occupations. They became financiers and money-lenders, though the mosaic code (Law of Moses) actually forbid it. They became physicians, dyers, silk-rearers, goldsmiths, and jewelers. In some of the larger cities, Jews established their own craft guilds and guild halls.

Jews began to gather in a street or quarter of each town, their solidarity reinforced by Gentile aversion. Homes grouped around the synagogue. Nearby were the school, bathhouse, workrooms, and hospital. Jewish females reigned in the home and frequently engaged in business. Betrothals among children became commonplace, just in case the parents died before the children were of age. At a period when the vast majority of Europeans were illiterate, schools of rabbinic learning sprang up.

The Golden Age in Spain

By the time Spain embraced Catholicism in the sixteenth century, Jews had long been established in communities there. Historians believe that Jews settled in Spain as early as the time of the Second Temple. Toward the end of the Visigothic Kingdom of Spain (466-711 C.E.), Jews of the Iberian peninsula faced severe persecution, causing dispersion and movement underground. In the Moorish invasion of the eighth century, Islamic tribes from northern Africa drove the Visigoths out. However, the Jews were allowed to stay, and Jewish life resumed. Other Jews from Africa were encouraged to come, to fill needs for artisans and other occupations.

LADINO

Known today as Judeo-Spanish, the traditional language of Sephardim—a form of medieval Spanish called Ladino—was primarily the language of literature. Jews continued to use this language even after leaving Spain in 1492. While its linguistic traditions held, its lexicon expanded to include words borrowed from languages native to the geographic areas where the Sephardim settled, such as Turkish, Greek, Italian, French, Hebrew, and even Serbo-Croatian. About 160,000 people speak the language today, primarily among older populations in Israel, New York, Seattle, and Miami.

During most of the 500 years of Moorish occupation (711-1212 C.E.), the Sephardim led a prosperous life. The tenth and eleventh centuries, for instance, became known as "The Golden Age." Spanish Jews became philosophers, physicians, diplomats, and scientists, and other well-respected professionals.

From the eleventh century until 1492, a growing Christian population challenged Moorish rule. Christian rule accommodated Jewish life until the ascendancy of Ferdinand and Isabella, the Castilian royal couple. In 1492 they vanquished the last Moorish stronghold. In the same year, they ruled that the Jews and the Moors must convert to Catholicism or leave Spain. About 100,000 Jews converted to Catholicism to remain in Spain and to save their wealth. These *Marranos*, or *Conversos*, did not get what they hoped for—30,000 of them died on the stake, burned as heretics during the Inquisition. Many of the remaining Conversos fled to other European nations, especially to the Netherlands. The center of Judaic gravity moved to the east, ending the western European chapter of Jewish history that began in the Middle Ages.

Flourishing in Africa and in the Turkish Empire

When expelled from Spain, many Jews found homes in northern Africa, where they became artisans, traders, financial agents, diplomats, physicians, and interpreters. A greater number went to the Turkish Empire, where trade was left to the Jews, Armenians, and Greeks. In a short time, Constantinople's Jewish community grew to be the largest in Europe, with about 30,000 people. But, this was rivaled and surpassed by Salonika in Greece, which remained a leading Jewish city for 400 years. The golden age of Jews in Turkey came to an end in 1574 with the death of Selim II.

Migration caused by expulsion from Spain created new Jewish centers in Palestine, most notably in Safed in the Upper Galilee. A century after the Inquisition, Palestine had at least eighteen Talmudic colleges and 21 synagogues.

THE GENEALOGIST'S TIMELINE OF JEWISH HISTORY

Before Common Era

1007	David rules over the tribe of Judah
586	Destruction of the First Temple and Babylonian Exile
539	Persians conquer Babylonia
516	Second Temple
332	Hellenistic Conquest
301	First Jews in Alexandria
200	Antiochus III becomes ruler of Judea
167	Antiochus IV's edict forces Jews to abandon practice of Judaism
63	Roman Conquest

Common Era

6	Judea becomes a Roman province
70	Destruction of the Second Temple
135	Bar Kokhba Revolt, eventually unsuccessful, to free Jerusalem from Roman rule; shortly thereafter, Roman Emperor Hadrian changes the name of Judea to Palestine
1264	Statute of Kalisz
1290	Expulsion from England
1306	Expulsion from France
1388	Privileges for Jews in Lithuania
1492	Expulsion of Jews from Spain
1495	Expulsion of Jews from Lithuania
1496	Expulsion of Jews from Portugal
1505	Return of Jews to Lithuania
1569	Poland's unification with Lithuania
1648	Chmielnicki uprising; Ukraine area, formerly Polish, is now Russian
1654	First Jewish immigrants arrive in New Amsterdam
1772-1795	The Partitioning of Poland
1791	Catherine the Great of Russia defines the Pale of Settlement
1791	Emancipation in France
1796	Emancipation in the Netherlands
1812	Emancipation in Prussia
1867	Emancipation in Austria
1881	Assassination of Russian Czar Alexander III brings on pogroms and spurs mass immigration

The Beginning of the Ghetto

Jewish life in northern and central Italy continued. In a large part of the country, Jews were restricted to money-lending, operating from Rome and surrounding areas. The population grew in the fourteenth century due to migrations from northern European persecutions and expulsions. Italy was perhaps the only European country in which persecution was never elevated into a system. Waves of refugees came from France, Germany, and Spain.

In 1555, Pope Paul IV ordered that Jews were to be strictly segregated in their own quarter, subsequently known as the Ghetto, imitating the original Jewish quarter at Venice, founded in 1516 near the old *geto* or "foundry." The ghetto system spread throughout Italy. From the mid-sixteenth century, Italy set the example of intolerance and the ghetto became a fixture of European Jewish life.

The Formation of Eastern European Jewry

Jews have lived in Eastern Europe since the early days of Christianity, primarily in communities around the Black Sea. By the early thirteenth century, there were Jewish communities in Poland. Immigrants from German towns came in the middle of the century. In 1264, Duke Boleslaw V the Pious issued the Statute of Kalisz, the oldest known set of privileges granted to Jews. In

YIDDISH: THE *MAMALOSHN*

The *mamaloshn* or "mother tongue" of Ashkenazic Jews is Yiddish, a mostly oral language based on medieval German dialects with Hebrew, Aramaic, Romance, and Slavic components. Early Yiddish began prior to 1250 in the valleys of the Moselle, Rhine, Main and Upper Danube rivers. As Jews migrated to the east and south, they took the language with them. Eastern European dialects began to develop in the period 1500-1750. This took on a written form after 1750 and a literary culture developed.

The western European dialect declined as a result of the Haskalah movement (Jewish Enlightenment) in the late eighteenth century to move toward national languages while it increased in eastern Europe.

1304, references were made to a Jewish quarter in Kraków. In 1388, Jews came to Lithuania because it granted economic privileges, only to be expelled in 1495. At that time, Poland had between 10,000-30,000 Jews.

Poland became a second haven for Jews where they could live according to their traditional values. Moving east to Poland presented them with economic opportunity versus persecution they faced in Germany and elsewhere. In 1264, King Boleslaw the Pious issued a model charter of protection and liberties for the Jews, giving them freedom of opportunity and security. Jews created new commercial avenues and provided necessary financing.

In 1354, Casimir the Great authorized Jews to rent estates. In 1388, Jews of Lithuania, Kraków, Lublin, and Posen received a similar charter. Poland certainly appeared as a land of promise. In 1500, the country was home to about 50,000 Jews and by 1650, half a million Jews. The majority of today's world Jewry descended from Poland and Slavic lands.

A large number of Jews in Poland were merchants, while others were craftsmen, manufacturers, and administrators of great estates. They hosted great fairs. A degree of self-government evolved, and the Jews elected the Chief Rabbi and judges answerable to the King. The *Kahal* or "community" was to contribute to taxes. And, each town had a yeshiva. Every father's ambition was to have a learned son or son-in-law.

The Partitioning of Poland

Between the years 1772 and 1795, this Polish homeland was divided and annexed by three surrounding countries—Austria-Hungary, Prussia, and Russia. This became known as the partitioning of Poland.

The First Partition in 1772 gave 83,000 square kilometers and 2.5 million people to Austrian Emperor Joseph II. It also gave 36,000 square kilometers and 1.5 million people to Frederick "The Great" Hohenzollern of Prussia, and 92,000 square kilometers and 1.3 million people to Russia's Catherine the Great. Prussia and Russia significantly added to their holdings in the Second Partition in 1793. Prussia took another 51,000 square kilometers and 1 million more people, while Russia grabbed 250,000 square

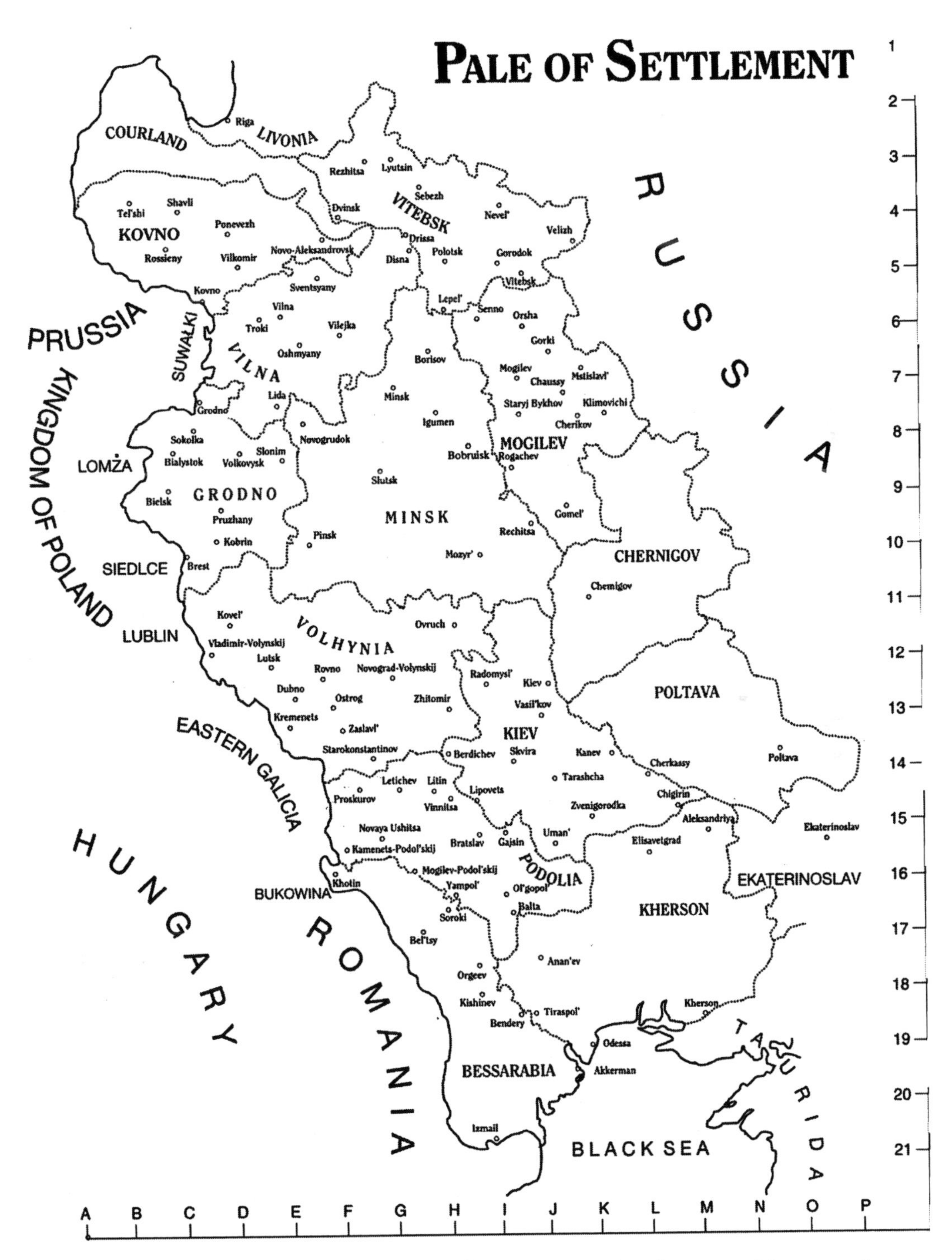

Jews were restricted to live in the Pale of Settlement. Map reprinted courtesy of Avotaynu, Inc.,
A Dictionary of Jewish Surnames from the Russian Empire

kilometers and with this land, another 3 million people. In 1795 with the Third Partition, Austria annexed 47,000 square kilometers and 500,000 people, Prussia another 48,000 square kilometers and a million more people, and Russia 120,000 square kilometers and 1.2 million people. With the Third Partition, the country called "Poland" ceased to exist and was not reconstituted until the end of World War I.

The partitioning is important for two reasons. First, the Jews of Poland were now living in different countries with different rules and regulations concerning Jews. Second, until the partitioning, Russia had no Jewish population to speak of.

The Pale of Settlement

Russia was the least favorably disposed to Jews and now ruled over the majority of them. Jews were confined to the newly acquired lands, now called the Pale of Settlement.

Under the reign of Nicholas I (1825-1855), one legal enactment after another adversely affected the Jewish population. He was more stringent than any Czar who preceded him. For example, one important decree extended conscription into the Russian Army for Jews for the first time—prescribing a 25-year minimum service period. Special taxes were imposed and the borders of the Pale narrowed, further restricting where a Jew could live.

The New Diaspora

With the 1881 assassination of Czar Alexander II, anti-Semitism ran rampant, demonstrated through terrifying pogroms. Anti-semitism, combined with economic opportunity and the desire to avoid conscription, paved the way for the mass migration to America.

3 What's in a Name? Jewish Surnames and Naming Patterns

There's an old story about an Ellis Island official asking a Jewish immigrant his name. The nervous immigrant replied "schon vergessen," Yiddish for "already forgot." And so the official entered his name as "Sean Ferguson," a surprising name for a Jewish immigrant. Even at the time of the mass wave of American immigration from 1880–1920, hereditary surnames among Eastern European Jews were relatively new—maybe a hundred years old or less. In their villages, they were known simply as "Yudel the tinsmith" or "Mendel, son of Mordechai." For millennia, Jews used a patronymic naming tradition.

ON THE BOOKSHELF
Alexander Beider, a mathematician and expert in onomastics, or naming, has produced two definitive books on Jewish surnames in eastern Europe: *Dictionary of Jewish Surnames from the Russian Empire* and *A Dictionary of Jewish Surnames from the Kingdom of Poland* (See Bibliography). These finely detailed dictionaries take the guesswork out of surnames.

DEFINITION
The term "patronymic" comes from the Latin for "father's name," while "matronymic" means "mother's name."

Surname Adoption Legislation

Surname adoption among Ashkenazic Jews took hold in Europe beginning in the late eighteenth century, forcing them to assume names that in a sense defied their patronymic naming tradition. This process occurred at different times throughout central and eastern Europe. Austrian Emperor Joseph II issued the first law of this type in 1787, making Austrian Jews the first Ashkenazic Jews to adopt surnames. The process was sometimes arduous and frequently contentious.

Krapivner (Orsha, Mstislavl', Vitebsk, Chigirin) T: see Krapivin. T: from the village Krapivna (Gajsin d., Vinnitsa d.) {*Kropivner*}.

Krapivnik T: from the village Krapivniki (Vilejka d., Disna d.) {*Krapivnikov*}.

Krapivnikov (Vilna, Ekater. gub.) T: see Krapivnik.

Krapivnitser (Vilna) T: from the village Krapivnitsa (Vilna d.) or Kropivnitsa (Białystok d.).

Krapivskij (Odessa, Chernigov gub.) T: see Kropivskij.

Krapotnitskij (Cherkassy) T: see Karapatnitskij.

Krapovenskij (Gomel') T: see Krapivin.

Kras (Elisavetgrad) F: see Kresil. A: beauty [Ukrainian] {*Krass; Krasyuk (Krysyuk)*}.

Krasavets (Proskurov) N: handsome man [Russian].

Krasavitskij (Gomel', Odessa) T: see Krasovitskij.

Krasel'shchik (Bobrujsk, Slutsk) O: see Krasil'shchik.

Krasel'shchikov (Gorki, Velizh) OS: see Krasil'shchik.

Krasenbaum (Cherkassy) A: see Karshenbojm.

Krasevich (Białystok) FS: see Krojn. AS: see Karas'.

Krashennyj (Uman', Odessa) N: painted [Russian].

Krashevich (Grodno, Zvenigorodka) FS: see Krojn. AS: see Karas'.

Krashinskij (Grodno gub.) T: see Kroshinskij.

Krashner (Kiev) T: see Kroshner. T: see Krasner.

Krashnik (Vitebsk gub.) T: see Krasnik. O: see Kraska.

Krashunskij (Lida) T: see Kroshinskij.

Krasik (Mstislavl', Mogilev, Cherikov) A: see Karas'.

Krasikov (Mstislavl') AS: see Karas'. T: from the village Krasikovo (Sebezh d.).

Krasil'chik (Bendery, Odessa) O: see Krasil'shchik.

Krasil'nik (Vasil'kov) O: see Krasil'shchik.

Krasilov (Novogrudok) FS: see Kresil. T: from the townlet Krasilov (Starokonst. d.) {*Kresilov, Krasilovskij, Krisilovskij*}.

Krasilovskij (Novograd, Zaslavl', Skvira) T: see Krasilov. T: from the village Krasilovka (Tarashcha d.).

Krasil'shchik (Kishinev) O: dyer [Russian] {*Krasel'shchik, Krasel'shchikov, Krasil'chik, Krasil'nik, Krasil'shchikov; Krasun; Krasil'skij*}.

Krasil'shchikov (Vitebsk, Gomel', Chernigov gub.) OS: see Krasil'shchik.

Krasil'skij (Kobrin, Lida) O: see Krasil'shchik(?).

Krasinshtejn (Zhitomir, Odessa) A: see Krasnoshtejn.

Krasinskij (Oshmyany, Brest, Minsk, Velizh, Vitebsk, Cherkassy) T: see Karasinskij. T: see Krasner.

Krasis (Zhitomir) FS: see Krojn.

Kraska (Orgeev) {*Krasko, Kraskin; Krasnik (Krashnik), Krasnikov, Krasnikovich*} O: dye [Russian, Belorussian]. A: flower [Ukrainian, Belorussian].

Kraskij (Troki) T: from the village Kraski (Sventsyany d.) {*Krasko*}.

Kraskin (Vitebsk, Riga, Gorki, Velizh) T: from the village Kraski (Vitebsk d.). O: see Kraska.

Krasko (Vilna, Shavli) O:, A: see Kraska. T: see Kraskij.

Kraslavskij (Taurida) T: see Kreslavskij.

Krasne (Tel'shi) N: see Krasnyj.

Krasnenker (Gajsin) T: from the village Krasnen'koe (Balta d.).

Krasner (Gomel', Borisov, Vilna, Bratslav, Mogilev-Pod., common in Litin) T: from the village Krasnaya (Novogrudok d., Lida d.) or Krasna (Białystok d.) or Krasnoe (townlet in the Yampol' d., village in the Vilejka d.) {*Krashner, Krosner, Krasinskij (Krisinskij, Krysinskij), Krasnov, Krasnovskij, Krasnyanskij*}.

Krasnik (Vilna, Borisov, Senno, Rezhitsa) O: see Kraska. T: from the village Krasnik (Borisov d., Pruzhany d.) {*Krashnik, Krasnikov, Krasnitskij*}.

Krasnikov (Bobrujsk, Taurida) T: see Krasnik. OS: see Kraska.

Krasnikovich (Ponevezh, Novo-Aleks.) OS: see Kraska.

Krasnits (Mozyr') T: from the village Krasnitsa (Chaussy d., Rogachev d., Cherikov d., Bykhov d.) {*Krasnitskij*}.

Krasnitskij (Bykhov, common in Kiev) T: see Krasnits. T: see Krasnik.

Krasnoborodov (Petersburg) NS: from 'krasnoborodyj' [Russian] red bearded.

Krasnobrodskij (Chigirin, Uman', Elisavetgrad) T: from the village Krasnyj Brod (Zvenigorodka d.).

Krasnofarber (Pruzhany) O: krasno-farber [Russian + Yiddish] one who deals with red dye.

Krasnogorskij (Odessa, Petersburg) T: from the village Krasnogorka (Balta d., Yampol' d.).

Krasnogur (Kovel', Kishinev, Odessa) N: krasno-(h)ur [Russian + Southeastern Yiddish] red hair. T: from the village Krasnogurka (Zhitomir d.).

Krasnokut_skij (Cherkassy, Chigirin, Aleksandriya) T: from the village Krasnyj Kut (Uman' d., Aleksandriya d.) {*Krasnokutskij*}.

Krasnokutskij (Cherkassy, Chigirin) T: see Krasnokut_skij.

Krasnolob (Uman', Ol'gopol') N: one having red forehead [Russian].

Krasnoper (Ostrog, Kremenets) A: see Krasnoperka.

Krasnoperka A: roach [Russian] {*Krasnoper, Krasnopiorko, Krasnopyurko*}.

Krasnopiorko A: see Krasnoperka.

Krasnopol' (Rovno, Kremenets, Tiraspol', Kamenets) T: from the village Krasnopol' (Ovruch d., Balta d.) {*Krasnopol'skij, Krasnopoler, Krasnopolin*}.

Krasnopoler (Kremenets) T: see Krasnopol'.

Krasnopolin (Kiev, Poltava gub., Aleksandriya) T: see Krasnopol'. T: from the village Krasnopol'e (Rechitsa d., Klimovichi d., Vitebsk d., Cherikov d.).

Krasnopol'skij (Mogilev, Zvenigorodka, Balta, Bratslav) T: see Krasnopol'.

Krasnopyurko (Pinsk) A: see Krasnoperka.

Krasnoroz (Tarashcha) N: from 'krasnorozhij' [Russian] red-faced. A: from 'krasnoroza' [Russian] red rose.

Krasnosel'skij (Slutsk, Starokonst., Ostrog, Kiev) T: from the village Krasnoe Selo (Bielsk d., Pruzhany d.) or Krasnosel'e (Ostrog d.) or Krasnoselka (Zhitomir d., Chigirin d., Starokonst. d., Zaslavl' d., Ostrog d., Ovruch d.).

Krasnoshanskij (Khotin) T: see Krasnoshenskij.

Krasnoshchek (Mogilev, Kiev) N: see Krasnoshchekij.

Krasnoshchekij (Ekater. gub.) N: having red cheeks [Russian] {*Krasnoshchek, Krasnoshchekin, Krasnoshchekov, Krasnoshchok, Krasnoshchoka*}.

Krasnoshchekin (Vitebsk) N:, NS: see Krasnoshchekij.

Krasnoshchekov (Mogilev, Kiev) N:, NS: see Krasnoshchekij.

Krasnoshchok (Vasil'kov) N: see Krasnoshchekij.

Krasnoshchoka (Ostrog) N: see Krasnoshchekij.

Krasnoshenskij (Khotin) T: from the village Krasnosheny (Orgeev d.) {*Krasnoshanskij; Krasnoshevskij (Krasnyshevskij)*}.

Krasnoshevskij (Kherson) T: see Krasnoshenskij(?).

Krasnoshtejn (Zvenigorodka, Vasil'kov, Vinnitsa, Bratslav, Balta, common in Odessa) A: krasno-shteyn [Russian + Yiddish] red stone {*Krasinshtejn*}.

Krasnostav (Rossieny) T: from Krasnostav (townlet in the Novograd d., village in the Slonim d.) or from the town Krasnystaw (district center in Lublin gub.) {*Krasnostavskij, Krasnostov*}.

Krasnostavskij (Slonim, Zaslavl', Slonim, Bendery) T: see Krasnostav.

Krasnostok (Vilna) T: from the village Krasnostok (Sokółka d.).

Krasnostov (Vilna) T: see Krasnostav.

Krasnov (Zvenigorodka, Uman', Vasil'kov, Cherkassy, Balta, Ol'gopol', common in Odessa) NS: see Krasnyj. T: see Krasner.

Krasnovets (Tiraspol', Orgeev) T: from the village Krasnovtsy (Lida d., Disna d.).

Krasnovskij (Gorki, Zvenigorodka) T: see Krasner.

Krasnyanskij (Białystok, Uman', Bel'tsy, Lipovets, Bratslav) T: see Krasner. T: from the village Krasnyany (Lida d., Sokółka d.).

Krasnyj (common in Pruzhany; Uman', Vasil'kov, Tarashcha,

338

Consulting one of the Beider dictionaries can quickly help you identify the origin of your surname. Reprinted with permission from A Dictionary of Jewish Surnames from the Russian Empire *by Alexander Beider (Teaneck, N.J.: Avotaynu, Inc., 1991).*

Surname Adoption in Galicia

By decree, Jews in the Hapsburg Empire—including the area known as Galicia (Austrian Poland)—had to adopt surnames by 1 January 1788. (This only applied to the former parts of eastern Poland that were ceded to Austria-Hungary; parts of Poland that formed western Galicia were not annexed until the third partition of Poland in 1795.) Jews were prohibited from creating names from places and from the Jewish (Yiddish) language. The law dictated that surname adoption would be carried out by local municipal authorities. Naming expert Beider described the process: a group of officials—one cavalry captain, one lieutenant, one auditor, and two noncommissioned officers—traveled from community to community to enforce surname adoption. Their mission consisted of preventing adoption of common German surnames among Jews—their priority was selection of unusual family names, ensuring each family in the same locality received a different name. This has obvious implications for the genealogist: a married son not living with his parents would have had to select a different family name from his father. If he lived with his parents, he would have had to select the same family name—or not. These priorities were not always enforced. Jews were able to select their own names, subject to approval by the Austrian officials. If they did not choose names on their own, they were assigned.

There was a clear distrust of the process among Jews, since it was interpreted as a means to collect taxes and/or draft into military service. There are stories of officials playing with the names: if bribed appropriately, officials gave the Jewish family a name like Rosenthal ("valley of roses"). If not, the family could receive a nonsensical or derogatory name like Eselkopf ("ass's head"). I am not exactly sure which category my paternal grandmother's maiden name, Zuckerkandel ("rock candy") or her mother's name, Seife ("soap"), falls into. I like to think they had too much integrity to resort to bribery.

Surname Adoption in Russia

Jews were prohibited from living in Russia as late as 1762. But when Russia annexed the eastern Polish territories in 1772, it began to have many Jews in its population. The number significantly increased with annexations in 1793 (Volhynia, Podolia, Kiev, and Minsk) and 1795 (Lithuania, Courland, and Grodno), the region of Bialystok in 1807, Bessarabia in 1812, and the Kingdom of Poland in 1815.

Since Jews did not typically carry hereditary names, the Russian government found it difficult to tax them. In an 1804 edict, Jews were required to have or assume a hereditary family name or sobriquet that had to be used uniformly in all transactions and registers. Another law in 1835 required each Jew of the Russian Empire must keep forever the hereditary or assumed family name without any change. Clearly, this new law indicated that the 1804 edict did not take hold as well as the Russian authorities had wanted or expected.

Surname adoption took place within the Jewish communities themselves. Though no formal description of the process exists today, many genealogists have gathered anecdotal information. At the 1998 Summer Seminar on Jewish Genealogy in Los Angeles, entertainer Theodore Bikel fascinated his audience with the recounting of how his family name came to be. His ancestor had to come up with a name, so he took a passage from a book, developed an acronym by taking the first letter of each word and gave birth to the name, Bikel.

Different communities used different methodologies to create distinctive naming patterns. For instance, surnames ending with *son* or *zon* were frequently found in parts of Vitebsk Gubernia. In Borisov, where my paternal grandfather's family is from, many surnames ended in *kind*, including a large number of matronymics.

Surname Adoption in Poland

After Napoleon's 1815 defeat, the largest portion of Poland was ceded to Russia and became officially known as the Kingdom of Poland. My maternal grandparents, and I'm sure countless others, referred to this area as Russian Poland.

In March 1821, the governor of the Kingdom of Poland decreed that surnames must be assumed and declared to the Polish authorities. This legislation called for the process to be completed within six months. The elders of the Jewish communities supervised the process. Each Jew was to carry a certificate of surname adoption, and if he did not use the name on the certificate, he would be punished. Six months came and went, and many, many Jews still did not have surnames. Although congregational boards replaced community elders as a body for surname enforcement in January 1822, they had even less influence. Substantial resistance protected the tradition-bound patronymic naming. In the years 1824–1825, any Jew who still had not adopted a surname was given one—with no say in the matter.

Given the situation, I was naturally surprised when I came across my maternal grandfather's name, Pryzant, in the early civil records of Ostrów Mazowiecka, Poland, at a time when the appearance of surnames was very rare. This led me to hypothesize that the family was not indigenous to Poland; in fact, family lore has it that the family moved eastward from France with Napoleon.

Attitude Towards Surnames

Surnames did not appear to be something that the Jewish population across eastern Europe used in everyday life. Spellings varied widely. According to Beider, the Jewish attitude towards forced surnames was in fact negative and largely ignored. Most people knew each other and, therefore, used nicknames. One example of this is told by one of the founding fathers of Jewish genealogy, Arthur Kurzweil. In his groundbreaking work, *From Generation to Generation,* he tells the story of his search for his great-grandfather, Julius Kurzweil. In a phone conversation with a man who appeared in a photograph with Julius, Kurzweil was astounded that the man did not recollect Julius—at least not in connection with the surname Kurzweil. It was not until Kurzweil asked if he knew "Yudl the tinsmith" that the man could recall him.

Nothing Is as Consistent as Change

In my maternal grandparents' 1918 New York City marriage record, my grandfather's mother's maiden name was entered as Turnsky. The first time I encountered this family in the Jewish records for the town of Zaręby Koscielne in Russian Poland, the name appeared as Dunsky. As I continued my research in these vital records I came across many variations: Donski, Dansky, Donicki, Doniczki, and even Donszczkow. In 1826 birth records for a pair of twins in the Polish town of Chęciny, I literally saw one of my surnames, Drewno, change from one birth record to Drobner in another.

Carol Skydell of Chilmark, Massachusetts shared the following with me: "When names were changed in the old country, it was usually to avoid conscription or some other unwelcome experience. In many cases we hear the stories of men buying the papers of younger or much older men in order to avoid conscription. In my own family research, we had one member buying the papers of another man, marrying and having three children under the assumed name, and as soon as he set foot in America where he had relatives and felt safe, reverted to his original name."

Categories of Names

Generally speaking, hereditary names fall into four categories: patronymic, occupational, nickname, or place name. Among Jews, however, there are a few others, including matronymic and abbreviated names. Still other names come from animals, birds, fish, and insects. The names reflect their local culture.

QUICK HIT
Russian Empire Surnames
Beider's dictionary can now be searched online at Ancestry.com <www.ancestry.com/search/rectype/inddbs/3173.htm>

In his first naming study, Beider conducted an analysis of selected Russian voter lists from the early twentieth century. He found that surnames based on place were most common (23.5%), followed by occupational (16.5%), artificial (fabricated, 15.9%), and masculine given name (15.1%). There are clear regional distinctions, though. For instance, place names were used by more than a third of the voting age men in cities and towns in Vilna, Vitebsk, Grodno, and Minsk Gubernias and nearly twice that in Kiev

The onomastics expert of Jewish genealogy, Dr. Alexander Beider, addresses the 20th International Conference on Jewish Genealogy, Salt Lake City, UT, July 2000. Courtesy Judy Salomon.

Gubernia! Occupational names occurred more frequently in Volhynia Gubernia and Bessarabia than elsewhere. Nearly a third of the men in Novogrudok, Minsk Gubernia used names based on a masculine given name and nearly 40% in Mogilev Gubernia used names based on a female given name.

Patronymic

The patronymic form was shaped by the particular locality. For instance, the Slavic version would add *–ovich*, *-vich*, or *–ov*, as in Kopelovich, Yankelovich, Rubinov, Davidov or the Polish *–wicz* as in Anschelewicz. Other Slavic suffixes were *–in*, *-sky*, *-uk*, *-chik*, *-chuk*, *-enko*, *-enok*, and *–an*. Germanic and Yiddish versions would add *–son*, *-zon*, or *–sohn*, like Levinson, Jacobson, or Josephson, or *–s* or *–kind* (used especially in Belarus and Lithuania) as in Elkind. The Romanian suffix is *-vici* as in Abramovici.

Surnames the same as a given name—like Marcus, Maier, Hirsch—were most common in Germany.

Occupational

How better to distinguish between two men named Mottel in the town than to say Mottel the tailor and Mottel the baker. The names stuck and became hereditary, passed down from one generation to another. So depending on where your ancestor was from, a tailor might have been known as Schneider, Chait, Portnoy, Kravetz, or Kroiter.

Nickname

Hereditary family names based on nicknames often describe a forebear's appearance (stature, hair, eyes, complexion, size), a characteristic or trait (strong, bold, brave), financial status, habits, or special skills. Some examples describing personal characteristics include: Klein ("small"), Gross ("large"), Lang ("long"), and Weiss ("white").

Place Names

The first time I looked up my maiden name of Krasner in a surname dictionary, I saw that it meant either "beautiful" or "fat."

In my mind, there's a big difference between the two. But it wasn't until I consulted with Beider that I learned:

> **Krasner** (Gomel', Borisov, Vilna, Batslav, Mogilev-Pod., common in Litin) T: from the village of Krasnaya (Novogrudok district, Lida district) or Krasna (Bialystok district) or Krasnoe (townlet in the Yampol' district, village in the Vilejka district.)

Now this made sense to me. My family came from the Borisov district, and Vilejka figured into my family history somehow.

Place names served as surnames in several ways: when someone was associated with or living near or a particular hill, brook, bush, dale, valley, island, bridge, meadow, and road, village and when the person was known as coming from a particular locality. Some examples include: Rosenthal ("rose valley"), Grunthal ("green valley"), Goldberg ("golden mountain"), Berliner ("from Berlin"), Danziger ("from Danzig"), and Krakower ("from Kraków").

Matronymic

My great-grandmother's maiden name of Dvorkin is an example of a surname based on a female given name, in this case, Dvora. Some other examples include: Shifrin (Shifra), Sorkin (Sorkin), Rivkin (Rivka), Malkin (Malka), and Chaikin (Chaike).

Names used as part of this practice included biblical names and names of Hebrew, Romance, Germanic, and Slavic origin. Other suffixes included *–l*, *-ka* or *–ko*, *-ash* or *–ush*, *-ovich*, *-ov*, *-ich*, *-uk*, *-chuk*, *-sky*, *-enko* and others.

Artificial Names

More than half of Poland's Jews adopted artificial names when authorities imposed the naming process. These names had no connection to the family's given names, place, occupation, or physical characteristics. Examples include Goldberg and Silverstein. According to Beider, this practice began in eastern Galicia after the first partioning of Poland in 1772. Words are typically derived from German or Yiddish.

Abbreviated Names

You might think at first that a name like Katz might imply an ancestor resembled a cat or had something to do with cats, yet the name itself is short for *Kohen Zedek* meaning "priest of righteousness." There are several Jewish surnames that fall into this category:

Segal—*Segan Levviyyah*, meaning "assistant to the Levites"

Schatz—*Sheliah Tzibbur*, meaning "minister of the congregation"

Other names represent a father's or other male name:

Bry—Ben Rabbi Israel

Basch—Ben Shimeon

Schach—Sabbatai Cohen

Other Names

Still other names reflect animals, birds, and fish, such as Sperling (sparrow) or Adler (eagle) or house signs, such as Rothschild. Some believe that hereditary names derived from house signs—a practice that developed during the fifteenth and sixteenth centuries in the heart of German Jewry, Frankfurt am Main—laid the groundwork for the artificial compounds names such as Teitelbaum and Hirschhorn, that appeared in the eighteenth and nineteenth centuries to the east.

SEE ALSO

See Chapter 8 for more on rabbinic surnames, Chapter 9 for more on Sephardic surnames, and Chapter 10 for Colonial America Jewish surnames.

QUICK TIP

Wide variations can exist for any given surname, as shown in the Turnsky example. This can certainly make research more challenging. When reviewing vital records and other surname lists, check for any Yiddish or Hebrew entries as they can often be very revealing—and consistent. Pay careful attention to parents' names and their patronymics, where available, so you can keep families together despite surname differences. Remember to keep an open mind.

Personal Names

In Ashkenazic tradition, children are named for the deceased. In Sephardic, children are named for the living. You can use the naming patterns to your advantage to create some hypotheses about whom someone was named for. Figure 1 shows an Ashkenazic example from my mother's family.

Even without knowing about the great-grandmother, you could assume that several children born around the same time to siblings are probably named for a common ancestor who died near the time the first child was born. In this case, you might have come up with two hypotheses: (1) Beila was Chaim Joseph's mother; or (2) Beila was his wife's mother. Research proved the first hypothesis.

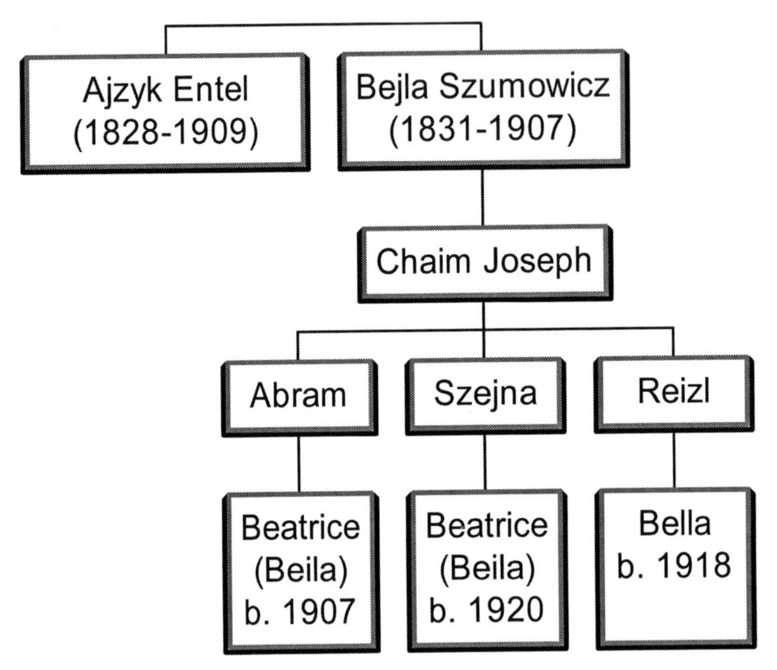

Understanding Ashkenazic tradition to name after the deceased can link you to the past.

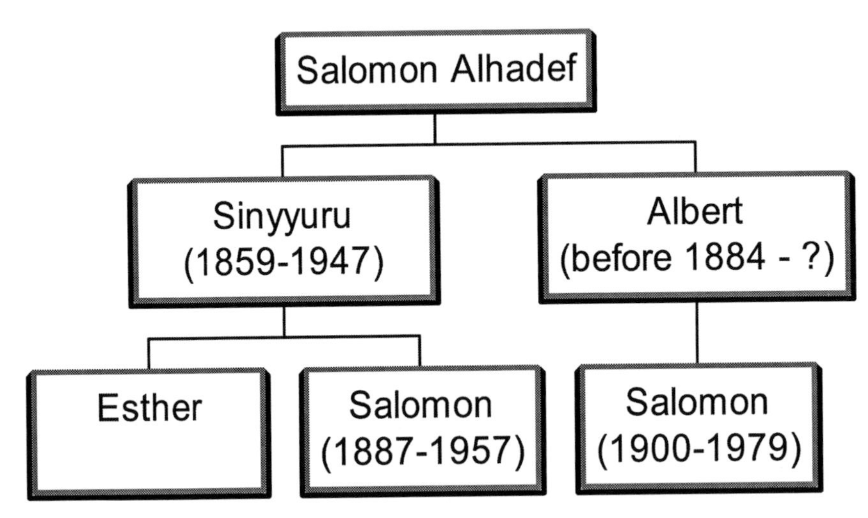

Understanding Sephardic tradition to name after the living can also link you to the past.

In the Sephardic tradition, the practice is to name after the living. Typically, the first-born son is named after the paternal grandfather and the second is named for the maternal grandfather. Similarly, the first-born daughter is named after the paternal grandmother and the second named after the maternal grandmother. The next child receives the name of a paternal uncle or aunt and the one after that, the name of a maternal uncle or aunt. Dan Kazez of Springfield, Ohio provided the following from his Turkish family tree for Figure 2.

Irrespective of the tradition or practice, analyzing given names can provide you with clues to preceding generations. It's always a good idea to ask relatives, "Who were you named for?" The repetition of the same name in two family lines can indicate there is some type of relationship between them. For instance, the name Moshe Aron repeats in my paternal grandfather's family, the Pryzant family. I met a woman at a business-related conference whose surname was Pryzant. We chatted a bit and she mentioned she had a relative named Moshe Aron and that her family came from the same town in Poland as mine. The dates worked out so that her Moshe Aron could have been named for my great-great-grandfather. I haven't found a definitive connection yet, but there may be something there.

ON THE BOOKSHELF

One guide to understanding given names is Rabbi Schmuel Gorr's *Jewish Personal Names: Their Origins, Derivation and Diminutive Forms.*

Known for his work on Jewish surnames, naming expert Dr. Alexander Beider has just written *A Dictionary of Ashkenazic Given Names: Their Structure, Pronunciation, and Migrations.* See the Bibliography for more information.

Amuletic Names

There is always a story about a sick child who is renamed Chaim or Chaia. Why? Because our ancestors believed this would trick the evil eye and bring good luck. Of course, those same names could be given to children to honor the deceased relatives who bore those names.

Tomes have been written about Jewish names and naming practices. I could only hope to give you a broad overview here. For more extensive reading and thorough treatment, you can't miss with Beider's books.

An understanding of your surnames can help you find your immigrant ancestors, the topic of the next four chapters.

PART II

Finding Your Immigrant Ancestors

4 Locating Your Ancestral Town

A year or so ago, a small volume in my local bookstore's Judaica section caught my eye. I don't recall the name of the book, but one image within it sticks in my memory. It showed Europe and America with the Atlantic Ocean between. The immigrants standing in America were dressed in dandy clothes, reaching out to their brethren in Europe as if to say "Come on over!"

Pinpointing your immigrant ancestor's home can be tremendously rewarding. It will also probably take lots of sleuthing to find it.

Where's Gubernia?

"My grandmother said she came from a place called Gubernia."

Yes, Grandma probably came from Gubernia, but which one? You see, *Gubernia* is the Russian word for "province"—it is not a town name. Nor is it from the Yiddish for "born" as I originally thought.

No matter which gubernia Grandma may have said she's from, chances are she was from a much smaller town, or shtetl, within the province. Such was the case with my maternal grandmother, Reizl Entel. I was told she said she was from "Łomża Gubernia" in Poland. Her New York City marriage record said she was from Łomża as well. For days, I agonizingly combed through handwritten Polish in the civil registrations of Jewish

Jewish immigrants in America say, "Come on over!" to their European brethren in this 1907 illustration by the Hebrew Publishing Co. Courtesy Miriam Weiner Archives.

vital records for Łomża, filmed by the Church of Jesus Christ of Latter-day Saints (LDS) and got nothing more than a headache. It was only after finding Grandma's Petition of Naturalization that I learned she came from "Austravah," known as Ostrów Mazowiecka, located in Ůomza Gubernia. Part of the difficulty was fully understanding that Łomża was both a gubernia and a city of sorts. Years later, while examining other records from Ostrów Mazowiecka, I discovered she wasn't from Ostrów Mazowiecka either—she had been born in Dąbrowa Michałka; "Ostrova" was the closest town where other relatives lived and one that offered a synagogue.

If you're like me and you've been led to believe that your family came from Warsaw, Vilna, Minsk or another very large city, chances are your family lived in a small town and used the city or province as a reference point.

How can you find the exact place where your family came from?

Home and Government Sources

The best place to begin your journey back to your ancestral town is with family stories and legends you can gather from relatives. Ask questions to determine the immigrant's original name, name used in America, date of immigration and place of entry, native town and country, and approximate date of birth. Look also for monikers associated with an ancestor. For example, a potential relative told me that her grandfather was called the "Match King of Russia." The town I was researching had two match factories—a possible connection.

It's also a good idea to ask what larger town or city was nearby. By focusing on "reference cities," you won't get caught up in the dizzying maze of constantly changing national borders and multiple towns with the same name.

- Family memorabilia, civil, and government sources can guide you to your ancestor's hometown.
- Ketubot (marriage certificates, which, depending on their source, could be printed in Hebrew, Yiddish, or Aramaic)—These often beautifully illustrated docu-

ON THE BOOKSHELF
The National Archives has a collection of documents, recording correspondence between more than 70,000 people with the Czarist government, called the Russian Consular Records. Avotaynu offers an index to these records on microfiche. See <www.avotaynu.com> for more details.

ments may contain very helpful information including the towns where the bride and groom lived and where marriage banns took place.

- Foreign-issued passports and U.S. passport applications—Rummaging through family papers, you may find an immigrant's passport. Hold onto it—this is a rare find. If you think your naturalized immigrant ancestor may have used a passport to travel before or during 1925, you can consult the LDS microfilms under "UNITED STATES - EMIGRATION AND IMMIGRATION" or National Archives microfilms M1371 (Registers and Indexes for Passport Applications 1810-1906), M1848 (Index to Passport Applications 1850-52, 1860-80, 1881, 1906-23), M1372 (Passport Applications, 1795-1905), and M1490 (Passport Applications, 1906-25) in Washington, DC and some regional branches. If you're looking for a paper copy of the passport and it was issued before 1925, you can write to NARA, Attn.: Old Military and Civil Records, 700 Pennsylvania Ave., NW, Washington, DC 20408-0001 or send an e-mail to inquire@nara.gov. Records issued after 1925 are held at the U.S. State Department, Research and Liaison Branch, 1111 19th Street, NW, Suite 200, Washington, DC 20522-1705.

- Old correspondence—My aunt had a black-lined postcard, a death notice, announcing the passing of her grandfather in Zaromb. It also provided the street address of my grandfather's oldest brother, Icek, who later perished in the Holocaust.

- Old photographs—My paternal grandmother came from Kozlów, Galicia. When looking through her old photo album, I saw a picture of three children with the photographer's name and address in nearby Zborów embossed on its cardboard frame. Not only did this help me broaden my research to another town, it also helped me to eventually identify the children in the picture.

.A POCZTOWA

NADAWCA:
Ostrów k Łomży
Ul Brokowska 6
W Pan Icek
Pryzant

M. Max Peretman
2321 Merman Ave
Coney Island Broklin
New-york Amerike.
U.S.A.

P. Z. G. № 76 — 10.000.000 — 26.

2027—85

This 1926 death notice postcard provided the address of my grandfather's oldest brother, Icek, in Poland. Icek and his family later perished in the Holocaust.

- Vital records—Clues to your town can be found in birth, marriage, and death records. You may have some of these within the family, such as marriage certificates for your immigrant family members. You can also find them through archival research. For instance, in civil registrations of Jewish vital records in Poland, village names can be found in the text or margin of the specific event's entry. While some U.S vital records may only cite birthplace very generally, such as Poland or Russia, it is useful to see if the information corroborates other evidence you have.

SEE ALSO
For more on naturalization records, see Chapter 5.

- Naturalization papers—Your family may have your immigrant ancestor's Certificate of Naturalization. The number on the certificate will help you to easily request the Declaration of Intention and the Petition for Naturalization that preceded it, listing the applicant's birthplace. These papers will also give you a clue as to the ship on which he or she came which could provide additional detail.

SEE ALSO
For a more detailed explanation of ship manifests, see Chapter 5.

- Ship passenger records—The birthplace was recorded for each arriving ship's passengers beginning in 1906. The name and address of the nearest relative left behind were added the following year. These entries, often citing the exact town, can be very enlightening. The entry for last place of residence may also lead you to areas where other family members lived.

QUICK TIP
Census Records on CD
Heritage Quest now provides all U.S. federal census records (1790-1920) on CD. See <www.heritagequest.com> for more details.

- Census records—U.S. federal and state census records can help you identify geographic origin. Entries are typically vague, but it is a good place to start. The Federal Census began recording an individual's birthplace in 1850. And, beginning in 1880, the census asked for birthplace of the individual's father and mother. The risk here is that the place name is often very general and doesn't specify a town.

- Military records—If you know the veteran's name, branch of service (Army, Navy, or Marine Corps), state from which the veteran entered service, and the war in

Reizl Entel's Petition for Naturalization identified her place of birth as "Austravah" which meant Ostrów Mazowiecka, Poland.

DUPLICATE (To accompany monthly report on Form 2206)

UNITED STATES OF AMERICA

PETITION FOR NATURALIZATION

ROSE PERLMAN

1864 60th St., Bklyn, NY

Austravah, Russia

Bella, Nov. 14, 1918; Lillian, Nov. 18, 1920; Irving, Jan. 20, 1926. All born and reside in Bklyn, NY.

Austravah, Russia

Bremen, Germany — New York, NY

Reizel Antel

June 6, 1914 — SS George Washington

AFFIDAVITS OF WITNESSES

Fanny Morgenstern

1860 60th St., Bklyn, NY

Bella Perlman

1864 60th St., Bklyn, NY

ROSE PERLMAN

BEST REPRODUCED COPY AVAILABLE

370

U. S. DEPARTMENT OF LABOR
NATURALIZATION SERVICE

ORIGINAL

No. 3569

UNITED STATES OF AMERICA

DECLARATION OF INTENTION

Invalid for all purposes seven years after the date hereof

United States of America, District of New Jersey, ss: In the 1 District Court of The United States

I, Max Krasner, aged 42 years, occupation Merchant, do declare on oath that my personal description is: Color white, complexion fair, height 5 feet 6 inches, weight 135 pounds, color of hair brown, color of eyes Grey other visible distinctive marks None

I was born in Borysow, Russia on the 21 day of May anno Domini 1876; I now reside at 171 Van Buren St. Newark, N.J.

I emigrated to the United States of America from Rotterdam Holland on the vessel Rotterdam; my last foreign residence was Borysow Russia; I am married; the name of my wife is Eva; she was born at Austria and now resides at Newark N.J.

It is my bona fide intention to renounce forever all allegiance and fidelity to any foreign prince, potentate, state, or sovereignty, and particularly to The Present Government of Russia, of whom I am now a subject; I arrived at the port of New York, in the State of New York, on or about the 20 day of August, anno Domini 1899; I am not an anarchist; I am not a polygamist nor a believer in the practice of polygamy; and it is my intention in good faith to become a citizen of the United States of America and to permanently reside therein: SO HELP ME GOD.

Max Krasner
(Original signature of declarant)

Subscribed and sworn to before me in the office of the Clerk of said Court this 19 day of May, anno Domini 1919

[SEAL]

W. B. Rice
Clerk of the United States District Court.

Max Krasner's Declaration of Intention shows he was born in Borisov, Russia.

which the veteran served, you should be able to find a family member's place of foreign birth in a military pension record. If the timeframe is after 1916, you'll also need to know entry and release dates, military ID number, Social Security number (1936 and later), whether the veteran was an officer or enlisted person, and date of birth.

QUICK TIP
Finding Your Ancestor in World War I Draft Cards
If your ancestor lived in a large city, you'll need the street address in order to locate the card.

- World War I Draft Registration Cards, 1917-1918—Twenty-four million men registered for Selective Service in 1917 and 1918. One or more of these men could be your immigrant ancestor. It doesn't matter whether he was naturalized or not. The registration card gives the exact place of birth (city/town, state/province, country) and can be accessed through the LDS Family History Library ("UNITED STATES – MILITARY RECORDS – WORLD WAR, 1914-1918") or through the National Archives.

DEFINITION
A *landsmanshaft* (plural *landsmanshaftn*) is a society formed by former residents of a particular geographic area like a town or *shtetl*. These societies also typically provided services to *landslayt*, people from the town, including burial. After World War II, many *landsmanshaftn* wrote and published memorial books, known as Yizkor books, about their towns and inhabitants.

ON THE BOOKSHELF
YIVO Institute for Jewish Research has a guide to its holdings of *landsmanshaft* records, which can include photographs, correspondence, bulletins, announcements, and more as well as a guide to its archives. See *Guide to YIVO's Landsmanshaftn Archives* by Rosaline Schwartz and Susan Milamed, and *Guide to YIVO Archives*, compiled and edited by Fruma Mohrer and Marek Web.

- Society affiliation—Often immigrants joined town-based societies, called *landsmanshaftn* in Yiddish. These societies traditionally offered cemetery plots. My maternal grandfather, Max Perlman (a.k.a Avram Mendel Pryzant), born and raised in Zaromb—the Yiddish name for the Polish village of Zaręby Koscielne—joined the Zaromber Progressive Young Friends Society, which started up in 1913, the year he arrived in America. He is buried in one of the Zaromber plots in Montefiore Cemetery in St. Albans, New York. You may have papers in the family—an obituary that lists a society affiliation, or a copy of a memorial or *Yizkor* book for the town that the society may have published. One note: All other documented evidence—marriage and death records, naturalization papers, etc.—on my grandfather said he was from Łomża. It was only his membership in the *landsmanshaft* and family stories that suggested otherwise.
- Obituaries—These local newspaper items, whether Jewish or secular, may indicate place of birth before

your immigrant ancestor came to America and/or membership in a *landsmanshaft*. These notices often contain much more information than a death certificate and may even communicate more accurate details.

- City Directories—Polish and Russian city directories can lead you to specific towns where your ancestors lived and worked. The Russian business directory, *Vsia Rossia*, was published in 1895, 1899, 1902, 1911-12, and 1923, though the 1923 edition has no surnames and therefore offers little genealogical value. The 1929 and 1930 Polish business directories are also helpful. Note that Galicia is included in the Polish directories. You can find these directories at libraries such as the New York Public Library, Library of Congress, and Harvard University Library, among others.
- Social Security Applications—The Social Security Death Index from the U.S. Department of Health and Human Services is available to the public through the FOIA. You can access the index using Internet sites, such as <www.myfamily.com>.
- Alien Registration Cards—All aliens were required to register after 1941. To obtain a copy of a registration, contact the Immigration & Naturalization Service, Freedom of Information, Room 5304, 425 I Street NW, Washington, DC 20536.
- Surname clues—If your surname is very unusual, you may want to consult Alexander Beider's *A Dictionary of Jewish Surnames from the Kingdom of Poland* and *A Dictionary of Jewish Surnames from the Russian Empire.* Some surnames are found only in a particular locality in eastern Europe.

Gazetteers

Naturally, you'll want to know as much about your ancestor's town as possible. It is not uncommon to find a town that has

QUICK HIT
Online Databases
Several sections of the Russian directory are available online on the JewishGen web site <www.jewishgen.org/databases> such as the 1895 entries for Kiev, Poltava, and Chernigov, the 1903 entries for Minsk Gubernia, and the 1911 entries for Mogilev Gubernia. The 1891 Galician directory is also available online at JewishGen.

SEE ALSO
See Chapter 13 for a listing of database resources on the JewishGen web site.

SEE ALSO
See the sidebar on the Freedom of Information Act at the end of this chapter for more information on Social Security Applications.

QUICK HIT
LDS Online Catalog
You can access the catalog at <www.familysearch.com>.

QUICK HIT
Entering the surname you are researching into one of the databases below can help you find towns where your ancestors may have lived.

JewishGen Family Finder <www.jewishgen.org/jgff>—Executing a search on this database will pull up all entries
cont. on pg. 43

1678 **Kozłów** WOJEWÓDZTWO TARNOPOLSKIE **Krasnosielce**

KOZŁÓW.

Miasteczko, pow. Tarnopol, sąd grodzki i sąd okręgowy Tarnopol, 4069 mieszk. (8 km) Jezierna, linja kol. Krasne-Tarnopol Kozłów k. Tarnopola Jezierna. Urząd miejski. 1 rz. kat., 1 gr. kat. Stow. przemysłowców. Targi: co czwartek.

Petite ville, distr. de Tarnopol, tribunal urbain et tribunal d'arr-t Tarnopol, 4069 habit. (8 km) Jezierna, ligne de Krasne-Tarnopol Kozłów k. Tarnopola Jezierna. Office municipal. 1 cath. 1 gr. cath. Assoc. d'industriels. Marchés: le jeudi.

Lekarze (médecins): Biener A. dr — Zarzycki Stef. dr. (chir).
Akuszerki (sages-femmes): Fastyk T.
Apteki (pharmacies): Blachowski S. — Kubrakiewicz W.
Bednarze (tonneliers): Lachocki W.
Blacharze (ferblantiers): Goldberg.
Bławaty (tissus): Barczak H. — Chrap S. — Hameldank I. — Korn Sz. — Lewinter M. — Lille R. — Nauman M. — Steinbruch N.
Cieśle (charpentiers): Krbkosz K.
Fryzjerzy (coiffeurs): Bürger J.
Kołodzieje (charrons): Mazur A. — Rosiecki B.
Kooperatywy (coopératives): ×„Nywa" — ×„Samopomoc".
Kowale (forgerons): Głożek P. — Kawok — Leszczyński J. — Myczak J.
Krawcy (tailleurs): Fenster E. — Pliszner M. — Winter J.
Murarze (maçons): Soczyński K.
Piasek i żwir — eksploatacja (exploitations des sables et graviers): Korn S.
Piekarze (boulangers): Petersill M. — Sass F.
Piwiarnie (brasseries-débit): Brossko K. — Kreindter M.
Różne towary (articles divers): Brandes W. — Burstin T. — Chrap M. — Finkiel I. — Flaum I. — Katz D. — Pakiet Z. — Pysiak A.
Rzeźnicy (bouchers): Ast M. — Czaczkies Z. — Jurkowski M. — Kleinrok Sz. — Teich M. — Zaremba J.
Skóry (cuirs): Beck Ch. — Chrap A. — Katz N. — Nusbaum I. — Zahnstecher Ch.
Stolarze (menuisiers): Teich W. — Wolkentreiber M. — Zukerkandel H.
Szewcy (cordonniers): Fajger M. — Federowski J. — Kaspryta J. — Strzałkowski I.
Tytoniowe wyroby (tabacs): Goldfeld M.
Wyszynk trunków (spiritueux): Adler B. — Baran N. — Goldfeld K. — Schor A.
Zboże (grains): Katz D. — Neuman M. — Siepa J.
Żelazne wyroby (quincailliers): Hamer S. — Marder J.

KOZOWA.

Miasto, pow. Brzeżany, siedziba sądu grodz. sąd okr. Brzeżany, 4913 mieszk. (2 km) linja kol. Potutory-Tarnopol Kozowa-Brzeżany Kozowa Krzywe. Urząd miejski, 1 rz. katolicki, 1 gr. katolicki. Przytulisko dla starców. Stow. kupieckie. Targi: co poniedziałek. Młyny, kamieniołomy.

Petite ville, distr. de Brzeżany, siège du trib. urbain, trib. d'arr-t Brzeżany, 4913 habit. (2 km) ligne de Potutory-Tarnopol ligne de Kozowa Brzeżany Kozowa Krzywe. Office municipal, 1 cath., 1 gr. cath. Asile de vieillards. Assoc. des commercants. Marchés: le lundi. Moulins, carrières de pierres.

Burmistrz (Maire): Piotr Traunfellner.
Straż ogniowa ochotn. Komendant (Corps des pompiers volont. Commandant): M. Zieliński.
Lekarze (médecins): Jurkiewicz A. dr. — Manacki A. dr. — Schimmel Szym. dr. — Sternberg Is. dr.
Lekarze weterynarji (médecins vétérinaires): Fuchs Izr.
Adwokaci (avocats): Ambach Abr. dr. — Fried Emil dr. — Kurzrock Marek dr. — Sobel Iron. dr. — Stadnyk Mik. dr.
Notarjusze (notaires): Traunfellner Piotr.
Właściciele ziemscy (propriétaires fonciers): Szeliski H. (720).
Akuszerki (sages-femmes): Burger S. — Fuhrman A. — Kusna K.
Apteki (pharmacies): Polisinka Sukc.
Bednarze (tonneliers): ta B. — Gore Szuster J.
Blacharze (ferblantiers): Migden M. — Rosenstrauch H.
Bławaty (tissus): Ast E. — Hochman L. — Jeki D. — Mandelberg N. — Rauch I. — Schmutz Ch. — Schmutz H. — Teller S. — Wasser N.
Flank S. — Goldberg K. — Himeldank I. — Kieselstein H. — Kieselstein O. — Kieselstein S. — Schmutz N. — Streusand I.
Budowlane materjały (matériaux de construction): Kieselstein J. — Rottenberg J.
Bydło — handel (marchands de bestiaux): Rothstein I.
Cegielnie (briqueteries): Szeliński H.
Cieśle (charpentiers): Gorsko W. — Lebonicki A.
Drzewo (bois): Karpen N. — Zwerling Ch.
Fryzjerzy (coiffeurs): Bürger L. — Furman A. — Goldfarb M.
Galanterja (merceries): Schleicher E.
Gliniane wyroby (poteries): Nestel M.
Herbaciarnie (débits de thé): Kuliczkowski P.
Jaja (oeufs): Zieliński T.
Kamieniołomy (carrières de pierres): Rzeszutko P. — Salamon W. — Storc J. — Studziński St. — Zieliński.
Kaszarnie (fabric. de gruaux): Abend A.
Kolonjalne artykuły (épiciers): Bajer Sz. — Isserles B. — Leber S. — Lewin B. — Schapira S. — Teitelbaum H.
Kołodzieje (charrons): Baran M. — Kawka G. — Kawka J. — Sigal B.
Kominiarze (ramoneurs): Pruski M.
Konie — handel (marchands de chevaux): Hochman R. — Fuchs M.
Kooperatywy (coopératives): ×„Wola".
Kowale (forgerons): Krynicki S. — Paka J. — Rygajło M.
Krawcy (tailleurs): Flank A. — Reichenberg A. — Reichenberg W. Sted M.
Maszyny rolnicze (machines agricoles): ×Spółdzielnia Maszynowa.
Młyny (moulins): Kurzrock M. i Rawicz Z. (mot) — Szeliski H. (wod.).
Murarze (maçons): Kiosowski A. — Krywda M.
Piekarnie (boulangers): Glanc R. — Menkes A. — Stadtmauer.
Piwo — hurt (bières en gros): Ratner Ch. — Saar A.
Powroźnicy (cordiers): Klein J.
Restauracje (restaurants): Durst J. Kraczyło Z. — Kurzrock D. — Sakolnicki P.
Różne towary (articles divers): Dreksler L. — Durst L. — Feigenbaum M. — Frühling S. — Glaserman K. — Goldenberg A. — Hammer J. — Hass M. — ×Kakol Jan — Liebling S. — Liebling T. — Mittelman W. — Rothstein J. — Schatten J. — Steinfink J.
Charmatz M. — Bajor B. — Goldfarb A. L. — Hasenhorn Sz. — Maczuga K. — Schapira M.
Rymarze (bourreliers): Hawryluk M. — Melles O. — Wojtyło.
Rzeźnicy (bouchers): Bajor F. — Bajor Jan — Bajor Jós. — Bajor K. — Bajor T. — Der J. — Flam I. — Fracht S. — Nestel — Spring S. Grosberg L. — Nachman M.
Skóry (cuirs): Jeckel G. — Juffe H. — Kronberg Sch. — Lindenman M. Gutstein I. — Witków W.
Skórzane wyroby (maroquiniers): Werfel O.
Sól (sel): Palek M. Sukc.
Stolarze (menuisiers): Akselrad B. — Eimer L. — Morgenstern I.
Studnie — budowa (forages de puits): Ottendreit W. — Rygajło M.
Szewckie przybory (fournitures pour chaussures): Rohatiner M.
Szewcy (cordonniers): Blacharski K. — Dobrowolski J. — Grubiak A. — Samborski Z. — Szuster L. — Trofimiak G. — Trofimiak M. Dąbrowski P. — Grubiak P.
Szklarze (vitriers): Glücker W. — Spring J.
Tytoniowe wyroby (tabacs): Jarosiński St.
Wyszynk trunków (spiritueux): Bartha Antoni — Kuliczkowski A. Karpen S. — Kurzrock R. — Rozmarin A. — Scharr A. — Stadtmauer D. — Steklosa M.
Zajazdy (auberges): Weksler K.
Zboże (grains): Becher M. — Bosen S. — Binder L. — Fränkel B. — Friedman M. — Halpern J. — Leitner I. — Rozmarin St. — Rotstein M. Kahane J. — Peczanik F.
Zegarmistrze (horlogers): Weinreb S.
Ziemiopłody (produits du sol): ×„Ceres", Spółdz. z o. o.
Żelazo (fers): Gewing A. — Nebel J. — Safier J. — Schächter S. — Werfel B.

KOZÓWKA.

Wieś i gmina, pow. Brzeżany, sąd pow. Kozowa, sąd okr. Brzeżany, 942 mieszk. (4 km) Kozowa, 1 gr. kat.

V-ge et commune, distr. de Brzeżany, tr. de distr. Kozowa, tr. d'arrond. Brzeżany, 942 habit. (4 km) Kozowa, 1 gr. cath.

Właściciele ziemscy (propriétaires fonciers): Leszczyński Stanisław dziert. (357) — Maramarosz Karol (Ułanicha 203).
Kooperatywy (coopératives): ×„Samopomoc". ×Kółko Rolnicze.
Kowale (forgerons): Wróblewski J.
Tytoniowe wyr. (tabacs): Jakubów T.

KOZÓWKA.

Wieś gmina, pow. Tarnopol, sąd pow. Mikulińce, sąd okr. Tarnopol, 1876 mieszk. (10 km) Proszowa Tarnopol.

V-ge et commune, distr. de Tarnopol, trib. de distr Mikulińce, trib. d'arr-t Tarnopol, 1876 habit. (10 km) Proszowa Tarnopol.

Właściciele ziemscy (propriétaires fonciers): Borowski hr. Jerzy (216) — Mochnacka Marja (185) — Sozański Stan. (235).
Akuszerki (sages-femmes): Szewczuk — Sobczyszyn.
Kooperatywy (coopératives): ×„Harasd".
Kowale (forgerons): Konopnicki A. — Poticha J. — Rosoliński J. — Wyspiański P.
Młyny (moulins): Buczkowski J.
Wyszynk trunków (spiritueux): Konopnicki M. — Sauberman G.

KRASIEJÓW.

Wieś i gmina, pow. Buczacz, sąd pow. Monasterzyska, sąd okr. Stanisławów, 1002 mieszkańców (2,5 km) Korościatyn Uście Zielone Monasterzyska, 1 gr. kat.

V-ge et commune, distr. de Buczacz, tr. de distr. Monasterzyska, trib. d'arr-t Stanisławów, 1002 habitants (2,5 km) Korościatyn Uście Zielone Monasterzyska, 1 gr. cath.

Właściciele ziemscy (propriétaires fonciers): Słonecki Adam (279).
Cieśle (charpentiers): Grand M.
Kooperatywy (coopératives): ×„Dobra Wola".
Kowale (forgerons): Duchniak S.
Krawcy (tailleurs): Jabłoń D. — Skrynnyk J.
Szewcy (cordonniers): Szajda D.
Wyszynk trunków (spiritueux): Münzer M.

KRASNA.

Wieś i gmina, pow. Zborów, sąd pow. Zborów, sąd okr. Złoczów, 650 mieszk. (4 km) Zborów Plaucza Mała.

V-ge et commune, distr. de Zborów, tr. de distr. Zborów, trib. d'arr-t Złoczów, 650 habitants (4 km) Zborów Plaucza Mała.

Właściciele ziemscy (propriétaires fonciers): Gozdawa Tyszkowski Ant., dzierż. (220).
Konie — handel (marchands de chevaux): Adler A.
Kooperatywy (coopératives): ×„Samopomicz", Sp. z o. o.
Kowale (forgerons): Lewicki J.
Szewcy (cordonniers): Cebry J.
Tytoniowe wyroby (tabacs): Cebrij J. — Lacher Ch.
Zboże (grains): Lach Ch.

KRASNE.

Wieś i gmina, powiat Skałat, sąd pow. Grzymałów, sąd okr. Tarnopol, 1722 mieszk. (24 km) Chorostków Touste, 1 rz. kat., 1 gr. kat.

V-ge et commune, distr. de Skałat, tr. de distr. Grzymałów, tr. d'arr-t Tarnopol, 1722 habit. (24 km) Chorostków Touste, 1 cath., 1 gr. cath.

Właściciele ziemscy (propriétaires fonciers): Siedlecka Wanda (276).
Bławaty (tissus): Nałukowy M.
Kasy pożyczk.-oszczędn. (caisses d'emprunt et d'épargne): ×Kasa Stefczyka.
Kooperatywy (coopératives): ×Kółko Rolnicze — ×„Medobir".
Kowale (forgerons): Susła B.
Krawcy (tailleurs): Sicewicz J.
Lasy — eksploatacja (exploitations forestières): Badian M. i Tilles S.
Młyny (moulins): Schönberg N.
Różne towary (art. divers): Seftel H.
Stolarze (menuisiers): Kolba M.
Wyszynk trunków (spiritueux): Ungar M.

KRASNE.

Wieś i gmina, pow. Złoczów, sąd pow. i sąd okr. Złoczów, 1593 mieszk. linja kol. Lwów - Podwołoczyska Krasne k. Lwowa, rz. kat., gr. kat. Tartaki, młyn.

V-ge et commune, distr. de Złoczów trib. de distr. et trib. d'arr-t Złoczów, 1593 habit. ligne de Lwów - Podwołoczyska Krasne k. Lwowa, cath., gr. cath. Scieries, moulin.

Właściciele ziemscy (propriétaires fonciers): Russocka hr. Hel. (151).
Akuszerki (sages-femmes): Majba E.
Bednarze (tonneliers): Skalski S.
Cieśle (charpentiers): Freundlich F. — Łaska D.
Kasy pożyczk.-oszczędn. (caisses d'emprunt et d'épargne): ×„Ukraińska Kasa", Spółdz. z o. p.
Kołodzieje (charrons): Gorczak St.
Kooperatywy (coopératives): ×Kółko Rolnicze, Sp. z o. o. — ×„Syla", Sp. z o. o.
Kowale (forgerons): Turkiewicz P.
Krawcy (tailleurs): Jaworski S. — Ponulak H.
Młyny (moulins): Russocka hr. H.
Murarze (maçons) Grypa W. — Łaska W.
Piekarze (boulangers): Bodakiewicz J.
Różne towary (articles divers): Ciokan — Niźnikowa L.
Rzeźnicy (bouchers): Baranicki P. — Moszczak S. — Tomaszewski J.
Stolarze (menuisiers): Majba J.
Szewcy (cordonniers): Dubiniak E. — Nadała M.
Ślusarze (serruriers): Ślusarz A.
Tartaki (scieries): Rozum A. — Russocka hr. H. — Zimand H.
Tytoniowe wyr. (tabacs): Jakubowska M. — Korczyński Z.
Wyszynk trunków (spiritueux): Ciokan M. — Krzyżanowska M. — Majer Ch.
Zajazdy (auberges): Augstreich Z.

KRASNOPUSZCZA.

Wieś i gmina, pow. Brzeżany, sąd pow. i sąd okr. Brzeżany, 252 mieszkańc. (10 km) Dunajów Pomorzany, 1 gr. kat.

V-ge et commune, distr. de Brzeżany, trib. de distr. et trib. d'arr-t Brzeżany, 252 habit. (10 km) Dunajów Pomorzany, 1 gr. cath.

Młyny (moulins): Konwent O. O. Bazyljanów (wod).

KRASNOSIELCE.

Wieś i gmina, powiat Zbaraż, sąd pow. Zbaraż, sąd okr. Tarnopol, 1025 mieszk. linja kol. Zbaraż-Łanowce Zbaraż, 1 gr. kat.

V-ge et commune, distr. de Zbaraż, tr. de distr. Zbaraż, trib. d'arr-t Tarnopol, 1025 habit. ligne de Zbaraż-Łanowce Zbaraż, 1 gr. cath.

Właściciele ziemscy (propriétaires fonciers): Malecki Wład. (253).
Kaszarnie (fabrication de gruaux): Humeniuk W.
Kooperatywy (coopératives): ×„Zhoda".
Młyny (moulins): Segal I. i Ska, dzierż.
Tytoniowe wyroby (tabacs): Chmiel G. — Rogocki P.
Wyszynk trunków (spiritueux): Balin S.

KRASNOSIELCE.

Wieś i gmina, pow. Złoczów, sąd pow. i sąd okr. Złoczów, 526 mieszk. (6 km) Zarwanica Złoczów, 1 gr. kat.

V-ge et commune, distr. de Złoczów, tr. de distr. et tr. d'arr-t Złoczów, 526 habit. (6 km) Zarwanica Złoczów 1 gr. cath.

Cieśla (charpentiers): Wasinta M.
Kamieniołomy (carrières de pierres): Sierota S.
Kołodzieje (charrons): Owczar M.

Polish and Russian directories can lead you to specific towns where your ancestors lived and worked. This page from the 1930 Polish business directory identified several family members from the former Galician town of Kozlów.

the same name as dozens of other towns. How do you know which one is yours?

Two useful books can help. Chester G. Cohen's *Shtetl Finder Gazeteer* primarily covers the Pale of Settlement area and geographically associates each *shtetl* to a "reference" city (Riga, Kovno, Vilna, Minsk, Mohilev, Grodno, Bialystok, Warsaw, Łódż, Pinsk, Brest-Litovsk, Lublin, Kraków, Lvov, Kiev, and Odessa). The native name (e.g., Polish or Russian name) and the Yiddish name for each shtetl are listed. For example, my grandfather's shtetl of "Zaromb" as he called it is listed under "Zaręby Koscielne," its Polish name.

The second book is far more geographically inclusive. Compiled by Gary Mokotoff and Sallyann Amdur Sack, the definitive *Where Once We Walked* lists more than 22,000 communities in central and eastern Europe where Jews lived before the Holocaust. It includes more than 15,000 alternate town names, since many of us only know the Yiddish name for our ancestral towns.

Latitude and longitude specifications help to identify exactly which town is yours. For example, there are fourteen listings for "Ostrów." Each of these entries suggests proximity to a larger city, provides the pre-Holocaust population, and the exact degree location. Where possible, references are made to source materials that include more information on the town, including: American Gathering/Federation of Jewish Holocaust Survivors, Central Archives for the History of the Jewish People, Chamber of the Holocaust, *Encyclopaedia Judaica, Guide to Unpublished Materials of the Holocaust Period, A Guide to YIVO's Landsmanshaftn Archive*, Hebrew Subscription Lists, and the LDS Family History Library Catalog.

Another source to try on the JewishGen web site is the JewishGen ShtetlSeeker <www.jewishgen.org/ShtetlSeeker>, an online database of more than 500,000 places in Eastern Europe, based upon the U.S. Board on Geographic Names. The site displays maps using links to MapQuest.

Maps

Good, detailed maps are sold through several booksellers, including Jonathan Sheppard <www.jonathansheppardbooks.com>

cont. from pg. 41

for the surname and identify other researchers interested in the same name.

Jewish Records Indexing – Poland <www.jewishgen.org/jri-pl>—Just enter your surname, click on Soundex code, and you'll receive a report that lists hits against your surname from nearly 1,000,000 Jewish birth, marriage, and death records from Poland. This is particularly helpful if you have very little information on your family's place of origin.

SEE ALSO

For more in-depth information on the JewishGen Family Finder and Jewish Records Indexing – Poland, see Chapter 13.

Ostrow (near Janow Lubelski), Pol.; pop. 18; 38 km SSW of Lublin; 51°00'/22°15'.

Ostrow (near Jaroslaw), Pol.; pop. 74; 38 km WNW of Przemysl; 50°01'/22°25'.

Ostrow (near Konstantynow), Pol.; pop. 2; 107 km S of Bialystok; 52°11'/23°20'.

Ostrow (near Lubartow), Pol.; pop. 24; 45 km NNW of Lublin; 51°36'/22°20'.

Ostrow (near Luninets), Byel.; pop. 3; 26 km SSE of Pinsk; 51°55'/26°13'.

Ostrow (near Miechow), Pol.; pop. 5; 32 km NE of Krakow; 50°14'/20°22'.

Ostrow (near Przemysl), Pol.; pop. 65; 6 km WNW of Przemysl; 49°48'/22°44'.

Ostrow (near Ropczyce), Pol.; pop. 27; 88 km WNW of Przemysl; 50°05'/21°35'.

Ostrow (near Sokal), Ukr.; pop. 41; 75 km N of Lvov; 50°29'/24°17'.

Ostrow (near Tarnopol), Ukr.; pop. 3; 82 km SW of Rovno; 50°20'/25°13'.

Ostrow (Nowogrodek), Byel.; pop. 8; 94 km N of Pinsk; 52°53'/25°59'.

Ostrowczyk Polny, *see* Ostrovchik Polny.

Ostrowek, Pol.; pop. 90; 94 km ENE of Warszawa; 52°19'/22°25'; COH, HSL.

Ostrowek (near Kalisz), Pol.; 88 km W of Lodz; 51°54'/18°09'; PHP1.

Ostrowek (near Sokolow), Pol.; pop. 44; 62 km NE of Warszawa; 52°33'/21°47'.

Ostrowek (near Wegrow), Pol.; pop. 56; 75 km NW of Lublin; 51°46'/21°52'; GUM3.

Ostrowek (near Wielun), Pol.; 75 km NW of Czestochowa; 51°21'/18°37'; PHP1.

Ostrowiec, *see* Ostrowiec Swietokrzyski. Ostrowiec usually refers to the town of Ostrowiec Swietokrzyski.

Ostrowiec (Lvov area), Pol.; pop. 53; 50 km NNE of Przemysl; 50°09'/23°09'.

Ostrowiec (Vilnius area), *see* Ostrovets.

Ostrowiec Kielecki, Pol. AMG, PHP1. This town was not found in BGN gazetteers under the given spelling.

Ostrowiec Swietokrzyski, Pol. (Ostrovitz, Ostrovitza, Ostrovtse, Ostrowiec); pop. 10,095; 88 km SW of Lublin; 50°56'/21°24'; AMG, COH, EDRD, EJ, FRG, GA, GUM3, GUM4, GUM5, GUM6, HSL, HSL2, LDL, PHP4, POCEM, SF, YB.

Ostrowik, Pol.; 56 km WNW of Bialystok; 53°25'/22°29'; HSL.

Ostrow Kaliski, Pol.; pop. 22; 88 km WSW of Lodz; 51°33'/18°13'.

Ostrow Krolewski, Pol.; pop. 2; 38 km E of Krakow; 50°01'/20°29'.

Ostrow Lubelski, Pol. (Ostrov Lubelski, Ostrova); pop. 1,267; 32 km NNE of Lublin; 51°29'/22°51'; GA, GUM3, GUM5, GUM6, HSL, HSL2, JGFF, LDL, LYV, POCEM, SF.

Ostrow Mazowiecka, Pol. (Ostrov Mazovyetska, Ostrow Mazowiecki); pop. 6,812; 82 km NE of Warszawa; 52°48'/21°54'; AMG, EDRD, EJ, GUM3, GUM4, GUM5, HSL, HSL2, JGFF, LDL, LDS, LYV, PHP1, PHP4, SF, YB.

Ostrow Mazowiecki, *see* Ostrow Mazowiecka.

Ostrowo, *see* Ostrow Wielkopolski.

Ostrow Polnocny, Pol.; 38 km NE of Bialystok; 53°16'/23°41'; SF.

Ostrow Poludniowy, Pol.; pop. 6; 38 km NE of Bialystok; 53°15'/23°42'.

Ostrowsko, Pol.; pop. 11; 75 km SSE of Krakow; 49°29'/20°06'.

Ostrow Szlachecki, Pol.; pop. 8; 38 km E of Krakow; 50°02'/20°29'.

Ostrow Volhynia, LDL. This pre-World War I community was not found in BGN gazetteers.

Ostrow Wielkopolski, Pol. (Ostrowo); pop. 170; 88 km NNE of Wroclaw; 51°39'/17°49'; CAHJP, HSL, JGFF, LDS.

Ostrowy, Pol. (Ostrovy); pop. 138; 32 km NNW of Czestochowa; 50°59'/19°04'; HSL, SF.

Ostrowy Baranowskie, Pol.; pop. 21; 101 km WNW of Przemysl; 50°19'/21°39'.

Ostrowy Tuszowskie, Pol.; pop. 1; 101 km WNW of Przemysl; 50°18'/21°39'.

Ostrozec, *see* Ostrozhets.

Ostrozen, Pol.; pop. 19; 75 km ESE of Warszawa; 51°48'/21°45'.

Ostrozhets, Ukr. (Ostrozec); pop. 624; 50 km W of Rovno; 50°40'/25°33'; AMG, COH, EDRD, GUM4, LDL, SF.

Ostrozske Predmesti, Cz.; pop. 53; 62 km ESE of Brno; 48°59'/17°24'.

Ostrusza, Pol.; pop. 6; 88 km ESE of Krakow; 49°47'/21°01'.

Ostruv; See listings below. *See also* Ostrov; Ostrow.

Ostruv (near Bobrka), Ukr.; pop. 54; 50 km SE of Lvov; 49°28'/24°16'.

Ostruv (near Kalush), Ukr.; pop. 26; 88 km SE of Lvov; 49°10'/24°38'.

Ostruv (near Kamenka Strumilovska), Ukr.; pop. 10; 45 km ENE of Lvov; 49°56'/24°36'.

Ostruv (near Lutsk), Ukr.; pop. 3; 69 km WNW of Rovno; 50°59'/25°33'.

Ostruv (near Lvov), Ukr.; pop. 89; 26 km SSW of Lvov; 49°40'/23°52'.

Ostruv (near Tarnopol), Ukr.; 120 km ESE of Lvov; 49°29'/25°35'; GUM4, GUM5.

Ostrykol, Pol. (Ostrykol Wloscianski); pop. 24; 88 km NW of Bialystok; 53°44'/22°26'; AMG.

Ostrykol Wloscianski, *see* Ostrykol.

Ostryna, Byel. (Astrin, Istrin, Ostrin); pop. 1,067; 195 km WSW of Minsk; 53°44'/24°32'; COH, EJ, GA, GUM3, GUM5, HSL, JGFF, LDL, LYV, SF, YB.

Ostrz, *see* Oster.

Ostrzeszow, Pol. (Schildberg); pop. 122; 75 km NE of Wroclaw; 51°25'/17°57'; CAHJP, HSL, JGFF, LDS.

Osveya, Byel.; pop. 700; 157 km WNW of Vitebsk; 56°01'/28°06'; HSL.

Osviet, LDL. This pre-World War I community was not found in BGN gazetteers.

Osvracin, Cz.; pop. 3; 120 km SW of Praha; 49°31'/13°03'.

Oswiecim, Pol. (Auschwitz, Aushvits, Oshpetzin, Oshpitsin, Oshvitsin, Oshvitzin, Oshvyentsim, Ospinzi); pop. 4,950; 50 km WSW of Krakow; 50°02'/19°14'; AMG, CAHJP, COH, EGRS, EJ, FRG, GA, GUM3, GUM4, GUM5, GUM6, HSL, HSL2, JGFF, LDL, LYV, PHGBW, PHP1, PHP2, PHP3, PHP4, POCEM, SF, YB. As the location of the infamous Auschwitz concentration camp, most sources refer to the camp rather than the town.

Osyakow, *see* Osjakow.

Osyetsk, *see* Osiek.

Oszczerze, Pol.; pop. 27; 69 km ENE of Warszawa; 52°18'/22°00'.

Oszczow, Pol.; pop. 44; 126 km NE of Przemysl; 50°33'/24°04'; GUM4, GUM5.

Oszlar, Hung.; 32 km SE of Miskolc; 47°53'/21°02'; HSL, HSL2.

Oszmiana, *see* Oshmyany.

Oszro, Hung.; 94 km ESE of Nagykanizsa; 45°53'/17°55'; HSL. This town was located on a pre-World War I map, but does not appear in contemporary gazetteers.

Osztopan, Hung.; pop. 22; 50 km ENE of Nagykanizsa; 46°31'/17°40'.

Otach Tyrg, *see* Ataki.

Otaci Sat, *see* Ataki.

Otaci Targ, *see* Ataki.

Otalez, Pol.; pop. 31; 94 km NE of Krakow; 50°21'/21°14'.

Otchakov, *see* Ochakov.

Oteni, Rom.; pop. 3; 139 km ESE of Cluj; 46°15'/25°15'.

Otfinow, Pol.; pop. 30; 62 km ENE of Krakow; 50°11'/20°49'.

Otinya, *see* Otynya.

Otiski Vrh, Yug.; pop. 1; 114 km NW of Zagreb; 46°35'/15°03'.

Otmet, Pol. (Ottmuth); 88 km SW of Czestochowa;

249

Gazetteers can help pinpoint your ancestral town.
Reprinted with permission from Where Once We Walked: A Guide to the Jewish Communities Destroyed in the Holocaust.

Use maps to locate your town and its surrounding area.
Reprinted with permission of Jonathan Sheppard Books.

and Avotaynu <www.avotaynu.com>. These include 1915 eastern Europe, 1916 Carpathia and Rumania, 1799 and 1817 Poland, the Austro-Hungarian Empire about 1875, Germany circa 1760 and 1875, 1845 Russia in Europe, and 1794 Czechoslovakia.

It's also worthwhile to check out the Geography and Map Division of the Library of Congress, which houses the world's largest and most comprehensive cartographic collection. I requested and received a detailed World War II map from the Library of Congress for one of the Russian towns I research, Borisov, indicating landmarks, streets, and rivers. If I knew my family's street address, I would have easily been able to pinpoint where they had once lived.

There are many resources at your disposal to determine exactly where your immigrant ancestor came from. And that is just the beginning of your journey to your ancestor's hometown.

QUICK TIP

Present-day travel atlases and road maps are useful to identify your ancestral towns and their surroundings. Avotaynu distributes several of these covering Poland, Czech Republic/Slovakia, Russia and Commonwealth of Independent States, and more.

FOR MORE INFORMATION

Library of Congress
Geography and Map Division
101 Independence Ave. SE
Washington, DC 20540-4650
E-mail: maps@loc.gov (please include name and full mailing address)
Fax: 202-707-8531

Jonathan Sheppard Books
<www.jonathansheppardbooks.com>
Box 2020
Plaza Station
Albany, NY 12220

Avotaynu
<www.avotaynu.com>
P.O. Box 99
Bergenfield, NJ 07621

The Freedom of Information Act

Reprinted with permission of
Family Chronicle Magazine

There is perhaps no better friend to the genealogist than the U.S. government's Freedom of Information Act (FOIA). Whether you're having a tough time locating naturalization records, or you need to verify a birthplace or parent's name, the FOIA can help. If your family members served in the U.S. military or had any dealings with the FBI, the FOIA can also help.

What Is It?

The Freedom of Information Act went into effect 4 July 1967 and affected access to twentieth century records. There is no restriction on records pertaining to yourself. However, you can get access to records about the deceased if you provide proof of death and about those still alive by submitting your request with authorization in the form of written, notarized permission. There is no restriction on records created more than 75 years ago, though there is a 72-year restriction on the Federal Census. The act requires federal government agencies and the armed forces to release records to the public on request unless the information is exempted by the Privacy Act of 1974 or for national security reasons. Records containing information on adoption, illegitimacy, or mental health remain closed except by court order.

The "Electronic Freedom of Information Act Amendments of 1996" bill addresses time limits and agency backlogs of FOIA requests. One major change under this set of amendments affecting family historians concerned the maintenance of agency reading rooms, requiring agencies to make three categories of records—final opinions rendered in the adjudication of administrative cases, specific agency policy statements, and administrative staff manuals that affect the public—routinely available for public inspection and copying. The new amendments added categories of reading room records and made most of them available electronically through Internet online access.

Hot links available from the National Archives and Records Administration (NARA) FOIA Electronic Reading Room include Holocaust Era Assets and the JFK Assassination Records Collection Database.

Types of Information

Naturalization—You can request a search for the record of an immigrant ancestor naturalized on or after September 27, 1906 by submitting a Freedom of Information Act Form G-639 (replacing G-641). You can request this form from the Immigration and Naturalization Service (INS) in one of three ways:

- Call 1-800-870-3676 to request the form be mailed to you.
- Download Form G-639 from the INS website and print a copy <www.ins.gov/graphics/formsfee/forms/g-639.htm>.
- Have the forms mailed to you by submitting an online request <www.ins.gov/exec/forms/index.asp>.

The request should adequately describe the specific records you want (e.g., Naturalization, Visa, Alien Registration Records) to enable the INS to conduct a search. The minimum information required is the alien's full name (with other alternate names or spellings) and the date and place (country) of birth. Other useful information to submit includes: name at time of entry into the U.S., Alien Registration Num-

U.S. Department of Justice
Immigration and Naturalization Service

OMB NO. 1115-0087
Freedom of Information/Privacy Act Request

The completion of this form is optional.
Any written format for Freedom of Information or Privacy Act requests is acceptable.

START HERE – Please type or print and read instructions on the reverse before completing this form.

1. Type of Request: *(Check appropriate box)*
   - ☐ Freedom of Information Act (FOIA) *(Complete all items except 7)*
   - ☐ Privacy Act (PA) *(Item 7 must be completed in addition to all other applicable items)*
   - ☐ Amendment *(PA only, Item 7 must be completed in addition to all other applicable items)*

2. Requester Information:

Name of Requester:		Daytime Telephone:
Address *(Street Number and Name):*		Apt. No
City:	State:	Zip Code:

By my signature, I consent to the following:
Pay all costs incurred for search, duplication, and review of materials up to $25.00, when applicable. *(See Instructions)*
Signature of requester:___________
☐ Deceased Subject - **Proof of death must be attached**. *(Obituary, Death Certificate or other proof of death required)*

3. Consent to Release Information. *(Complete if name is different from Requester)(Item 7 must be completed)*

Print Name of Person Giving Consent:	Signature of Person Giving Consent:

By my signature, I consent to the following: *(check applicable boxes)*
☐ Allow the Requester named in item 2 to see ☐ all of my records or ☐ a portion of my record. If a portion, specify what part *(i.e. copy of application)*
____
(Consent is required for records for United States Citizens (USC) and Lawful Permanent Residents (LPR)

4. Action Requested (*Check One*): ☐ Copy ☐ In-Person Review

5. Information needed to search for records:
   Specific information, document(s), or record(s) desired: *(Identify by name, date, subject matter, and location of information)*
   ____
   ____
   Purpose: *(Optional: you are not required to state the purpose for your request; however, doing so may assist the INS in locating the records needed to respond to your request.)*
   ____

6. Data NEEDED on SUBJECT of Record: *(If data marked with asterisk (*) is not provided records may not be located)*

* Family Name	Given Name:		Middle Initial:
*Other names used, if any:	* Name at time of entry into the U.S.:		I-94 Admissions #:
* Alien Registration #:	* Petition or Claim Receipt #:	* Country of Birth:	*Date of Birth or Appx. Year
Names of other family members that may appear on requested record(s) *(i.e., Spouse, Daughter, Son):*			
Country of Origin *(Place of Departure)*:	Port-of-Entry into the U.S.		Date of Entry:
Manner of Entry: *(Air, Sea, Land)*	Mode of Travel: *(Name of Carrier)*		SSN:
Name of Naturalization Certifications:		Certificate #:	Naturalization Date:
Address at the time of Naturalization:		Court and Location:	

Form G-639 (Rev. 7-25-00)N

Form G-639 can get you passenger and naturalization papers from the INS.

Act of June 29, 1906 as amended May 25, 1932

UNITED STATES OF AMERICA

No. 169320

PETITION FOR CITIZENSHIP

the US District Court of Eastern District of NY at Brooklyn, NY

Nathan Fine, hereby filed, respectfully shows:

residence is 1857 - 55th St., Brooklyn, NY (2) My occupation is tailor

born in Minsk Russia on June 11, 1876 My race is Hebrew

my intention to become a citizen of the United States on June 1, 1927 in the US District

Eastern District, at Brooklyn, NY

married. The name of my wife is Ida

on December 1898 at Vilna Russia; she was

Vilna Russia on July 10, 1876; entered the United States

New York, NY on June 1903 for permanent residence therein, and now

1857 - 55th St., Brooklyn, NY I have 5 children, and the name, date,

birth, and place of residence of each of said children are as follows: Meyer, Sept. 15, 1899, Vilna, Poland, resides in Dover, NJ. David, Feb. 4, 1904, New York, NY and resides in Dover, NJ. , Sept. 12, 1907; Anna, Apr. 4, 1909; Sarah, May 25, 1911. Last three born York, NY and reside at 1857 - 55th St., Brooklyn, NY.

residence was Minsk Russia I emigrated to the United States of

Rotterdam Holland My lawful entry for permanent residence in the United States

New York, NY under the name of Nochim Shawise

June 30, 1901 on the vessel Potsdam

believer in or opposed to organized government or a member of or affiliated with any organization or body of persons teaching disbelief in or opposed government. I am not a polygamist nor a believer in the practice of polygamy. I am attached to the principles of the Constitution of the United States to the good order and happiness of the United States. It is my intention to become a citizen of the United States and to renounce absolutely and and fidelity to any foreign prince, potentate, state, or sovereignty, and particularly to

State of Russia

at this time I am a subject (or citizen), and it is my intention to reside permanently in the United States. (8) I am able to speak the English language. continuously in the United States of America for the term of five years at least immediately preceding the date of this petition, to wit, since

June 30, 1901 and in the County of Kings

next preceding the date of this petition, since January 1, 1925, being a residence within said county of at least preceding the date of this petition.

not heretofore made petition for citizenship: Number , on

and such petition was denied by that Court for the following reasons and causes, to wit:

denial has since been cured or removed.

and made a part of this, my petition for citizenship, are my declaration of intention to become a citizen of the United States, and the affidavits of the two verifying witnesses required by law. petitioner, pray that I may be admitted a citizen of the United States of America, and that my name be changed to

petitioner being duly sworn, depose and say that I have read this petition and know the contents thereof; that the same is true of except as to matters herein stated to be alleged upon information and belief, and that as to those matters I believe it to be true; and that this petition my full, true name.

x Nathan Fine
(Complete and true signature of petitioner)

AFFIDAVITS OF WITNESSES

Sobsey, occupation housewife

1756 - 58th St., Brooklyn, NY, and

Goldstein, occupation salesman

1857 - 55th St., Brooklyn, NY

duly, and respectively sworn, deposes and says that he is a citizen of the United States of America; that he has personally known and has been United States with

Nathan Fine, the petitioner above mentioned, since ~~June 1, 1927~~

knowledge the petitioner has resided in the United States continuously preceding the date of filing this petition, of which this affidavit is a date last mentioned, and at Brooklyn, in the County of Kings

the above-entitled petition is made, continuously since June 1, 1927, and that he has personal knowledge that the all such periods has been a person of good moral character, attached to the principles of the Constitution of the United States, and well disposed to the good order and happiness of the United States, and that in his opinion the petitioner is in every way qualified to be admitted a citizen of the United States.

Sobsey (Signature of witness) x Cecil Goldstein (Signature of witness)

sworn to before me by the above-named petitioner and witnesses in the office of the Clerk of said Court at Brooklyn, NY

day of July, Anno Domini 1932 I hereby certify that

declaration of intention No.

of such petitioner, has been by me filed with, attached to, and made a part of this petition on this date.

(SEAL)

Deputy Clerk.

The Freedom of Information Act provided me with Nathan Fine's Petition of Naturalization, indicating he traveled under the name of Nathan Shawise. Apparently, he used his wife's cousin's ticket.

ber, Petition Number, and Name on Naturalization Certificate. If the search takes more than two hours and duplication of documents is for more than 100 pages, there is a charge if fees exceed $14.

NARA's Freedom of Information Act reading room is located at the National Archives at College Park (Archives II) facility. To file an FOIA request for NARA operational records of any NARA organizational unit nationwide except the Office of the Inspector General, write to: NARA FOIA Officer, National Archives at College Park, 8601 Adelphi Road, Room 4400, College Park, MD 20740-6001.

Send your completed G-639 form to:

INS
FOIA
Room 5304 425 I Street, NW
Washington DC 20536

Social Security—The Social Security Death Index from the U.S. Department of Health and Human Services is available to the public through the FOIA. You can access the index using Internet sites, such as <www.myfamily.com>. However, you will probably want to request the actual social security application (using Form SS-5) from the FOIA Officer. The form will include the applicant's address, date and place of birth, father's name and mother's maiden name, sex, race, and in some cases, employment information. The original application is a registration for future benefits. To receive a copy of the original application, you must supply proof of death (usually in the form of a death certificate) and your relationship to the deceased. The fee is $7.00 if you include the decedent's social security number and $16.50 if you don't.

To request copies of applications for social security numbers (Form SS-5) for people who are deceased, address your request to:

QUICK TIP

Genealogist Harriet Rudnit of Glenview, Illinois, says, "I submitted an FOIA form to get my grandfather's naturalization papers. So far they haven't found anything, but the request was honored. Be sure to ask for all documents—petition for naturalization, naturalization, and any other relevant papers when you write."

Form SS-5
TREASURY DEPARTMENT
INTERNAL REVENUE SERVICE

U. S. SOCIAL SECURITY ACT
APPLICATION FOR ACCOUNT NUMBER

135-09-8790

Nathan (EMPLOYEE'S FIRST NAME) Harold (MIDDLE NAME) Seifer (LAST NAME) 160
(MARRIED WOMEN: GIVE MAIDEN FIRST NAME, MAIDEN LAST NAME, AND HUSBAND'S LAST NAME)

46 Goldsmith Av. (STREET AND NUMBER) 3. Newark (POST OFFICE) N.J. (STATE)

Metropolitan Life Ins. Co. (BUSINESS NAME OF PRESENT EMPLOYER) 5. 1172 Raymond Blvd. Newark, N.J. (BUSINESS ADDRESS OF PRESENT EMPLOYER)

45 (AGE AT LAST BIRTHDAY) 7. Mar. 3 14,1891 (DATE OF BIRTH: (MONTH) (DAY) (YEAR) (SUBJECT TO LATER VERIFICATION)) 8. Austria (PLACE OF BIRTH)

Solomon Seifer (FATHER'S FULL NAME) 10. Anna Lindeman (MOTHER'S FULL MAIDEN NAME)

SEX: MALE M FEMALE (CHECK (✓) WHICH) 12. COLOR: WHITE W NEGRO OTHER (CHECK (✓) WHICH) (SPECIFY) 1-1

IF REGISTERED WITH THE U.S. EMPLOYMENT SERVICE, GIVE NUMBER OF REGISTRATION CARD --

IF YOU HAVE PREVIOUSLY FILLED OUT A CARD LIKE THIS, STATE -- (PLACE) (DATE)

Nov. 25, 1936 (DATE SIGNED) 16. Nathan H. Seifer (EMPLOYEE'S SIGNATURE, AS USUALLY WRITTEN)

DETACH ALONG THIS LINE

Form SS-5 provides your family member's original Social Security application, such as this one for my grandmother's cousin, Nathan Seifer (born as Seife).

Social Security Administration Office of
Central Records
Operations FOIA Workgroup
P.O. Box 17772
300 N. Greene Street
Baltimore, Maryland 21290

Mark both the envelope and its contents: "FREEDOM OF INFORMATION REQUEST" or "INFORMATON REQUEST." The SSA advises not to include a return envelope.

Military Service—The public has the right to access certain military service information without the veteran's authorization or that of next-of-kin. This includes: name, service number, rank, dates of service, awards and decorations, city/town and state of last known address, including date of the address. If the veteran is deceased, information can include place of birth, geographic location of death, and place of burial. There are two caveats to bear in mind: (1) the National Personnel Records Center places emphasis on providing information for veteran benefits, not on genealogical searches; and (2) a 1973 fire destroyed millions of military records and damaged millions more. Eighty percent of Army records for 1912-1959 is gone as is 60 percent of Air Force records for 1947-1963.

Using Form 180, which you can download from <www.nara.gov/regional/mpr.html>, you can request twentieth century service records for soldiers serving in the U.S. armed forces from the National Personnel Records Center, 9700 Page Boulevard, St. Louis, MO 63132.

Federal Bureau of Investigation—Under the FOIA, you can request information from the FBI. If you're looking for information on significant historic events, celebrities, or gangsters, you can download files from the FBI's electronic reading room.

QUICK HIT
The electronic reading room can be accessed through the Internet at <www.nara.gov/foia/readroom.html>.

Standard Form 180 (Rev. 3-99)
Prescribed by NARA (36 CFR 1228.162(a))

Authorized for local reproduction
Previous edition unusable

OMB No. 3095-0029 Expires 7/31/2002

REQUEST PERTAINING TO MILITARY RECORDS

To ensure the best possible service, please thoroughly review the instructions at the bottom before filling out this form. Please print clearly or type. If you need more space, use plain paper.

SECTION I - INFORMATION NEEDED TO LOCATE RECORDS (Furnish as much as possible.)

1. NAME USED DURING SERVICE (Last, first, and middle)	2. SOCIAL SECURITY NO.	3. DATE OF BIRTH	4. PLACE OF BIRTH

5. SERVICE, PAST AND PRESENT (For an effective records search, it is important that ALL service be shown below.)

	BRANCH OF SERVICE	DATES OF SERVICE		CHECK ONE		SERVICE NUMBER DURING THIS PERIOD (If unknown, please write unknown)
		DATE ENTERED	DATE RELEASED	OFFICER	ENLISTED	
a. ACTIVE SERVICE						
b. RESERVE SERVICE						
c. NATIONAL GUARD						

6. IS THIS PERSON DECEASED? If "YES" enter the date of death.
☐ NO ☐ YES ______

7. IS (WAS) THIS PERSON RETIRED FROM MILITARY SERVICE?
☐ YES ☐ NO

SECTION II - INFORMATION AND/OR DOCUMENTS REQUESTED

1. **REPORT OF SEPARATION** (DD Form 214 or equivalent). This contains information normally needed to verify military service. A copy may be sent to the veteran, the deceased veteran/s next of kin, or other persons or organizations if authorized in Section III, below. NOTE: If more than one period of service was performed, even in the same branch, there may be more than one Report of Separation. Be sure to show EACH year that a Report of Separation was issued, for which you need a copy.

☐ An **UNDELETED** Report of Separation is requested for the year(s) ______

This normally will be a copy of the full separation document including such sensitive items as the character of separation, authority for separation, reason for separation, reenlistment eligibility code, separation (SPD/SPN) code, and dates of time lost. An undeleted version is ordinarily required to determine eligibility for benefits.

☐ A **DELETED** Report of Separation is requested for the year(s) ______

The following information will be deleted from the copy sent: authority for separation, reason for separation, reenlistment eligibility code, separation (SPD/SPN) code, and for separations after June 30, 1979, character of separation and dates of time lost.

2. **OTHER INFORMATION AND/OR DOCUMENTS REQUESTED** ______

3. **PURPOSE** (OPTIONAL - An explanation of the purpose of the request is strictly voluntary. Such information may help the agency answering this request to provide the best possible response and will in no way be used to make a decision to deny the request.) ______

SECTION III - RETURN ADDRESS AND SIGNATURE

1. **REQUESTER IS**

☐ Military service member or veteran identified in Section I, above
☐ Legal guardian (must submit copy of court appointment)
☐ Next of kin of deceased veteran ______ (relation)
☐ Other (specify) ______

2. **SEND INFORMATION/DOCUMENTS TO**
(Please print or type. See instruction 3, below.)

Name ______
Street ______
City ______

3. **AUTHORIZATION SIGNATURE REQUIRED** (See instruction 2, below.)
I declare (or certify, verify, or state) under penalty of perjury under the laws of the United States of America that the information in this Section III is true and correct.

Signature of Requester (Please do not print.) ______
Date of this request ______ Daytime phone ( )
E-mail address ______

This form is available at *http://www.nara.gov/regional/mprsf180.html* on the National Archives and Records Administration Web Site

Standard Form 180 can get you military service records from the National Personnel Records Center in St. Louis.

From the FBI's electronic reading room at <http://foia.fbi.gov/room.htm> you can click on a series of names and events and download FBI files. You can choose from a consolidated alphabetical list, a list of famous people, gangsters, historical events, and more.

Says Memphis, Tennessee, researcher Richard Wanderman, Jr., "I was recently able to acquire and download the FBI file (actually, 32 downloads) of Benjamin "Bugsy" Siegel, who is the first cousin of my great-grand-aunt's husband. In it, I was able to discover his parents' names and a few other things. I know it's a bit weird, but I was able to get his FBI record due to the FOIA."

Hilary Henkin of Atlanta, Georgia, used the FOIA to request FBI records as well. She reports, "Family lore says one of my relatives was watched by the FBI for many years because of his political beliefs. I wrote to the FBI for a copy of his file, under the FOIA. About six months later, I received a letter telling me that those records had been destroyed as per normal policy. I appealed the decision and recently received a second letter that the records had indeed been destroyed."

Patience Is a Virtue

Though the 1996 amendments require agencies to fulfill requests within a 10 to 20 day period, researchers are aware that this deadline is not always met. Says Carol Skydell, "The Social Security Administration has never met the legal requirement of getting back to me within the allowable time, but they do get back, eventually."

Worth the Wait

Harry Stein of Tucson, Arizona, sums up the benefits of pursuing federal agencies for information under the FOIA. "I define success as getting what I asked for if it was available. If it was not available, I received a complete explanation. Most agencies have a Freedom of Information Act office to execute Freedom of Information Act requests. I have used it with the military services, Immigration and Naturalization Service, and several federal courts. Many others have recovered unclassified information from the FBI."

While your request may not provide the information you want, as in Henkin's example, it's certainly worth the price of a stamp or a quick look online.

5 Passenger and Naturalization Records: Crossing to the "Other Side"

Great Uncle Hillel Meyer was the first Krasner family member to leave Russia and come to America. He left to avoid conscription into the Russian Army. He traveled from Hamburg to New York in 1896 and went to Newark, New Jersey, to join his maternal cousins, the Dvorkins. Two years later, Meyer's sister, Chaike, followed but traveled from Rotterdam. The year after that, my 19-year old grandfather also came through Rotterdam. My great-grandparents, Mordechai and Breina, and their daughter, Hesia, completed the migration in 1901 aboard the *S.S. Statendam* from Rotterdam. Mordechai and Breina left behind two married daughters and their families.

My maternal grandmother traveled on the North German Lloyd ship, *S.S. George Washington,* with her mother, aunt, and cousins from Bremen to New York. The ship was one of the last steamers to make the Atlantic journey in 1914 before World War I. It wasn't long before my grandmother and one of her cousins were seasick. My great-grandmother made them both a bed on the stairs of the deck from the pillows and *perineh* (feather bed) they brought with them from Poland. My great-grandmother desperately wanted them to recuperate. She was afraid that the girls might be deported if they were sick upon their arrival in America.

New York Harbor, with the Statue of Liberty and Ellis Island, epitomizes immigrant entry. In the 100-year span between 1820 and 1920, nearly 24 million immigrants sailed or steamed into the United States through the New York harbor. The remainder went to Boston (2 million); Baltimore (1.5 million); Philadelphia (1.2 million); New Orleans (710,000); San Francisco (500,000); Key West, Florida (130,000); Portland-Falmouth, Maine (120,000); Galveston, Texas (110,000) or other ports like Passamaquoddy, Maine; New Bedford, Massachusetts; Providence, Rhode Island; and Charleston, South Carolina. Others still headed to one of Canada's two main ports: Halifax, Nova Scotia or Quebec City in Quebec.

Ira Glazier, Director of the Center for Immigration Research at the Temple-Balch Institute in Philadelphia, told me during a 1999 interview, "People went places where they had relatives or townspeople. There wasn't a great deal of choice. Destinations were determined by the network, by the chain."

Ship passenger records literally mark the rite of passage. They provide insights into family relationships, physical characteristics, area of settlement, ancestral town, and more. The records were developed at the port of embarkation and therefore represent, for the most part, original surnames.

How do you go about finding passenger records for your family?

Ports of Emigration and Their Passenger Records

Hamburg—Hamburg-Amerika Line

The Hamburg Passenger lists, accessible through the LDS Family History Centers (see Locality index, Hamburg, Germany—"Emigration and Immigration"), represent the most significant collection of departure lists—486 rolls of microfilm. They cover 1850-1934 with a break between 1915-1919. Nearly one-third of all central and eastern European immigrants appear on these lists. Indices simplify the search process. Passengers either took the direct route from Hamburg to America or indirect, cheaper routes through other European ports like Glasgow in Ireland or Southampton in England where they'd have to change ships.

QUICK TIP
Because the lists were compiled in German, you may need to search for Germanic spellings of your surnames. For instance, I needed to look for Dworkin instead of Dvorkin.

Direct passage indices include a consolidated 15-year index for the period 1856-1871 and then as part of the "regular indices," 1854-1934. The regular index is arranged by year or part of a year.

Indices for the indirect route cover the years 1854-1910 and are arranged by year and by the first letter of the surname. Review these carefully as parts of an alphabetical list may show up elsewhere where there was more room to record.

QUICK HIT

You can begin to access emigration lists online at: <www.hamburg.de/LinkToYourRoots/english/welcome.htm>. As of November 2000, only the years 1890-1893 are included in the site's database.

Bremen—Nord-deutscher Lloyd (North German Lloyd)

Many emigrants from Austria-Hungary and Poland embarked on their journeys to America from the port of Bremen in northern Germany. A bombing raid on the city destroyed many of the original records, however some do remain. The LDS church has filmed some abstracts and indices, listed under "Namenskartei aus den 'Bremer Schifflister' 1904-1914." Also, some lists are available online at <db.genealogy.net/maus/gate/shiplists. cgi?lang=en>.

Rotterdam—Holland-America

If your ancestors came to America on ships named the Amsterdam, Edam, Leerdam, Haardam, Niew Amersterdam, Noordam, Pennland, Potsdam, Ryndam, Rotterdam, Spaarndam, Statendam, Veendam, Volendam, Warszawa, Werkendam, Westernland, or Zaandam during the years 1900-1940, you'll find the often-overlooked Holland-America Line Passenger lists/Rotterdam Departure lists helpful. JewishGen offers an InfoFile on these records at <www.jewishgen.org/infofiles/hollam.txt>.

Other frequent ports for Jewish immigrants included Southampton and Liverpool in England, Cherbourg and LeHavre in France, and Antwerp in Belgium.

Canadian ports offered safe haven for many Jewish immigrants, especially when the American quota system was put in place in 1924. By 1895, the United States and Canada established a system of joint inspection of immigrants crossing by land. U.S. commissioners of immigration were placed in Quebec, Halifax, Montreal, Victoria, and Vancouver. A popular crossing point was St. Albans, Vermont, where immigrants from Montreal and Quebec were processed. My great-uncle Moshe Aron Pryzant left Zaręby Koscielne, Poland, in 1923, immigrated to Montreal, crossed into America through St. Albans in 1927, and made his way down to New York to join my grandfather.

The Hamburg-Amerika Line's S.S. Kaiserin Auguste Victoria.

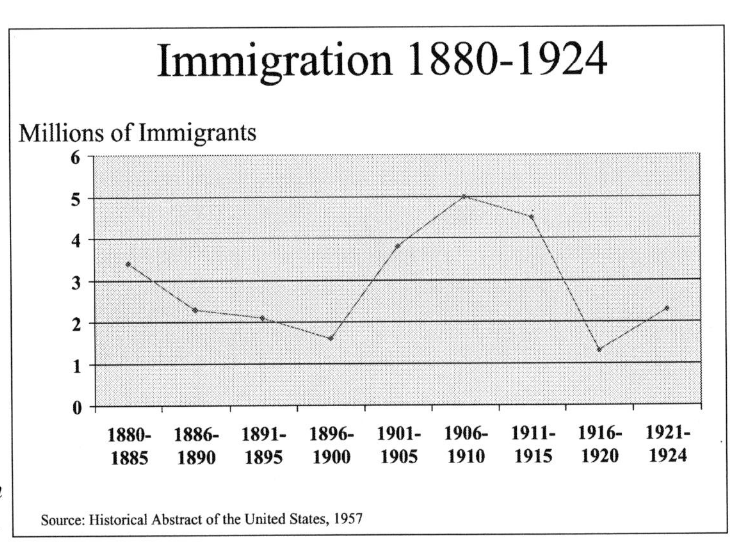

The Mass Wave of Immigration 1880-1924.

Ports of Immigration and Their Passenger Records

Beginning in 1820, the U.S. government required ship captains to submit a passenger list or manifest for passengers brought aboard at any foreign port and arriving at an American port. The National Archives holds the lists in microfilm and original form. The following port arrivals are indexed:

Baltimore	1820–1952
Boston	1848–1891
	1902–1920
New Orleans	1853–1952
New York	1820–1846
	1897–1902
	1902–1943
	1944–1948
Philadelphia	1800–1948
San Francisco	1893–1934
Miscellaneous ports	1820–1924

New York

Most American Jewish families with eastern European roots can point to immigrant ancestors who made the crossing during the heyday of immigration between 1880–1920, spurred by Russian pogroms, promises of economic prosperity (the *Goldene Medina*), and escape from Russian Army conscription that could last 25 years.

Indices. You will need to learn and use the Soundex coding system (see sidebar) used by the U.S. government to group similar sounding names together.

You can access these indices through the microfilm holdings of the Church of Jesus Christ of Latter-day Saints (LDS) at your local Family History Center, through the National Archives, at major public libraries like the New York Public Library (see U.S. History, Local History and Genealogy Division), and from Heritage Quest.

These indices take the form of microfilmed index cards. The early cards that form the 1897-1902 index are arranged in alphabetical order by surname and then alphabetical by given

QUICK HIT

Ellis Island Records

Searching New York passenger records has never been easier. Using the prompts at <www.ellisislandrecords.com>, you can search for your ancestors and click on to see the ship's manifest. You may need to try several name variations. You will still most likely want to work with the National Archives to get copies of appropriate manifests.

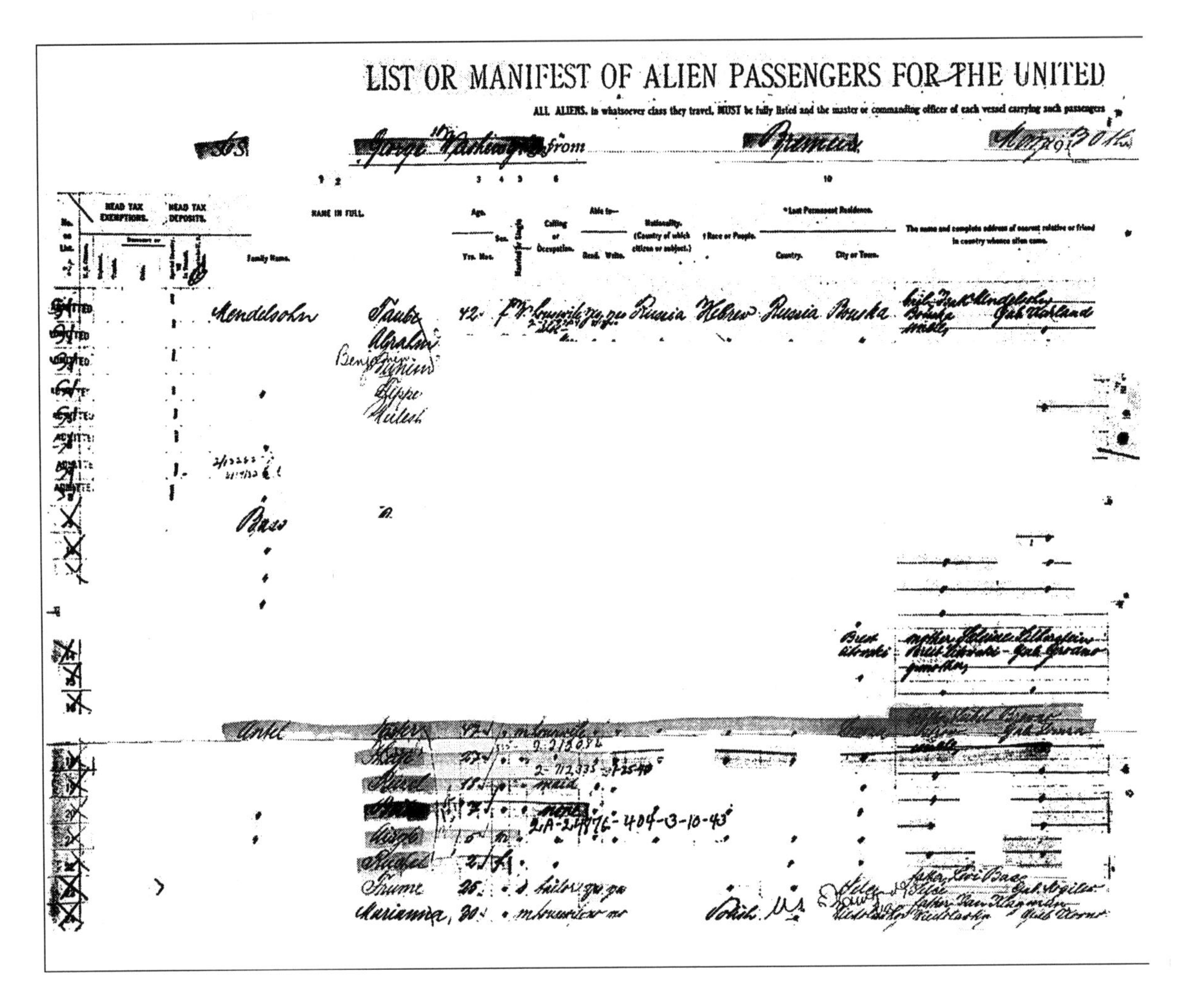

LIST OR MANIFEST OF ALIEN PASSENGERS FOR THE UNITED

ALL ALIENS, in whatsoever class they travel, MUST be fully listed and the master or commanding officer of each vessel carrying such passengers

S.S. Georg Washington from Bremen

HEAD TAX EXEMPTIONS. HEAD TAX DEPOSITS. NAME IN FULL. Family Name. Age. Yrs. Mos. Sex. Calling or Occupation. Able to— Read. Write. Nationality. (Country of which citizen or subject.) †Race or People. *Last Permanent Residence. Country. City or Town. The name and complete address of nearest relative or friend in country whence alien came.

Mendelsohn Taube 42 f Russia Hebrew Russia

Reizl Entel traveled on the S.S. George Washington *from Bremen to New York,*

STATES IMMIGRATION OFFICER AT PORT OF ARRIVAL.

must upon arrival deliver lists thereof to the immigration officer. This (white) sheet is for the listing of STEERAGE PASSENGERS ONLY.

Arriving at Port of New York, JUN 08 191[illegible], 191

111

SUPPLEMENTAL INFORMATION REQUIRED BY NATURALIZATION ACT APPROVED JUNE 29, 1906.

12 No. on List.	13 Final Destination. (Intended future permanent residence.) State.	City or Town.	14 Whether having a ticket to such final destination.	15 By whom was passage paid? (Whether alien paid his own passage, whether paid by any other person, or by any corporation, society, municipality, or government.)	16 Whether in possession of $50, and if less, how much?	17 Whether ever before in the United States; and if so, when and where? If Yes— Year or period of years.	Where?	18 Whether going to join a relative or friend; and if so, what relative or friend, and his name and complete address?	19	20 Whether a Polygamist.	21 Whether an Anarchist.	22	23 Condition of Health, Mental and Physical.	24 Deformed or Crippled. Nature, length of time, and cause.	25 Height. Feet.	Inches.	26 Complexion.	27 Color of— Hair.	Eyes.	28 Marks of Identification.	29 Place of Birth. Country.	City or Town.
1.	N.Y.	New-York	yes	son	200 no	—	—	son [illegible] 56 [illegible], New York brother	No	No	No	No	good	No	5	2	fair	blk	br	none	Russia	[illegible]
2.	"	"	"	brother	—	—	—		"	"	"	"	"	"	5	3	"	"	"	"	"	"
3.	"	"	"	"	—	—	—		"	"	"	"	"	"	5	2	"	"	"	"	"	"
4.	"	"	"	"	—	—	—		"	"	"	"	"	"	4	6	"	"	"	"	"	"
5.	"	"	"	"	—	—	—		"	"	"	"	"	"	4	5	"	"	"	"	"	"
6.	"	"	"	"	—	—	—		"	"	"	"	"	"	4	2	"	"	"	"	"	"
7.	"	"	"	"	—	—	—		"	"	"	"	"	"	—	—	"	"	"	"	"	"
8.	[illegible]				—	—	—	husband Samuel [illegible]	"	"	"	"	"	"	—	—	"	"	"	"	"	"
9.	D.C.	Washington	"	husband [illegible]	—	—	—	[illegible], Washington	"	"	"	"	"	"	5	1	"	br	br	"	"	[illegible]
10.	"	"	"	father	—	—	—	father	"	"	"	"	"	"	4	1	"	"	"	"	"	"
11.	"	"	"	"	—	—	—		"	"	"	"	"	"	—	—	"	"	"	"	"	"
12.	"	"	"	"	—	—	—		"	"	"	"	"	"	—	—	"	"	"	"	"	"
13.	"	"	"	"	—	—	—	husband [illegible]	"	"	"	"	"	"	—	—	"	"	"	"	"	"
14.	N.Y.	New-York	"	husband	—	—	—	[illegible], New York	"	"	"	"	"	"	4	11	"	"	"	"	"	[illegible]
15.	"	"	"	father	—	—	—	father	"	"	"	"	"	"	4	—	"	"	"	"	"	"
16.	"	"	"	"	—	—	—	[illegible], New York	"	"	"	"	"	"	4	1[illegible]	"	"	"	"	"	[illegible]
17.	"	"	"	[illegible]	—	—	—	husband	"	"	"	"	"	"	[illegible]		"	"	"	"	"	"
18.	"	"	"	husband	—	—	—	brother	[illegible]						5	[illegible]	"	"	"	"	"	"
19.	"	"	"	brother	—	—	—		"	"	"	"	"	"	5	2	"	"	"	"	"	"
20.	"	"	"	father	—	—	—	father	"	"	"	"	"	"	—	—	"	"	"	"	"	"
21.	"	"	"	"	—	—	—		"	"	"	"	"	"	—	—	"	"	"	"	"	"
22.	"	"	"	"	—	—	—	brother [illegible] 1551	"	"	"	"	"	"	—	—	"	"	"	"	"	[illegible]
23.	D.C.	Washington	"	brother	—	—	—	33 St. N.W. Washington	"	"	"	"	"	"	5	3	"	"	"	"	"	[illegible]
24.	Mass.	East Cambridge	"	husband	[illegible]	yes	[illegible]	husband [illegible], East Cambridge, Mass.	"	"	"	"	"	"	5	2	"	"	bl	"	"	[illegible]
25.	"	"	"	father	—	"	[illegible]	father	"	"	"	"	"	"	—	—	"	"	"	"	"	[illegible]

one of the last German steamers to arrive in the U.S. before World War I.

Name in Full	Age Years	Age Months	Sex	Calling or Occupation	Country of which they are Citizens	Native Country	Intended Destination or Location, State or Territory	State of passengers other than Cabin, whether Citizens of the United States	Transient, In Transit or intending protracted sojourn	Location of Compartment or Space occupied forward, amidships or aft	Number of pieces of Baggage	Port of Embarkation	Date and Cause of Death
Katharina [illegible]	11½		f	none		Russian	Elisabethpol	no	[illegible]	D		Hamburg	
[illegible] Kirvengart	20		m	merchant 2-109329		German	N.Y.	"	"	a		"	2 – 1
Georg Ury	22		"	"		"	"	"	"	"		"	
Faie Pikus	18		f	none		Russian	"	"	"	C		"	18 – 11
Antonina [illegible]	20		"	"		"	Pittsburg	"	"	"	1	"	
[illegible]	17		"	"		"	N.Y.	"	"	"		"	
Leiser [illegible]	18		m	sailor		"	"	"	"	B	1	"	
Bina Aronowitz	23		f	none		"	"	"	"	D		"	
Chame Dusher	11		"	"		"	"	"	"	C		"	
Schmul "	45		m	weaver		"	"	"	"	C		"	
Claire [illegible]	45		f	none		"	"	"	"	"		"	
Motel "	16		m	"		"	"	"	"	"		"	
Leiser "	7		"	"		"	"	"	"	"		"	
Taube "	6		f	"		"	"	"	"	"		"	
[illegible]	17		m	shoemaker		"	"	"	"	B		"	
Hillel Krassner	22		"	"		"	"	"	"	"		"	
Adam Kaczorowsky	18		"	labourer		"	Bayonne City	"	"	"		"	
Barbara "	16		f	none		"	"	"	"	D		"	
Anton Pinkewitz	21		m	labourer		"	Chicago	"	"	B		"	
[illegible]	21		m	"		"	Buffalo	"	"			"	

Great Uncle Hillel Meyer Krasner took the direct route from Hamburg to America in 1896. The index indicated he was from Minsk, even though the ship's manifest did not.

name. Many of them are very difficult to read. On these cards you'll find information on name, age, number of family members traveling together, group, list, sex, citizenship, steamer name, steamer line, and date of arrival in New York. Depending on the year, the fields may appear differently from card to card. Between 1897 and 1908, the cards used similar formats. But beginning in 1909, cards began to use a somewhat truncated system.

Timeframe	Format
1909-1911	Name, LN (Line), PG (page), VOL (volume), Vessel, Day/Mo/Year
1911-	Name, Age/Sex, LN, PG, VOL
1937-	Name, Age/Sex, Mo/year, LN, PG
1940s	Code, Vessel, Day/Mo/Year Name, Age/Sex, CR#
1940s	Code, Vessel, Day/Mo/Year Name, Age/Sex, VOL

Ship Manifests. Not much genealogical information appeared on ship manifests before 1893. But you can get the date and place of embarkation and arrival, the passenger's name, and country of origin.

After 1893, questions posed to the passenger included: name, age, sex, marital status, occupation, ability to read and write, nationality, last residence, seaport for landing in the United States, final destination in the United States, by whom was passage paid, whether the person had been in the United States before, name and address of relative the passenger was going to join in the United States, and condition of health. After 1906, the questioning expanded again to include name and complete address of the nearest relative or friend in the country the passenger left, and his height, color of hair and eyes, identifying marks, and country and city of birth.

Naturalization Records

I will never forget the trip my father and I took to the Bergen County Courthouse to get a copy of his mother's naturalization papers. My father had kept her Certificate of Citizenship

QUICK TIP

New York Passenger Lists are available from Heritage Quest and through the LDS Family History Centers. Major collections include:

T-519—Index to Passenger Lists, 16 Jun 1897-30 Jun 1902 (115 rolls)

T-621—Soundex Index, 1 Jul 1902-31 Dec 1943 (755 rolls)

T-612—Book Indexes to Passenger Lists, 1906-1942 by ship line (807 rolls)

Available finding aids at the Archives will help you locate the specific reel number within the series that you need.

DEFINITION

For genealogical purposes, dates are usually written as day, three-letter abbreviation for month, and four-digit year, such as "16 Jun 1897." If you adopt this method, you'll never have to wonder about the day, month or century with which a particular year was associated.

DEFINITION

"Group" means page number of the ship's manifest.

"List" means line number on a page. The line number should not exceed 30.

DEFINITION

You'll typically see a column header of "Race" on ship manifests. That column may say either "Hebrew" or "Mosaic" to indicate Jewish immigrants.

The S.S. Statendam *brought Mordechai and Breina Krasner to America in 1901.*

The American Line's S.S. St. Louis.

The Red Star Line's S.S.Vaderland *appears on the left and is compared to the historic Christopher Columbus ship, the* Santa Maria.

MANIFEST Port MONTREAL, CANADA AUGUST 15, 1927

Family name
PRYZANT

Given name
MOSES

Age 40 Yrs Mos Sex Male M. S. Occupation Presser Place of birth Corenby, Poland

Nationality Poland Race Hebrew Read Write Language or exemption Yiddish

Last permanent residence 3477 Colonial Ave., Montreal Destination Town New York State New York

Passage paid by Self Ever in U.S. No

Going to join Relationship Name Complete address
Father-in-law, Nehemnia Edel, 159 Monroe Street,

Purpose in coming and Time remaining in U.S. Permanent Canadian National 73325 Height 5 ft. 3 in. Complexion Medium Hair Brown Eyes Brown

Name and address of nearest relative or friend in country whence alien came
Wife, Rebecca, 3477 Colonial Avenue, Montreal

C.I.V. No. 181 Place of issue Montreal, P.Q. Polish Quota July 7, 1927

Seaport of landing Quebec Date of landing June, 1923 Name of S.S. Casandra

Recorded by Previously examined at Montreal, P.Q. Date 5-22-25 Previous disposition Quota Present disposition, P. K.

U.S. Department of Labor, Immigration Service

Great-uncle Morris Pryzant crossed into the United States from Canada at the popular St. Albans, Vermont entry point.

for years. We handed it to the clerk, who then disappeared into a back room. She returned with a huge book and showed us the Declaration of Intention ("first papers") and Petition for Naturalization. My father's eyes welled up when he saw his own name listed on the petition. He then told the clerk, "That's me!" The clerk could have cared less. But it was a very emotional moment for my father and me.

QUICK TIP
The 1920 Census records can give you an indication of whether your family member was naturalized. You'll typically see a column that uses a code of "Na" for Naturalized, "Pa," for first papers filed, and "Al" for Alien. You'll also find a year of naturalization.

Naturalization papers can provide a wealth of information, depending on the year recorded. In general, the later the year, the more information. My grandmother's 1927 Petition for Naturalization indicated her birthplace and date, name of the ship and its arrival date in New York, her husband's name, his birth and naturalization dates and places, their residence, their children and their children's birth dates and birthplaces. Names of witnesses can also be helpful in identifying close friends, neighbors, and family members. (An interesting sidenote: In her petition, my grandmother renounced citizenship to the Republic of Poland, when, in fact, the part of Galicia she was from was then located in Ukraine, U.S.S.R. When she had lived there herself, it was part of the Austro-Hungarian Empire.)

SEE ALSO
The sidebar on the Freedom of Information Act in Chapter 4 provides details on how to acquire records from the INS.

Before 1906, naturalizations could take place in any federal, state, county, or local court. There was no systematic approach to naturalization yet, so the information in these records varies greatly. In 1906, the federal government set up the Immigration and Naturalization Service. You can contact the INS in Washington to get a copy of your ancestor's naturalization papers.

You can pay a visit or write to the courthouse where you think the records may be filed. You can also check the National Archives branch in the region where your ancestor may have applied. In addition, check the LDS Family History Center Catalog locality section by [State, County]—"Naturalization and Citizenship."

Typically, an immigrant would wait five years before filing his or her first papers. Between 1855 and 1922, wives and children became citizens when the husband and father did. After 1922, women had to file their own papers.

Now that you know where your ancestors lived and when they arrived, it's time to dig deeper and explore European records.

ORIGINAL

12358

UNITED STATES OF AMERICA

PETITION FOR NATURALIZATION

To the Common Pleas Court of Bergen County at Hackensack, N. J.

The petition of Eror Krasner hereby filed, respectfully showeth:

First. My place of residence is 173 Ridge Rd., North Arlington, N. J.

Second. My occupation is Housewife

Third. I was born on the 9th day of May anno Domini 1893 at Koslov, Poland

Fourth. I emigrated to the United States from Rotterdam, Netherlands on or about the 15th day of August 1913, and arrived in the United States, at the port of New York on the 2nd day of September 1913, on the vessel Ryndam

Fifth. I declared my intention to become a citizen of the United States on the ... day of ... anno Domini ... Omitted Act Sept. 22, 1922

Sixth. I am married. My husband's name is Max ... he was born on the 20th day of May anno Domini 1876 Russia ... and now resides at with me.

Seventh. I have ... children, and the name, date, and place of birth, and place of residence of each of said children is as follows:
...ton, born Oct 31, 1919 at Newark, N.J., lives with me. Husband Nat. July 30, 1926 at Newark, N.J.
...rry " July 7, 1923 " N. Arlington, N.J. " " Height 5-3
...man " July 23, 1925 " " " " " " Hair Brown
Eyes Brown
Comp. Fair
Marks None

Eighth. I am not a disbeliever in or opposed to organized government or a member of or affiliated with any organization or body of persons teaching disbelief in or opposed to organized government. I am not a polygamist nor a believer in the practice of polygamy. I am attached to the principles of the Constitution of the United States, and it is my intention to become a citizen of the United States and to renounce absolutely and forever all allegiance and fidelity to any foreign prince, potentate, state, or sovereignty, and particularly to THE REPUBLIC OF POLAND of whom at this time I am a subject, and it is my intention to reside permanently in the United States.

Ninth. I am able to speak the English language.

Tenth. I have resided continuously in the United States of America for the term of five years at least immediately preceding the date of this petition, to wit, since the 2nd day of September anno Domini 1913, and in the State of New Jersey continuously next preceding the date of this petition, since the 19th day of May anno Domini 1918, being a residence within this State of at least one year next preceding the date of this petition.

Eleventh. I have not heretofore made petition for citizenship to any court.

Attached hereto and made a part of this petition are my declaration of intention to become a citizen of the United States and the certificate from the Department of Labor together with my affidavit and the affidavits of the two verifying witnesses thereto, required by law. Wherefore your petitioner prays that he may be admitted a citizen of the United States of America.

Era Krasner
(Complete and true signature of petitioner.)

Dated Act Sept. 22, 1922 V
Declaration of Intention No. ... and Certificate of Arrival from Department of Labor filed this 8th day of December, 1927

AFFIDAVITS OF PETITIONER AND WITNESSES

State of New Jersey
County of Bergen } ss:

The aforesaid petitioner being duly sworn, deposes and says that he is the petitioner in the above-entitled proceedings; that he has read the foregoing petition and knows the contents thereof; that the said petition is signed with his full, true name; that the same is true of his own knowledge, except as to matters therein stated to be alleged upon information and belief, and that as to those matters he believes it to be true.

Era Krasner
(Complete and true signature of petitioner.)

Robert Gordon, occupation Reporter, residing at Newark, N. J.
Dorcas M. Fleming, occupation Home Duties, residing at N. Arlington, N. J.

each being severally, duly, and respectively sworn, deposes and says that he is a citizen of the United States of America; that he has personally known Eror Krasner, the petitioner above mentioned, to have resided in the United States continuously preceding the date of filing his petition, since the 1st day of June anno Domini 1922, and in the State in which the above entitled application is made continuously since the 1st day of June anno Domini 1922; and that he has personal knowledge that the said petitioner is a person of good moral character, attached to the principles of the Constitution of the United States, and that the petitioner is in every way qualified, in his opinion, to be admitted a citizen of the United States.

Robert Gordon
(Signature of witness.)
Dorcas M. Fleming
(Signature of witness.)

Subscribed and sworn to before me by the above-named petitioner and witnesses in the office of the Clerk of said Court this 8th day December, anno Domini 1927

[SEAL]

James McIntosh, Clerk.
By Albert Sangiorgi, Deputy Clerk

"That's me!" exclaimed my father when he saw his name on his mother's Petition for Naturalization at the Bergen County Courthouse in Hackensack, New Jersey.

FOR MORE INFORMATION

Ellis Island Immigration Museum
<www.ellisisland.com>

The Mariners' Museum
100 Museum Drive
Newport News, VA 23606
<www.mariner.org>

The Steamship Historical Society of America
University of Baltimore
Baltimore, MD 21201
Photographs of ships.

Passenger Ships of Your Immigrant Ancestors
<www.kinshipsprints.com>

Ship Passage-Related Mailing Lists
Emigration-ships—a mailing list for anyone who wants to discuss the ships his or her ancestors arrived on or post passenger lists for any ships. To subscribe, send "subscribe emigration-ships" for mail mode or "subscribe emigration-ships-digest" for digest mode to <majordomo@genweb.net>.

IMMI-GRAND—for those attempting to do genealogical research whose grandparents or parents came to America after 1875. To subscribe, send "subscribe" to <immi-grand-l-request@rootsweb.com> (mail mode) or <immi-grand-d-request@rootsweb.com> (digest mode).

TheShips—for anyone interested in the ships on which our ancestors came. Subjects include emigration/immigration, ports of entry, ports of departure, ship descriptions and history, and passenger lists. You can search the ShipsList Digest Archive at <www.cimorelli.com/ShipsList/digest> to see if the ship you're interested in has been discussed. To subscribe, send "subscribe" to <theshipslist-l-request@rootsweb.com> (mail mode) or <theshipslist-d-request@rootsweb.com> (digest mode).

THE SOUNDEX CODING SYSTEM

In the 1930s, the U. S. federal government introduced a system for coding surnames based on sounds, appropriately called the Soundex. It assigned a numerical code for consonants and disregarded vowels. Consonants with similar sounds were grouped together. Surname codes consisted of the first letter of the name followed by three digits. If a surname had two consecutive letters that received the same numerical code, only one was used as in the example of my grandmother's name, Zuckerkandel, Z262. The "c" and the "k" would bear the same code of "2;" so only one was used.

Passenger arrival indices, naturalization record indices, and census records (1880-1920) rely on the Soundex system. It is not foolproof, though. For example, it doesn't group the sounds SH and SCH together, a problem for finding some German names. And the name you're researching may have been entered or read incorrectly, giving it a Soundex code you wouldn't know to look for. That was the case with the ship arrival record for my Zuckerkandel grandmother, whose name appeared as Zuckenkandel (Z252).

Many genealogical software programs have utilities that can easily Soundex code names for you. To code names from the JewishGen web site, go to <www.jewishgen.org/jos>.

Soundex Coding Guide

Code	Key Letters and Equivalents
1	b, p, f, v
2	c, s, k, g, j, q, s, z
3	d, t
4	l
5	m, n
6	r

The Daitch-Mokotoff (D-M) Soundex System

The Daitch-Mokotoff Soundex System was created by Jewish genealogy pioneers Randy Daitch and Gary Mokotoff to accommodate Slavic and Yiddish surnames not served well by the federal Soundex system. The system is used with specific Jewish genealogy search engines on JewishGen like the JewishGen Family Finder or for town names in reference works like Gary Mokotoff's and Sallyann Amdur Sack's gazetteer, *Where Once We Walked.*

The D-M Soundex system works similarly to the federal system in that it includes the first letter of the surname and then a numeric code. However, it uses six digits instead of three. For a detailed explanation of the exact coding system, see pages 419-420 in *Where Once We Walked* or the JewishGen Infofile at <www.jewishgen.org/infofile/soundex.txt>.

Both systems are used in Heritage Quest's Soundex Reference Guide which provides coding for over half a million surnames.

6 European Records

It was Presidential election day in 1996, and I was working from home since my son had no school. The phone rang late in the afternoon, and I was very surprised to learn that the caller was Yale Reisner of the Ronald S. Lauder Foundation Genealogy Project at the Jewish Historical Institute of Poland in Warsaw, Poland.

Yale had remembered my comment to him at the summer seminar on Jewish genealogy that my grandfather was from Zaromb. Now he was calling to tell me that the birth, marriage, and death records for the town had been found and were in the hands of the Jewish Historical Institute (JHI) in Warsaw. He asked if I were interested in learning more about the records. My response was a resounding yes!

I thought, what were the odds of my being home that day to receive such a call? Clearly this was *beshert*, pre-destined. Eventually, the Jewish Records Indexing – Poland project worked with the JHI to create an inventory of all the records so that the indices could be accessible through the Internet.

Many records were destroyed during the Holocaust, but many were not. So after you've exhausted American record sources, you may find yourself ready, willing, and able to begin researching European records. Thanks to books from Miriam Weiner, database projects like Jewish Records Indexing – Poland, and increased filming by the Mormons, finding and using European records has never been easier.

ON THE BOOKSHELF
Locating and Deciphering Polish Records
Miriam Weiner published a groundbreaking inventory of records in the Polish archival system in *Jewish Roots in Poland: Pages from the Past and Archival Inventories.* This is the definitive guide to archival holdings in Poland.

Once you have records in hand either from the LDS Family History Library films, the archives themselves, or from private researchers, you may find yourself a little intimidated. Not to worry—reading the records becomes less daunting when you use Judith Frazin's *A Translation Guide to 19th-Century Polish-Language Civil Registration Documents, Second Edition;* Jonathan Shea's *Russian Language Documents from Russian Poland;* or Jonathan Shea's and William Hoffman's *Following the Paper Trail: A Multilingual Translation Guide.*

QUICK HIT
Check the Jewish Records Indexing – Poland web site <www.jewishgen.org/jri-pl> for the most up-to-date news of towns in the database.

QUICK TIP
Direct Contact With the Archives and Local Offices
If you have a very targeted inquiry, let's say, you're interested in obtaining records for a handful of individuals, writing a letter yourself directly to the archives may be your best bet. Warren Blatt's "Writing to Poland: Vital Records in Poland" and "Vital Records in Poland" are available on the JewishGen web site <www.jewishgen.org>.

SEE ALSO
Jewish Records Indexing - Poland
For more in-depth information on this database, see Chapter 13.

The Pale of Settlement

Poland

Polish State Archives and Local Offices. Headquartered in Warsaw, the Polish State Archives consists of branch offices throughout Poland. One important arm of the archival system in Warsaw is the *Archiwum Glowne Akt Dawnych* or Archives of Ancient Acts (AGAD), which houses vital records more than 100 years old for towns formerly in Poland (eastern Galicia) and now in Ukraine. Local civil records offices, known as the *Urząd Stanu Cywilnego* or USC, generally hold vital records from the 1890s through the

AN OVERVIEW OF JEWISH VITAL RECORDS OF RUSSIAN POLAND*

YEARS	1808-1825	1826-1867	1868-1898	1899-1917	1918-1942
Type	Roman Catholic Civil Transcripts	Separate Jewish Registers			
Language	**Polish**		**Russian**		**Polish**
Location	Records older than 100 years are kept in regional branches of the Polish State Archives. Many of these records have been microfilmed by the Mormons (LDS)**, usually up to around 1865 or later for some towns.			Records less than 100 years old are typically kept in the town's Civil Records Office (Urząd Stanu Cywilnego).	
JRI-Poland Indexing Status	Limited***	Shtetl CO-OPs	Polish State Archives Project	Not Available	

* Applies to records in localities within the semi-autonomous region under Russian rule known as the Kingdom of Poland (Congress Poland). The area covered forms almost half of present-day Poland.

** May be viewed at LDS Family History Centers around the world. A list of available towns and types of records on microfilm may be downloaded from the JRI-Poland web site at <www.jewishgen.org/jri-pl>.

*** The majority of Jewish vital records in this period are patronymic (do not have surnames).

POLSKA RZECZPOSPOLITA LUDOWA POLSKA

URZĄD STANU CYWILNEGO w Ostrowi Mazowieckiej

Województwo ostrołęckie

Odpis skrócony aktu małżeństwa

I. DANE DOTYCZĄCE OSÓB ZAWIERAJĄCYCH MAŁŻEŃSTWO

	Mężczyzna	Kobieta
1. Nazwisko	ENTEL	DREWNO
2. Imię (imiona)	CHAIM	ESTERA TAUBA
3. Nazwisko rodowe	ENTEL	DREWNO
4. Data urodzenia	20 LAT	23 LATA
5. Miejsce urodzenia	OSTRÓW MAZOWIECKA	OSTRÓW MAZOWIECKA

II. DANE DOTYCZĄCE DATY I MIEJSCA ZAWARCIA MAŁŻEŃSTWA:

1. Data 2[illegible] września 1886 roku

2. Miejsce OSTRÓW MAZOWIECKA

III. NAZWISKO NOSZONE PO ZAWARCIU MAŁŻEŃSTWA

1. Mężczyzny ENTEL

2. Kobiety ENTEL

3. Dzieci ENTEL

IV. DANE DOTYCZĄCE RODZICÓW

A. Ojciec 1. Imię (imiona)	Ajzyk	Zelik
2. Nazwisko rodowe	Entel	Drewno
B. Matka 1. Imię (imiona)	Bejla	Chaja Rejza
2. Nazwisko rodowe	Szumowicz	Mularżewicz

V. ADNOTACJE O USTANIU LUB O UNIEWAŻNIENIU MAŁŻEŃSTWA:

Miejsce na opłatę skarbową

Poświadcza się zgodność powyższego odpisu z treścią aktu małżeństwa Nr 26/1886

Ostrów Mazowiecka data 1993-03-23

Z-ca KIEROWNIKA Urzędu Stanu Cywilnego

Wanda [illegible]

Pu-M-13 zam. 799/DW [illegible]
Sp-nia „Poligrafika" [illegible] (… szt.) f. A5

An extract from the USC office in Ostrów Mazowiecka, Poland: the 1886 marriage of my maternal great-grandparents, Chaim Entel and Estera Tauba Drewno. The beauty of the extract is that it's legible and typed. The downside is that it doesn't include the signatures and names of witnesses shown on the original record.

It took place in the town of Ostrow on the 11th/23rd day of August in the year 1863 at the 10th hour of the morning, came (presented himself) the Jew Zelek Herszkowicz Drewno, butcher, age 24 years, living here in Ostrow, together in the presence of witnesses, the Jews Leyzor Ickowicz Szkolnik, age 30, and Herszk Ejzykowicz Gelbort, day laborer, age 61 years, both living here in Ostrow, and showed us a female child born here in Ostrow on the 4th/16th day of the current month and year at 2 at night, from his wife, Chaja Rojza Majorowna, 20 years of age, to whom, during the religious ceremony, was given the name Estera Taube. This document was read to those present . . .

Translated by Barbara Krasner Khait, 28 Dec 1990

Use of the narrative style: the 1863 birth record of my maternal great-grandmother, Estera Tauba Drewno, Ostrów Mazowiecka, Poland.

1940s. Theoretically, records that have aged beyond 100 years are transferred to one of the Polish State Archives branches.

Naczelna Dyrekcja Archiwów Państwowych
00-950 Warszawa
skr. Poczt. 1005
ul. Długa 6
POLAND

Archiwum Główne Akt Dawnych (AGAD)
00-263 Warszawa
ul. Długa 7
POLAND

According to noted expert Miriam Weiner, a unique USC office in Warsaw holds books of Jewish vital records from eastern Galicia, dating from the late 1890s to 1943, when registration ceased. Access to the Jewish holdings is restricted by law, but research requests for specific records are permitted.

Civil registration of births, marriages, and deaths in what was then called Russian Poland (that part of Poland annexed by Russia during the Partitioning of Poland) began in 1808. Records used the Napoleonic format—a narrative style with very flowery and formal language. Before 1826, Jewish registrations were included with those of Roman Catholics and all other religions. Beginning in 1826, each religious community registered vital events separately. From 1808 through 1867, records were written in Polish; afterwards, they were written in Russian until 1918 when Poland re-emerged. Alphabetical indices often appear after the records and serve as a useful search aid.

Former Soviet Union

State Archives and Local Offices of the former Soviet Union. State archives exist for areas of the former Soviet Union in Ukraine, Belarus, Lithuania, etc. Local town hall records are housed at *Otdel Zapisi Aktov Grazhdanskogo Sostoyaniya* or the ZAGS office. In Ukraine, for instance, these offices are under the jurisdiction of the Ministry of Justice and each local ZAGS office reports to an *oblast* (administrative division or province) ZAGS archive. By law, the metrical books are retained in the ZAGS offices for a period of

LIETUVOS RESPUBLIKA
VILNIAUS MIESTO SAVIVALDYBĖS
CIVILINĖS METRIKACIJOS SKYRIUS

Nr. 6172

1997 m. rugsėjo mėn 23 d.

GIMIMO PAŽYMA

Pažymima, kad pil. Chana Bastunska
(vardas, pavardė)

gimė 1938 m. gruodžio mėn. 11 d.

Apie tai 1938 m. gruodžio mėn. 17 d. civilinės būklės aktų įrašų knygoje įrašyta Nr. 85

Tėvai:

tėvas Jankel Bastunski
(vardas, pavardė)

motina Taiba Bastunska
(vardas, pavardė)

Gimimo vieta Vilnaus m. Lietuvos Respublika

Skyriaus vedėjas

(parašas)

VILNIAUS MIESTO SAVIVALDYBĖS CIVILINĖS METRIKACIJOS SKYRIUS

The birth record extract for Chana Bastunska from the Vilnius Archives. Courtesy of Judy Baston.

75 years. Books older than that are transferred to the appropriate state archive, such as:

National Archives of the Republic of Belarus
26 Kozlova Street
220038, Minsk
BELARUS

Central State Historical Archives of Ukraine in Kiev
252601, Kyiv-110
Solomianska St. 24
UKRAINE

Central State Historical Archives of Ukraine in Lviv
290008, Lviv
Sobornaya Pl. 3-a
UKRAINE

Estonian State Historical Archives (for records before 1917)
J. Liivi 4
202400 Tartu
ESTONIA

Estonian State Archives (for records after 1917)
Maneezhi 4
15019 Tallinn
ESTONIA

Central State Historical Archives
Slokas iela 16
LV-1007 Riga
LATVIA

Lithuanian State Historical Archives
Gerosios Vilties 10
2009 Vilnius
LITHUANIA

Records from Russia tend to follow a tabular format with no indices.

ON THE BOOKSHELF

Do You Have Roots in Ukraine or Moldova?

In *Jewish Roots in Ukraine and Moldova,* Weiner again lists town-by-town and archive-by-archive holdings of records pertaining to the Jewish population in Ukraine and Moldova. These records include, but are not limited to, birth, marriage, death, divorce, census, tax and land ownership. Use this very important reference book to determine what records exist, what years are covered, and which archival repository holds them.

From the Polish inventory, I found that records for my grandmother's town of Kozlów, once belonging to the former Polish area of the Austro-Hungarian empire known as Galicia and now in Ukraine, are located in the Polish State Archives AGAD office in Warsaw. Available records for the town include birth records from 1877-1888, 1926-1928, and 1937; marriage records from 1937; and death records from 1925-1931 and from 1933-1938. From Weiner's Ukrainian inventory, the entry for the same town includes the listings from the Polish inventory, adds a USC holding for death records from 1896-1942 (the unique USC mentioned above), and then lists holdings in the Lviv State Archives. Among them are marriage records from 1877-1939 and land records from 1785-1788 and 1846-1879.

I hired private researchers in Warsaw and Lviv to access and extract records from these collections that pertained to my family. The result? Hundreds of records were found. Had I waited, I'd be able to access indices from the Jewish Records Indexing – Poland project, now working on eastern Galician records from AGAD.

"REVISION TALES"

Another great source of genealogical information is a series of tax lists called *Reviskie Skazki* in Russian, or literally translated, "revision tales." This peculiar name described the process used by the officials to verify or revise the information they orally received from the field enumerators. The lists, a direct result of Czar Peter the Great's 1718 decree that replaced landholding with households as a unit of taxation, were intended to be a census, counting everyone—except a civil servant, soldier, and fifteen other exempt categories. There were ten lists in all, some lasting several years from start to finish because of Napoleonic invasion or widespread famine. The lists were primarily used as a basis for taxation and army draft.

The fifth revision, decreed in 1794 to be completed by 1795, is the first list of interest to us. Entries may be in Polish if the towns were part of the annexation. Surnames—the adoption of which was not decreed until 1809— may not appear in these lists, though members of the household are grouped together.

The official schedule of the revisions were:

Fifth Revision—1795
Sixth Revision—1811
Seventh Revision—1816
Eighth Revision—1833
Ninth Revision—1850-1851
Tenth Revision—1858

LDS Holdings

Check the LDS catalog at your local Family History Center for localities whose revision lists have been filmed. I found 68 screens under "Minsk, Taxation" that enumerate holdings for the Fifth through the Tenth Revision. Lists are organized by province or *gubernia*, then district or *uyezhd*, and then by town or *derevnia*. Pay particular attention in the catalog for notations of Jewish records, since the lists for many other classes—peasant, Polish nobility, Russian noblemen, churchmen/clerics, foreigners, single homesteaders, petty bourgeois, "Old Believers" and others—were filmed. You can also consult the JewishGen Infofile, "Jewish Records from Belarus at the LDS Family History Library," at <www.jewishgen.org/infofiles/by-rec.txt>. Lists can still be found at archives throughout the former Soviet Union for other localities besides Belarus, including Lithuania and

Десятая Ревизская Сказка 1874 года [illegible] 20 дня о мещанах евреях Борисовского уезда Логойского Еврейского общества

Семейства	Мужеский пол — Мещане	По последней ревизии состояло	Из того числа выбыли — когда	Ныне на лицо — Лет
1	Меир Юдов Сарканъ [illegible] N 73 [illegible]	былъ пропущенъ		38
2	Мовша Евсеевъ Гедемъ	былъ пропущенъ		50
	его сыновья 1. Сроль	былъ пропущенъ		27
	2. Абрамъ къ N 87	былъ пропущенъ		18
3	Аронъ Янкелевъ [illegible]	былъ пропущенъ		55
	его сынъ Янкель къ N 36	былъ пропущенъ		23
4	Хаимъ Мееровъ [illegible] къ N 68	былъ пропущенъ		41
5	Гершонъ Рубиновъ Капеловичъ къ N 24	былъ пропущенъ		44
6	Мордухъ Ицковъ Краснеръ къ N 27	былъ пропущенъ excluded		36
7	Мовша [illegible] [illegible] къ N 3	былъ пропущенъ		40
8	Берка Вульфовъ Вайнштейнъ къ N 16	былъ пропущенъ		48
9	Аронъ Янкелевъ [illegible] къ N 105	былъ пропущенъ		27
10/11	Евель Янкелевъ [illegible] къ N 15	былъ пропущенъ		33

573

Десятая Ревизская Сказка 1874 года [illegible] 20 дня о мещанкахъ еврейкахъ Борисовского уезда Логойского Еврейского общества

Семейства	Женский пол — Мещанки	Во время [illegible]	Ныне на лицо — Лет
	его жена Геня Евсеевна		37
	Мовши жена Маргола [illegible]		46
	Сроля жена Итка		27
	его жена Ривка [illegible]		51
	его жена Сора Аронова		22
	его жена [illegible] [illegible]		39
	его жена Фрума Вульфова		45
	его жена Брайна Гилькова		34
	его жена Шейна Ицкова		43
	его жена [illegible] Ицкова		20
	его жена Лея Хаимова		26
			11

Tenth Revision List entry for Morduch Itzkov Krasner and his wife, Brayna [sic] Gilkova. Minsk Province, Borisov District, Logoisk, 1875.

ON THE BOOKSHELF
Lithuanian Records
If you're interested in researching families from Lithuania, refer to *Jewish Vital Records, Revision Lists and Other Jewish Holdings in the Lithuanian Archives* by Harold Rhode and Sallyann Amdur Sack.

SEE ALSO
Many online databases can jump start your European research, thanks to JewishGen and geography-specific special interest groups. See Chapters 13 and 15 for detailed information.

QUICK TIP
For the area of the former Lviv, Ivano-Frankivsk, and Ternopil oblasts, formerly in Galicia and now in Ukraine, records are located at the unique USC in Warsaw, mentioned above.

QUICK TIP
Direct Access to Records of the Former Soviet Union
You may want a former native to do your letter writing for you to archives in the former Soviet Union.

QUICK TIP
LDS Holdings of Jewish Interest
The Family History Library has filmed many Jewish vital records, particularly for Poland and Hungary. Check the catalog to see if birth, marriage, and death records for your town and/or its surrounding area have been filmed. You can find a listing of films pertaining specifically to Jewish records at <www.jewishgen.org/jri-pl> for Poland and throughout central and eastern Europe in the appendices to *The Encyclopedia of Jewish Genealogy.*

At the 20th International Conference on Jewish Genealogy in Salt Lake City, July 2000, the LDS Family History Department presented to the International Association of Jewish Genealogical Societies a CD containing an index to all known Jewish holdings of the Family History Library—more than 3,000 record groups representing more than 10,000 films, fiche, and books. Look to JewishGen for the online version at <www.jewishgen.org>.

Ukraine. To access these, you'll need to either contact the archives directly or use private researchers.

What You'll Find in the Lists

Sections of the list are categorized by class of resident. Jews represented one class and are clumped together, separate from the Christian populations. Look for the word *yevreyski* which is Russian for "Jewish." One researcher I know spent hours copying pages from the 1816 revision only to find that it was not for the Jewish population.

Information on males in the household, "Male Poll," is found on the left side of the page; females, "Female Poll," is on the right. In the Tenth Revision, for example, you'll find six columns for the males and four for the females. For the males, the five column entries tell you: (1) family number in the Ninth Revision; (2) family number in the Tenth Revision; (3) name, including the patronymic, allowing you to go back one generation (particularly useful when many family members have the same given name); (4) age at the last revision; (5) "omitted from the above numbers," indicating the additive nature of the list; and (6) age at the current revision. Depending on locality, the Female Poll can include four or five columns, capturing much of the same information as the Male Poll with the exception of age in the last revision. Surnames or maiden names are not given for females.

Lists were not intended to represent the entire population, but rather to be supplemental to previous enumerations. Males, as heads of household, were counted for taxation purposes, and therefore many sought to flee from the enumerator or "reviser." In some instances, dramatically more women were counted than men, the latter having magically disappeared from town. The process appeared to be rather slipshod, though it was probably common for the enumerator to be followed into town by the local police force.

Private Researchers and Research Groups

There are a number of private researchers who can extract records for you in both the Polish State Archives system as well as in various archives throughout the former Soviet Empire. Word-of-mouth seems to work the best in determining which researcher could be right for you. Some are more expensive than others. Some are more credible. Some have strong relationships with repository directors. Do not expect that you will get photocopies of all your family's records as if you were using a microfilm at your local Family History Center. Record extracts may be all that you can get, and while not copies of the original record, will certainly provide you with vital information.

In addition to individual private researchers, private research firms can help you locate vital records from eastern European archives.

FAST Genealogy Service

Headquartered in Maryland, FAST primarily specializes in Russia, Belarus, and the Baltic areas.

FAST Genealogy Service
8510 Wild Olive Drive
Potomac, MD 20854
Bfeldbly@CapAccess.org

Routes to Roots

This is Miriam Weiner's company, with offices in Ukraine and Poland. Routes to Roots offers archival research and customized tours to Poland, Ukraine, Belarus, and Moldova. Weiner, who was the first Jewish Certified Genealogist, prepares a client report with her findings, analysis, and conclusion.

Routes to Roots
136 Sandpiper Key
Seacaucus, NJ 07094
<www.routestoroots.com>
mweiner@routestoroots.com

1	2					3					4			5	6
Liczba porz. Fortlaufende Zahl	Urodzenia Der Geburt					Obrzezania lub nadania imienia Der Beschneidung oder Namens-Beilegung					Dziecięcia des Kindes			Urodzenie ślubne, rzekomo ślubne lub nieślubne Eheliche, angeblich eheliche oder uneheliche Geburt	Imię i nazwisko ojca jakoteż jego stan, zatrudnienie i miejsce zamieszkania Vor- und Zuname des Vaters, sowie Stand u. Beschäftigung und dessen Wohnort
	dzień Tag	miesiąc Monat	rok Jahr	miejsce Ort	numer domu Haus-Nr.	dzień Tag	miesiąc Monat	rok Jahr	miejsce Ort	numer domu Haus-Nr.	Imię Name	Płeć Geschlecht: męska männlich	żeńska weiblich		
	[illegible]	Mai	1892	Kozłów	78	[illegible]	Mai	1892	Kozłów	429	Seife Chawe	—	1	unehelich	Henoch Zuckerkandel [illegible] in Kozłów

Use of the tabular style: the 1892 birth record of my paternal grandmother, Chawa Seife, daughter of Henoch Zuckerkandel (and Pesia Seife), Kozlów, Galicia, Austria-Hungary.

Outside the Pale

Austria

If you're interested in records from the former Austro-Hungarian province of Galicia, you'll need to contact archives in either Poland or Ukraine. Whether your family lived in Galicia or you know you had relatives in Vienna, it's a good idea to check out the LDS Family History Library films for Jewish Vienna. They include metrical books for 1826-1938 and circumcision books from 1870-1914. You'll find them listed under "AUSTRIA, NIEDERÖSTERREICH, WIEN, JEWISH."

If the area you're researching is in present-day Austria, you can write to the Austrian National Archives at:

Österreichisches Staatsarchiv
Abteilung I: Haus-, Hof- und Staatsarchiv
Bibliothek
Minoritenplatz
A-1010 Vienna
AUSTRIA

The LDS Family History Library has also filmed Austrian Military records. They are not very easy to use, because the records are organized by regiment. The films cover 1740-1922.

Croatia

Archives. Croatia's Central State Archives, Hrvatski Drzavni Arhiv, is located in the capital city of Zagreb. Vital records before 1860 are held by the twelve Croatian Regional (Historical) Archives in Varazdin, Zagreb, Bjelovar, Pazin, Rijeka, Karlovac, Zadar, Split, Dubrovnik, Sisak, Slavonski Brod, and Osijek. Some archives have records after 1860 as well, and this varies from one region to another.

In 1945, all church vital records, and Jewish records as well, were released to the civil authorities and deposited with the City Register Offices. It could take some time to locate the appropriate office. There are 400 municipalities within 21 counties in Croatia. As an example, many offices exist within Zagreb.

QUICK TIP
When researching Galician records, be sure to search records by the mother's maiden name. Due to heavy taxation, Jewish couples often married only through a religious ceremony, not a civil one. Therefore, children of the couple were considered to be illegitimate, and their vital events were recorded using the mother's maiden name. It is not uncommon to come across marriage records where the bride and groom are in their 50s and 60s.

ON THE BOOKSHELF
Suzan Wynne's *Finding Your Jewish Roots in Galicia: A Resource Guide* is a must-have resource if you have Galitzianer roots. Also be sure to have on hand Miriam Weiner's *Jewish Roots in Poland* and *Jewish Roots in Ukraine and Moldova.*

To request records, you can write to:

Central State Archives
Marulicev trg 21
10000 Zagreb
CROATIA

Croatian State Archives of Zagreb
Opatica 29
10000 Zagreb
CROATIA

Croatian State Archives ofVarazdin
Trstenjakova 7
42000 Varazdin
CROATIA

The Records. You will find greater linguistic diversity and, therefore, perhaps some linguistic challenges among Croatian records. Births, marriages, and deaths could be recorded in Croatian, Slovene, Serbian, German, Hungarian, Latin, or Italian.

QUICK TIP
The LDS Family History Library has filmed some Jewish vital records for Croatia from as early as 1792 to as late as 1939, depending on the area. These are listed in the Summer 1999 issue of *Avotaynu* and can also be found in the online LDS catalog at <www.familysearch.com>.

QUICK HIT
The JewishGen Infofile on Croatia can give you the benefits of first-hand knowledge in working with Croatian records. See <www.jewishgen.org/infofiles/Croatia.htm>.

Czech Republic

Known as the Kingdoms of Bohemia and Moravia before 1918, several repositories in the current Czech Republic offer an array of records. These records have not been filmed by the LDS Family History Library at this time.

The Archives. The Czech State Archives holds birth, marriage, and death records, tax records, registration lists, and *Familianten* lists.

Civil recordkeeping began in 1784. The vital records are written in German, and since they are written in old Gothic script, they may pose some challenges to the American user. If you are requesting records by mail, you can ask for a translation. If you are researching on site, a catalog of archival holdings, organized by town name, can help you.

The Registers of Jews, developed to accommodate both the restrictive population policy and taxation, list fathers, mothers and all children. There are several registers.

The *Familianten* order, issued by Hapsburg ruler Charles VI in 1726, restricted the number of resident Jewish families and was enforced until 1848. With this order, only the first-born son of each Jewish family was allowed to marry. The order resulted in migration. In fact, by 1900 almost half of the Jews in Hungary were of Bohemian or Moravian descent.

E. Randal Schoenberg and Julius Mueller, authors of the JewishGen Infofile on Czechoslovakia <www.jewishgen.org/BohMor/czechguide.html>, point out: " One other result of the *Familianten* laws was that the government kept very good records of which families lived in which towns. *Familianten* lists were collected in the Book of Jewish *Familianten* (also called *Mannschaftsbücher* in Moravia). Records were collected in 1799 and in 1811 and updated until about 1830. Each record comprised the name of county, registration number of the family in the whole land, the registration number of family in the county (set up in 1725), name of the father, his wife, his sons and a few other family details. These records provide a very good resource for researchers investigating their family histories. For some families, up to three generations are included."

The *Familianten* books can be accessed at the Czech State Archives. For Moravia, the surviving books are available from the various regional archives, the Czech State Archives, or the Jewish Museum in Prague.

To request records, you can write to:

Czech State Archives
PhDr. Lenka Matusikova
tr. Milady Horakove 133
CZ-166 21 Praha 6
CZECH REPUBLIC
e-mail:arch@mvcr.cz

Jewish Museum of Prague
Jáchymova 3
110 00 Praha 1
CZECH REPUBLIC
telephone: +42-2-2481 00 99
fax. +42-2-2310 681
e-mail: zmp@ecn.cz

France

Archives and Vital Records. France is divided into 97 *Departements.* Records have been kept since the French Revolution. Vital record registers for the years prior to 1893 are located in the

QUICK TIP
Says Roseanne Leeson, "The most important thing in attempting to do research in France is that you must know the community your ancestors came from. This is imperative! And, this kind of research must take place on this side of the ocean. Records in France are not centralized nor indexed, but are filed by community, even in the departmental archives."

Archives Departementales at the *chef-lieu* in the district, usually the principal town. Unfortunately, you can't access these records by mail; you can only view them while on site—and you can't get a photocopy either.

For records after 1893, you can write to the appropriate *Mairies* or town hall in the town where the birth, marriage, or death took place. You must declare yourself as a descendant. Be as specific as you can about names and dates, and be sure to include an International Reply Coupon from your local post office for response.

Exceptions exist but the good news is that the LDS Family History Library has filmed the civil registers from as early as 1792, so you can view them at your local Family History Center. Roseanne Leeson of Los Altos, California has been researching her roots in Alsace and has found the films to be the most useful source.

Census Records. If your family lived outside Paris and its surrounding area, the civil census records may be of use to you. They began in 1836 and continued every five years until 1936 and irregularly thereafter. Census records before 1893 are held by the Archives *Departementales*. After 1893 they are held in the *Mairies*. In either case, they are not indexed or microfilmed.

If your family lived in Paris, you can access a separate set of census records. You will, though, need to know the exact district or *arrondissement*—the city has 20 of them, each with its own *Mairie*. Records prior to 1893 are held by the Archives de la Ville de Paris.

To locate the appropriate town hall for post-1893 records, write to:

Tribunal de Grande Instance
Greffe de l'Etat Civil
2, Boulevard du Palais
75001 – Paris
FRANCE

Micheline Gutmann, author of the JewishGen Infofile on French records, notes that the Archives of Paris before 1860 were destroyed. "Some (about one-third) of the records have been reconstructed from other sources. So, in that case, you have to look for an existing reconstruction at the Archives."

If your family came from the Alsatian region, the 1784 census list may be of interest to you. It lists head of household, wife, and children. You can order microfilms from the LDS Family History Library and use an index to help you. This index was created by a fellow Jewish genealogist and can be obtained through Avotaynu at <www.avotaynu.com> or through the Cercle de Généalogie Juive, at <www.genealoj.org/document.html>. The index contains four separate lists: family name, first name, maiden name, and village, which essentially reproduces the census.

Notarial Records. If you're looking for Jewish marriage records before 1792, notarial records (*actes notaries*) provide the only source. Such sources are particularly important in the Alsace region, because eighteenth century Jews were required to marry before a notary.

FOR MORE INFORMATION

Les familles Juives en France lists *departement* by *departement*, town by town, all the known civil sources for Jewish genealogy in France, from the 1500s to 1815.

JewishGen Infofiles on France
<www.jewishgen.org/infofiles/fr-1.txt>
<www.jewishgen.org/infofiles/fr-2-3.txt>
<www.jewishgen.org/infofiles/fr-4.txt>
<www.jewishgen.org/infofiles/fr-5-6.txt>

Cercle de Généalogie Juive
<www.genealoj.org>

Germany

Vital Records. Some 2,000 microfilm reels with German-Jewish vital records are available from the LDS Family History Library. Check its catalog at either your local Family History Center or the online catalog at <www.familysearch.com>.

Family trees, family histories, community records. Established in 1955, the Leo Baeck Institute (LBI) is dedicated to the study of history of German-speaking Jewry, including Austria. It has offices in New York, London, and Jerusalem. The institute's Family Research Division has thousands of family trees, community records, and more. The institute publishes *Stammbaum*, a journal for German Jewish genealogy.

If you're going to visit LBI in New York (part of the Center for Jewish History), the institute requests that you complete the Family Research Application Form available from its web site at <http://users.rcn.lbi1/famappl.htm>.

The Leo Baeck Institute
15 West 16th Street
New York, NY 10011
Lbi1@lbi.com
lbifamily@usa.net (for Family Research Division)

ON THE BOOKSHELF

The best guide for those seeking their German ancestry is *Germanic Genealogy: A Guide to Worldwide Sources and Migrations.* It contains a special chapter for the Jewish researcher.

Another book that deals specifically with German-Jewish resources is *Library Resources for German-Jewish Genealogy* by Angelika G. Ellmann-Krüger with Edward David Luft. It lists lots of library sources that can enhance your basic research.

QUICK TIP

Our Ancestors Moved Around More Than We Think

Be sure to check neighboring towns for your surnames. Marriage often led to families moving around. Here's one example: When my great-grandfather Joseph Chaim Pryzant married Chana Donsky, he moved from Ostrów Mazowiecka to Zaręby Koscielne, where she lived.

Also be sure to note migration patterns. For instance, during the first half of the nineteenth century, Belarussian Jews were encouraged to move to Ukraine for greater economic opportunity. Also, many families from Galician towns along the front during World War I took refuge in cities such as Vienna. Understand the possible migration patterns for the geographic area you research, as you may find vital records in areas well beyond the immediate locale.

QUICK TIP

When Vital Records Don't Exist

Notary records, resident lists, land records, and tax or revision lists—all can provide extremely useful information. In fact, resident or tenant registers are sometimes more revealing than the vital records themselves. In one set I used for Ostrów Mazowiecka, listings for my family name all family members, and for each, include mother's first and maiden names, place and date of birth, military service, and date of emigration. These entries often refer back to specific vital records, providing the place, year, and record number. Though vital records exist for this town, I was not able to find my maternal grandmother's birth record. The tenant register entry for her at least told me she was born in Dąbrowa Michałka in 1896.

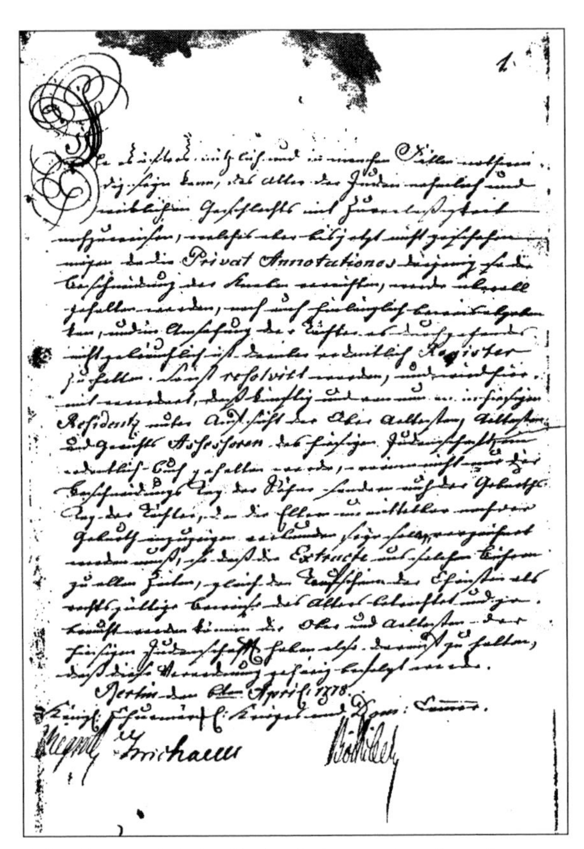

The decree of 6 April 1788 that assigned to the Elders of the Jewish Community of Berlin the obligation to keep a reliable record of all Jewish births within the city. Courtesy of Leo Baeck Institute.

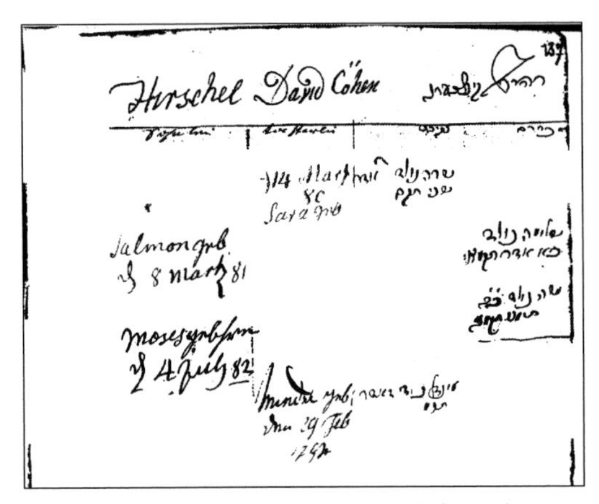

A tabular format 1792 birth record from the Jewish Community of Berlin. Courtesy of Leo Baeck Institute.

Hungary

Jews and other religious communities were required to keep their own vital records for the government beginning in 1851. The civil registration process began in 1895. The LDS has filmed many Hungarian-Jewish vital records, so be sure to consult the LDS Family History Library catalog before contacting the Hungarian National Archives directly. If needed, you can request records by contacting:

National Archives
Bécsi kapu tér 2-4
1014 Budapest
HUNGARY
telephone: 00361 356 58 11

Romania

Similar to the archival systems of other eastern European countries, the National Archives holds records older than 75 years, while the local city and town Vital Records Office (Oficiul Starii Civile) holds the more recent ones. Civil registration began in 1831 in Wallachia, in 1832 in Moldova, and in 1895 in Transylvania (as part of Hungary).

You can write to the Romanian National Archives at:

Achivelor Statului
Bulevardul Gh. Gheorghui-Dej 29
Bucurest 1
ROMANIA

Slovak Republic

A 1999 publication, *A Guide to the Slovak Archives*, by Zuzana Kollarova and Jozef Hanus, written in both Slovak and English, covers the central archives, seven state regional archives, two municipal archives of Bratislava and Kosice, 37 state district archives, and some 20 additional government or semi-government archives. You can write to the Slovak Central Archives at:

Statny Ustredny Archiv
Drotarska cesta 42
817 01 Bratislava
SLOVAKIA

Records may be in Slovak, Hungarian, Hebrew, German, or Latin.

QUICK HIT

Avotaynu's microfiche, "Index to Jewish Vital Statistics Records of Slovakia"
<www.avotaynu.com>

The Central Union of Jewish Religious Communities in Slovakia
<www.angelfire.com/hi/ZNO/index.html>

7 Israeli Records

"My Dad's mother moved to Jerusalem where she is buried. As a young child, I used to write Jewish letters to her," wrote my then 90-year-old grandmother's first cousin, Evelyn, in 1993. American-born Evelyn had never met her father's mother, Dina Himmeldank Zuckerkandel, from Galicia.

I figured Dina died in Palestine sometime between the time Evelyn could write (maybe 1909 or later) and 1928, when my aunt was born and named for her. This was the starting point for my research in what has been called the best single source of Jewish genealogical data—Israel.

No matter where your roots are from, your research will probably take you to Israel at some point. Maybe someone in your family immigrated there before or after World War II. Maybe you'll look for records from your European or Middle Eastern ancestral town. No matter—Israeli archives, agencies, and repositories can help you.

ON THE BOOKSHELF

The definitive guide to research in Israel is Sallyann Amdur Sack's *A Guide to Jewish Genealogical Research in Israel*, co-authored with the Israel Genealogical Society. The book describes a variety of archives, libraries, and agencies and their holdings, including detailed appendices listing Yizkor Books, *landsmanshaftn*, archival and library holdings, and more. While intended to be an onsite research guide, it can help you understand the kinds of resources you can request by mail, e-mail, or the Internet.

Resources on People and Places in Israel

Chevrot Kadisha—Burial Societies

I wrote to the *chevrot kadisha* or burial societies to find Dina's burial information. As Sallyann Sack points out, no commercial funeral homes exist in Israel. These burial societies take care of everything.

The largest and oldest society in Jerusalem is called the General Ashkenazi Chevra Kadisha. You'll need to know the deceased's family and personal name to effectively search its computerized files. You may need the deceased's father's name as well if the name is common. The further back in time you go, the more likely it will be that only the name and patronymic were recorded, such as Menachem ben Mordechai.

Other important societies include the Chassidic Burial Society and the Kehillat Yerushalayim Burial Society, both in Jerusalem, and the Chevra Kadisha of Tel Aviv/Jaffa.

I wrote to these societies searching for any information on Dina. Unfortunately, my search turned up nothing.

QUICK HIT
A JewishGen infofile lists *chevrot kadisha* and burial societies at <www.jewishgen.org/infofiles/il-chevk.txt>, organized by city/town.

Jewish Agency Search Bureau for Missing Relatives
P.O. Box 92
91920 Jerusalem
ISRAEL

Batya Unterschatz is an icon of Jewish genealogy; some call her the "miracle worker." She has helped many researchers. More importantly, she has helped families find relatives in Israel—often with great emotional impact. When Batya speaks at a Summer Seminar on Jewish genealogy, there's not a dry eye in the room—the impact of bringing together siblings who were separated for 50 years or more is so dramatic. She maintains a database of more than one million names from individuals from the immediate post-World War II era looking for family.

If you're looking for relatives, you can't go wrong by contacting Batya at the Search Bureau for Missing Relatives. Her database is linked into the Ministry of the Interior's database, so searches are very thorough. Donations are appreciated.

SEE ALSO
The Search Bureau can help you find connection to Holocaust era survivors and their families. See the sidebar in Chapter 11.

Israel State Archives
Prime Minister's Office
Kiryat Ben Gurion
Jerusalem 91919
ISRAEL

These archives hold documents from the Ottoman Period, British Mandate Period, and modern period, including population registers, consular records, migration records, and department of health birth and death registration for 1919-1948. According to Sack, vital records are held at the Ministry of the Interior.

Municipal Archives

Jerusalem Municipality Historical Archives
Municipality of Jerusalem
P. O. Box 775
91007 Jerusalem
ISRAEL

Haifa Municipal Archives
2 Herman Street
35026 Haifa
ISRAEL

Resources on the World's Jewish Communities

Yad Vashem—Martyr's and Hero's Remembrance Authority
Hall of Names
P.O.B. 3477
Jerusalem 91034
ISRAEL
FAX- 972 2 6419534
<www.yad-vashem.org.il>

Accessing Yad Vashem's Hall of Names and its library is a must for anyone pursuing Holocaust-related research. Work is in progress to digitize Pages of Testimony and to create a master database, a "List of Lists," to house about 18 million occurrences of names and accompanying data from about 10,000 lists. Yad Vashem hopes to enable searches of the database from the Internet.

SEE ALSO
For more in-depth information, turn to Chapter 11 on Holocaust Research.

Central Archives for the History of the Jewish People
P.O. Box 1149
91010 Jerusalem
ISRAEL
<http://sites.huji.ac.il/archives/>

The Archives has a large collection of birth, marriage, death, and burial registers from Germany and sporadic registers from France, Italy, and Poland. Such registers came into existence from about the end of the eighteenth century. You can also access circumcision registers, voting lists, tax lists, and more. Private collections and papers of local and international Jewish organizations

QUICK TIP
Most of the vast resources of the Central Archives for the History of the Jewish People is organized by geographic location. Be sure you know the location you're researching to be most productive.

augment the vital records. Austrian, South American, Latvian, and Moroccan materials are included as well as others.

The Archives also houses several hundred family trees and genealogies, catalogued by the main family name.

Inventories and registers cover a millennium, comprising thousands of pages of summaries and lists.

The Archives believes in the importance of microfilming Jewish archival materials held outside Israel as a protective measure. Prague, Łódż, Lvov, and Amsterdam community archives are among the largest filmed by the Archives so far.

Diaspora Research Institute
Tel Aviv University
Carter Building
Ramat Aviv
Tel Aviv 69978
ISRAEL
Telephone: 972-3-640-9799 or 972-3-640-9462
Fax: 972-3 640-7287
e-mail: mrozen@ccsg.tau.ac.il

The institute researches the history of the Jewish people in all parts of the world at all periods of time and includes the Goldstein-Goren Centre for the History of the Jews in Romania, established in 1987. Prior to that, the Institute focused on Holland, Islamic countries, Italy, Poland, and the former Soviet Union. Romania was home to a large and flourishing Jewish community in the Diaspora. The institute also houses digitized videos of Jewish community records from Salonika and Athens.

Jewish National and University Library
Hebrew University
Givat Ram Campus
P.O. Box 503
Jerusalem 91004
ISRAEL

According to Sack, the purpose of this library is to serve as an "impetus to and a record of the cultural rebirth of the Jewish People in its homeland." Its roots began in 1893 as the Midrash Abarbanel Library established by B'nai B'rith. It became part of Hebrew University in 1918.

The Department of Manuscripts and Archives offers betrothal and wedding contracts, *mohel* registers (of circumcisions), consular files, and card files for *pinkassim* or register books of Jewish communities.

The Microfilm Room holds *pinkassim* for a great variety of major Jewish communities in the Diaspora, including Vienna, Prague, Salonika, Florence, and many others. It also houses the Montefiore censuses of the Jews of Palestine taken in 1839, 1849, 1855, 1866 and 1875. More than 25,000 immigrant name changes made during Palestine's British Mandate Period of 1918-1948 were listed in the *Palestine Gazette* and can be found at the library.

Though vital records for my ancestral Galician shtetl of Kozlów (now in Ukraine) are not available before 1877, the Jewish National and University Library holds *chevra kadisha* records for the town for the period 1815-1948. At one time or another, the road will lead to Israel.

PART III

Special Topics in Jewish Genealogy

8 Rabbinic Research

"Ever since I was little, I was told I was descended from Moses Isserlis, the ReMa, a prominent rabbi in sixteenth century Kraków," says Marty Isserlis of Basking Ridge, New Jersey. Isserlis has come to know about his prestigious ancestor by working through cousins in Israel and reaching out to experts.

Generally speaking, if you've got a rabbinic line in your ancestry, chances are you've known about it for years. This is the kind of oral tradition that gets passed down from generation to generation. There's been a lot of scholarly debate about whether all Ashkenazic Jews are descended from Rashi, who is a descendant of King David, and the validity and interrelationships between rabbinic lines. While few of us may have some direct involvement, the discussion is lively and at times fascinating.

If you've been told that you're descended from a particular rabbi or a rabbi from a particular town, it's definitely worth your while to check it out. While a connection can't be guaranteed, rabbinical line genealogies are documented and have been for hundreds of years. Rabbinic descent in a way is genealogical nirvana.

Rabbinic Lines

Some classic rabbinical lines include the names of Katzenellenbogen, Horowitz, Luria, Spira, Treves, Landau, Katz, Rabinowitz, Walsh, and more. In addition to these names are acronyms like MaHaRaSHaL (**M**orenu **h**a-**R**av **S**hlomo **L**uria) and well-known figures, such as:

BeSHT Baal Shem Tov—Israel ben Eliezer (1700-1760), founder of Chassidism, born in Podolia.

GRA Gaon of Vilna (also known as *Vilner Gaon*)—Elijah ben Solomon Zalman (1720-1797), talmudist of Vilna and highly distinguished rabbi to whom many claim descent.

MaHaRaL—Rabbi Judah Lowe ben Bezalel (1525-1609), Chief Rabbi of Moravia, kabbalist and scholar. Prominent in Prague, he was reputed to be a descendant of King David. His family came from Worms and his descendants include: Brill, Dubnow, Kaunitzer, Brandeis, and Low.

MaHaRaM—Could indicate one of a number of great sages: MaHaRaM Lublin, MaHaRaM Padua (and founder of the Katzenellenbogen family), MaHaRaM A"SH (R. Meier Eisenstadt, author of *Panim Me'irot*) and MaHaRaM Schick (R. Moses, progenitor of that large rabbinical family).

MaHaRaSHaL—Rabbi Solomon ben Jehiel Luria (1510-1573), who officiated in several Lithuanian and Polish communities including Lublin.

Rashi—Rabbi Solomon ben Isaac (1040-1105), Talmudic commentator of Troyes, France. Several lines claim descent from Rashi, and his descendants are often the subject of many genealogical research articles. Descendants include: Treves, Luria, Katzenellenbogen, Heilprin, and Zarfati.

Shirley Rotbein Flaum of Houston, Texas, researches the Chassidic rabbinic line of Rotbajn/Rotbein, Walden, and Kestenberg of Poland, descendants of Rashi through the MaHaRaSHaL, and his descendant, Rabbi Benjamin Ozer ("Even HaOzer").

They are also descendants of Rabbi Meir Eisenstadt ("Panim Me'irot") and other major rabbis.

She says, "The surname Rotbein is very rare. As far as I know, I am the only person researching this line. My father was the only survivor of a very large Chassidic family from Łódż. When I was a young girl, he told me just once about the existence of a long line of rabbis. I never forgot his words. Like other children of survivors, I had scant knowledge of my ancestry—no more than a few names scribbled on a piece of paper. I decided to try to solve the mystery of my ancestry and posted a message on the Internet. A fellow researcher volunteered to look up Rotbein in *Otsar Harabanim* ('Treasure of the Rabbis'). The appearance of Rotbein rabbis in this source was the major clue that led to hiring a rabbinical researcher, who quickly uncovered the existence of a prominent and ancient rabbinical line."

Research Tips

The first source to check is Neil Rosenstein's two-volume definitive work, *The Unbroken Chain.* He consulted many sources to depict and describe the massive genealogies of major rabbinical lines.

Another good source of biographical information is the *Encyclopaedia Judaica*, which is available in major and some local libraries.

Though perhaps lesser known, many other sources are available in English, including individual web sites with rabbinic genealogy. There is more rich literature to help you further, mostly in Hebrew. The books listed in the bibliography can get you started. You can find them in good Judaica collections at libraries and institutions like the New York Public Library, Jewish Theological Seminary, and YIVO Institute for Jewish Research in New York City.

It's also a good idea to check memorial books or Yizkor books for your ancestral town. You'll read more about these sources in Chapter 11. Suppose your family's oral tradition says you're descended from the Belzer Rebbe, a Chassidic rabbinical leader. Make sure you research the town of Belz to find out more about the Rebbe, using memorial books and the *Encyclopaedia*

QUICK TIP
The *Encyclopaedia Judaica* is available on CD. See <www.virtual.co.il/vj/advertising/judaica>.

UNBROKEN CHAIN 37 CHAPTER II - SAMUEL FAMILY

b

DESCENDANTS OF
R. ELIJAH son of R. ZVI HIRSCH (APTER) KATZENELLENBOGEN

THE SAMUEL FAMILY of LONDON AND PHILADELPHIA

ANCESTRY:

G1. R. Meir of Padua.
G2.1. R. Samuel Judah Katzenellenbogen.
G3.3. R. Saul Wahl.
G4.1. R. Meir Wahl.
G5.2. R. Moses Katzenellenbogen.
G6.6. R. Saul.
G7.3. R. Jacob Katzenellenbogen, the Martyr.
G8.2. R. Zvi Hirsch (Hirschel) Apter, died 1704.
G9.1. R. Elijah (Eliezer Hirschel) Apter, died 1736/7.[29]

G10.1. Lieb.
G10.2. Michla, married Sander, A.B.D. Lesla, later head of the Jewish Council (Parnas) at Krotoschin. She died in 1737.
G10.3. Joseph (called Ducist or Ducit) of Posen, died in 1759.

G11.1. Eliezer.
G11.2. Samuel, dropped the name Katzenellenbogen, and was called Samuel Samuel. He died in 1758 at Krotoschin.

G12.1. Daughter.
G12.2. Esther, married Phineas Halevi Phillips, who settled in England from Germany in 1775. He was the son of Jonas Phillips, who died in London in 1794. Esther died at Krotoschin in 1822. He lived at Little Tulse Street, Goodman's Fields, London.

Phineas regularly attended the great fairs in Germany, periodically travelling to England before settling there. He carried on an extensive business in gums and indigo. He was held in high esteem by the reigning prince. Phineas was always provided with a special *inschutzbrief* (Letter of Protection) on his journeys throughout Germany. On one occasion, favoring the horticultural tastes of the prince, the Jewish merchant brought him a collection of Dutch bulbs, which the latter appreciated throughout his life.

Phineas held the post of Chief of the Jewish community of Krotoschin. He was the progenitor of the Phillips Family London. (See below - Branch II.)

G12.3. Moses Samuel, born in 1740 (or 1742), initially settled in Liverpool, died in England in 1839.[30] He married Rachel, daughter of Jonas Phillips, as did his sister Esther

29. See D.K. and New York Public Library manuscript *PWO (Samuel) by Sandford A. Moss (1939). See also **Records of the Samuel Family** by Joseph Bunford Samuel (Philadelphia, 1912).

30. See **Genealogical Notes Upon the Family of Baron Henry de Worms, Sometime Member of Parliament for East Toxteth** by Bertram B. Benas (1940); Hannah F. Cohen **Changing Faces** (London, 1937), which contains paintings of both Moses and his wife.

Neil Rosenstein's Unbroken Chain *details the genealogy of rabbinic families. Reprinted with permission.*

Judaica, and contact other researchers interested in the town. Since the Yizkor books are written mostly in Hebrew or Yiddish, don't stop there. Be sure to check out the other Hebrew sources listed in this chapter.

Check to see if your ancestor has written texts. These may have been published or left only in manuscript form and located in some library or archive. Often their approbations offer up some genealogical detail.

DEFINITION
An approbation is text authored by a respected person or persons, such as a prominent rabbi or rabbinical family relative. It appears before the book's text begins. The approbation is considered to be a "seal of approval."

David Kershen of Yeshurun Library in Jerusalem suggests looking for *megilot yochasin*, scrolls of family genealogies that appear at the beginning or end of certain rabbinic works, and adds, "Another not sufficiently tapped source is the title page, especially of rabbinic works of the 18th and 19th centuries."

Also, *prenumeranten* ("prior numbers") lists can be an important source. These are lists of people who ordered prepaid copies of a book prior to its publication. Such donations were considered a *mitzvah* or "good deed," and in return, the names of the advance subscribers were published in the book. The lists typically appeared between 1850-1910 but could span from the late eighteenth to the mid-twentieth centuries.

Says Werner Frank of Calabasas, California, who recently lectured on rabbinic genealogical research at the 20th International Conference on Jewish Genealogy in Salt Lake City, "Because of the rabbinical families' practice of marrying amongst themselves, there also exists a rich body of interlocking information that forms large genealogical networks. These marriages tend to tie together multiple rabbinical families that cover wide geographic areas, from Italy in the south, Poland to the east, and France to the west. A unique aspect to this rabbinical family genealogy is the presence of a daughter's name and her marriage partner, who invariably is also a rabbi. The availability of female names and their associated progeny is unusual in Jewish genealogy, since most early sources only track the male lines."

Tracing a rabbinic line may seem much easier than tracing the typical eastern European family because many rabbinic families bore hereditary surnames well before legislation forced widespread Jewish surname adoption. You may find, though, that the son-in-law of a well-known rabbinic family may have assumed his wife's surname in order to enhance his own *yichus* or lineage.

CASE STUDY: FOLLOWING THE TRAIL OF RABBI LANGFUS

Robert Heyman of Australia relied on networking and several sources to help him track down his ancestry from Rabbi Chaim David Langfus of Bedzin. He says, "I knew for several years that my great-great-great-great-grandfather was Rabbi Chaim David Langfus of Bedzin. I was told that by an Israeli cousin, who has since passed away. I've confirmed all this through the LDS records. I had no idea then what kind of family he was a part of.

"That came when I had my article 'Where Did My Kestenbergs Originate' published in *Avotaynu.* I mentioned that my great-great-great-grandfather was Shmuel Yaakov Kestenberg, who married Hendl Langfus, daughter of Chaim David Langfus. A Langfus cousin read this accidentally, and called me, and gave me a chapter of the memoirs her grandfather wrote, in which he stated that Rabbi Chaim David Langfus was the son of Rabbi Yitzchak of Zychlin, and his mother was the sister of the famous Rabbi Yitzchak of Warka, and Rabbi Yitzchak of Warka was nine generations removed from Rabbi Mordechai Jaffe, author of *HaLevush.* The memoirs mentioned Rabbi Yosef Levinstein, ABD* Serock, famous as a rabbinic genealogist. I obtained his book, *Dor v'Dor v'Dorshav,* as well as Nathan Tzvi Friedman's *Otzar Harabanim* from Robinson Bookseller's in Tel Aviv. I couldn't get any more information other than Rabbi Yitzchak of Warka's father was Rabbi Shimon of Dzialoszyn, known as 'Baal HaRachmanut.' I searched the Judaic sections of the Library of Congress and of Harvard University for Rabbinic texts, as well as YIVO. I found several texts about Rabbi Yitzchak of Warka, and some writings of Rabbi Yosef Levinstein. Chaim Friedman in Israel graciously offered to go through his material on Rabbi Levinstein, but came up empty. I searched the journals for which Rabbi Levinstein wrote, and again came up empty. One text on Rabbi Yitzchak described his father as the paternal grandson of Rabbi Yitzchak of Kalisz. I searched the book *Toldot Yehudei Kalisz,* and while it mentions several ancient Rabbis of Kalisz, this one was not mentioned. All sources mention that Rabbi Shimon of Dzialoszyn was a direct descendant of Rabbi Mordechai Jaffe, but I have yet to find one to give a generation count like my cousin's memoirs.

"Recently a Kalisz cousin in Israel found my listing in the JewishGen Family Finder, and told me that the picture of Rabbi Shimon's grave is in the Brzeziny Yizkor Book (have yet to check that); it mentions his father's name as Yosef. He also gave me some material about Rabbi Langfus, which confirms his relationship to Rabbi Yitzchak of Warka, and says that Rabbi Langfus's paternal grandfather was a Rabbi with the initials 'mem alef.' The 'mem' I'm pretty sure is Moshe, based on the fact that that was the name of his firstborn son."

---

*"Av bet din," literally father of rabbinical court.

CASE STUDY: THE KROCHMAL RABBIS

I have known Michael Tobias of Glasgow, Scotland, for many years as we share an ancestral town in Poland. He's been instrumental in the creation of the Jewish Records Indexing – Poland project and has lent his talents to other web-based indexing projects for other geographies. He recently told me of his research efforts on his rabbinic line. Here is his story:

"My mother's maiden name is Cromwell. How English can you get? She was born in Liverpool, England. Both of her parents were born in Łódż, Poland. I have recently located my grandfather's birth record in the Łódż records from the Polish State Archives. The surname in Poland was Krochmal. My grandfather was Mendel Krochmal—a famous name as you will see.

"There are two famous Krochmal rabbis. Krochmal is not a common name. We are wondering if there is a connection. There was Rabbi Nachman Krochmall (1785-1840) who lived most of his life in what is now Ukraine. He was, in turn, a descendant of Rabbi Menachem Mendel Krochmal (1600-1661), who was Chief Rabbi of Moravia until his death.

"I have managed to locate copies of the late Paul Jacobi's* work on this family. It is an interesting story. Nachman Krochmal was a Kohen, but his ancestor, Menachem Mendel, was not! It appears that a female descendant of Menachem Mendel married a Kohen and he adopted her surname as she came from a more illustrious family.

"Menachem Mendel Krochmal, son of Abram, was born in Kraków in 1600 and his line can be traced back two or three generations earlier around Kraków. One of his daughters-in-law, Bella Mireles, was descended from the famous Horowitz / Ha-levy family. If we can trace back to that line, then we go back to Spain around 1020. It will be difficult to prove our connection, because there is a lack of documents.

"My great-grandfather Abram Krochmal [notice the Abram-Mendel father-son link] was apparently born in Warsaw around 1868, and we know his father was called Pinkus. We are hoping we can somehow trace this line back to Nachman and hence back to Menachem Mendel.

"Our Krochmal family never claimed to be anything other than Yisroel. To be descended from Nachman or his father means our Krochmals should be Kohanim.

"I have been in touch with several other Krochmal families around the world. Many of them claim descent from Rabbi Nachman. Apart from that I am doing research in the Czech Republic to try to locate records for Rabbi Menachem Mendel's family. I am trying to locate more info on Rabbi Nachman, and in particular, the death record of his son, Abram, in Frankfurt, Germany.

"I have to say this little 'twist' in my family research only started earlier this year, and I find it really exciting!"

* Paul Jacobi's work on rabbinical families has been incorporated into the Family Tree of the Jewish People genealogy database at Beth Hatefusoth in Tel Aviv. See Chapter 13 for more details on this database.

9 Sephardic Research

Several years ago, I worked with a fellow whose surname was Askenazi. Not knowing any better, I assumed he had Ashkenazic, or eastern European, roots. During a lunchtime conversation, he shattered my naïve assumptions: his family was actually from Turkey, and they were Sephardic. This inconsistency, or so it seemed to me, led me on a journey to more fully understand Sephardic genealogy.

Sephardic Jews, or literally "Spanish" Jews (*spharad* is Hebrew for "Spanish"), represented about 90 percent of the world's Jewish population in the 1300s. By 1700, that percentage declined to 50 percent. By 1930, the numbers further reduced to less than 10 percent, mostly from the Middle East. Now Sephardic and Middle Eastern Jews represent 25 percent of the Jewish population and about 60 percent of the state of Israel.

The Second Diaspora

The migrations caused by the Inquisition can be especially important to the genealogist. The Jews who left Spain at this time typically took one of two routes. The first went east to Islamic lands, communities along the northern rim of the Mediterranean, and up into the Balkans and the former Yugoslavia. This was the larger of the two movements and included some 200,000 Jews. Ten thousand Sephardic Jews eventually settled in Romania, particularly in Wallachia, Transylvania, and Dobrodgea.

The second route was somewhat circuitous. Sephardim migrated through Portugal to northern Europe, usually as Marranos. Those who followed this route formed secret communities in Holland, the Spanish-held Netherlands, and towns in southern France. Coinciding with the age of exploration, many eventually migrated to the New World, to Brazil, Curaçao, Surinam, and New Amsterdam.

Surname Adoption

Within the Jewish community the patronymic surname system of *x ben y* or *a ibn b* (e.g., Abraham ben Solomon) was insufficient to differentiate individuals, especially in the big towns. As a result, Sephardim adopted permanent surnames as early as the eleventh century, as a concoction of Hebrew, Arabic, and Spanish. Their Ashkenazic counterparts did not adopt surnames until some 400 years later in the late eighteenth and throughout the nineteenth centuries when required by legislature. A typical Sephardic Jew's first name was in Hebrew and the surname in either Hebrew or Arabic. Usually forced religious conversion resulted in Spanish names after the expulsion.

Sephardic surnames had their roots in symbolic meanings, professions and occupations, birthplace, and patronymics. A good example of symbolic meaning origin is the surname Maimon. The father of the famous philosopher Maimonides (1135-1204) was named Asher ("fortunate"), and was also known as Maimon (Arabic for "fortunate"). The son was first known as Moshe ben Maimon and then as Maimonides (son of Maimon, using the Greek ending *-ides* for "son of"). Other examples include Shalom, which means "peace" or "greetings" in Hebrew. This became Benveniste or Benvenisti in Spanish. Haviv, which means "dear" in Hebrew and Habib, which has the same meaning in Arabic, became Caro in Spanish.

Professional and occupational examples include Hazan ("cantor"), Alfakar ("potter" in Arabic), and Gabai ("synagogue official").

A very popular source for surnames was town or city or origin, among them: Alcalay (from Alcola), Spinoza or Espinoza (from Spinoza), Bejerano (Bejar), Ghirondi or Gheron (Gherona),

Cordovero (Cordoba), Saragossi (Saragossa), Montefiore, Montalban, Alfandari, Aftalion, and Barzilai.

Patronymic examples include names like Nachmanides and Davidon, and again, Maimonides.

The second diaspora led to the creation of many surname variations. For instance, Professor Lavoslav Glesinger published a list of the Sephardi surnames in former Yugoslavia that included those that appear to be Ashkenazic but, in fact, have Sephardic roots: Aserovic (Ashkenazi: Usherovici), Abramovic (Abramovici), Samuelovic (Smilovici), and Kahanovic (Kahanovici). Yugoslavia also is home to Sephardic surnames such as Levi, Albahari, Ruben, Papo, Farchi, Semo, Gaon, Koen, Alfandari, Albala, Almosnino, Almuli, Finci or Finti, Pijade, Demayo or Mayo, Musafia, Eskenazi, Ben Zion, and others. These are also common surnames among Sephardim in Romania.

Sephardic Jews were living in Italy and France by the year 1300. The Spanish surname Hazan, for instance, became Cantorini in Italy. Rofe was a common surname among physician (Hebrew, *rofeh*) families. Dayan ("rabbinical judge"), Sassoon, and others were common in France.

ON THE BOOKSHELF
Excellent sources of Sephardic surnames include Dan Rottenberg's *Finding Our Fathers,* Rabbi Malcom Stern's *Americans of Jewish Descent: A Compendium of Genealogy* and *First American Jewish Families: 600 Genealogies 1654-1988, Third Edition.*

SEE ALSO
See Chapter 3 for more on given name practices among Sephardim.

Traditional Sources Still Apply

Interviews with relatives, ship passenger records, vital records, and naturalization records can help you research your Sephardic roots. Just because "Sephardic" implies Spanish, it doesn't mean your ancestors won't show up in Ashkenazic territories. The "father of Jewish genealogy," Arthur Kurzweil, tells of Sephardim in his family's hometown in the Galicia province of the Austro-Hungarian Empire. Sephardic communities existed in Lithuania, Vienna, Kraków, and other Ashkenazic centers. If your Sephardic family lived in these Ashkenazic places, try researching these traditional sources.

Special Sources and Networking

Jeff Malka of the Washington, DC area began researching his roots around 1996. At that time, organized Sephardic genealogical research was nascent. Since Malka's mother's family had

Ashkenazic roots, he used all the networking tools offered by the JewishGen web site. Sephardic material was starkly absent. He says, "There was maybe a message once every three weeks on the Sefard Forum. Now, there are two to four messages every day. While we still have a long way to go, the Internet has helped us make great networking strides." Inspired by his JewishGen experiences, Malka developed his own web site <www.orthohelp.com/general/sefardim.htm#web> featuring links to Sephardic sites, family genealogies, history, and more.

Etsi: Sephardi Genealogical and Historical Society

<www.geocities.com/EnchantedForest/1321>

Etsi (Hebrew for "my tree") is a Paris-based society that focuses on Sephardic genealogy and history. It covers the Ottoman Empire (Turkey, Greece, Palestine, Syria, Libya, Egypt, etc.), North Africa (Algeria, Morocco, Tunisia), Spain, Portugal, Gibraltar, and Italy. Etsi also includes a research group called the Special Interest Group of the Ottoman Empire. Founded in 1998, the society publishes the quarterly journal *Etsi,* the only journal dedicated to Sephardic genealogy. It supports and encourages all research work on Sephardic genealogy and history, especially archives records, cemetery records, and *ketubot* (Jewish marriage contracts).

The journal's articles in the past have included topics like "Sephardic Genealogical Information Available from Ottoman, Balkan, and Levant Postal History," "Sephardic Genealogical Investigations in Amsterdam," "Bibliography: The Sephardis of Romania," and "Archives: The Move of the Jewish Cemetery of Fez, Morocco." The journal is "a must" for genealogists with Sephardic ancestry interests.

Online Discussion Group for Sephardic Genealogy Research

The Sefard Forum newsgroup provides researchers interested in Sephardic ancestry with a convenient way to post messages and inquiries. More than 350 people subscribe from more than 20 countries. Go to <www.jewishgen.org/infofiles/SefardForum.htm> to learn more about the forum and how to subscribe.

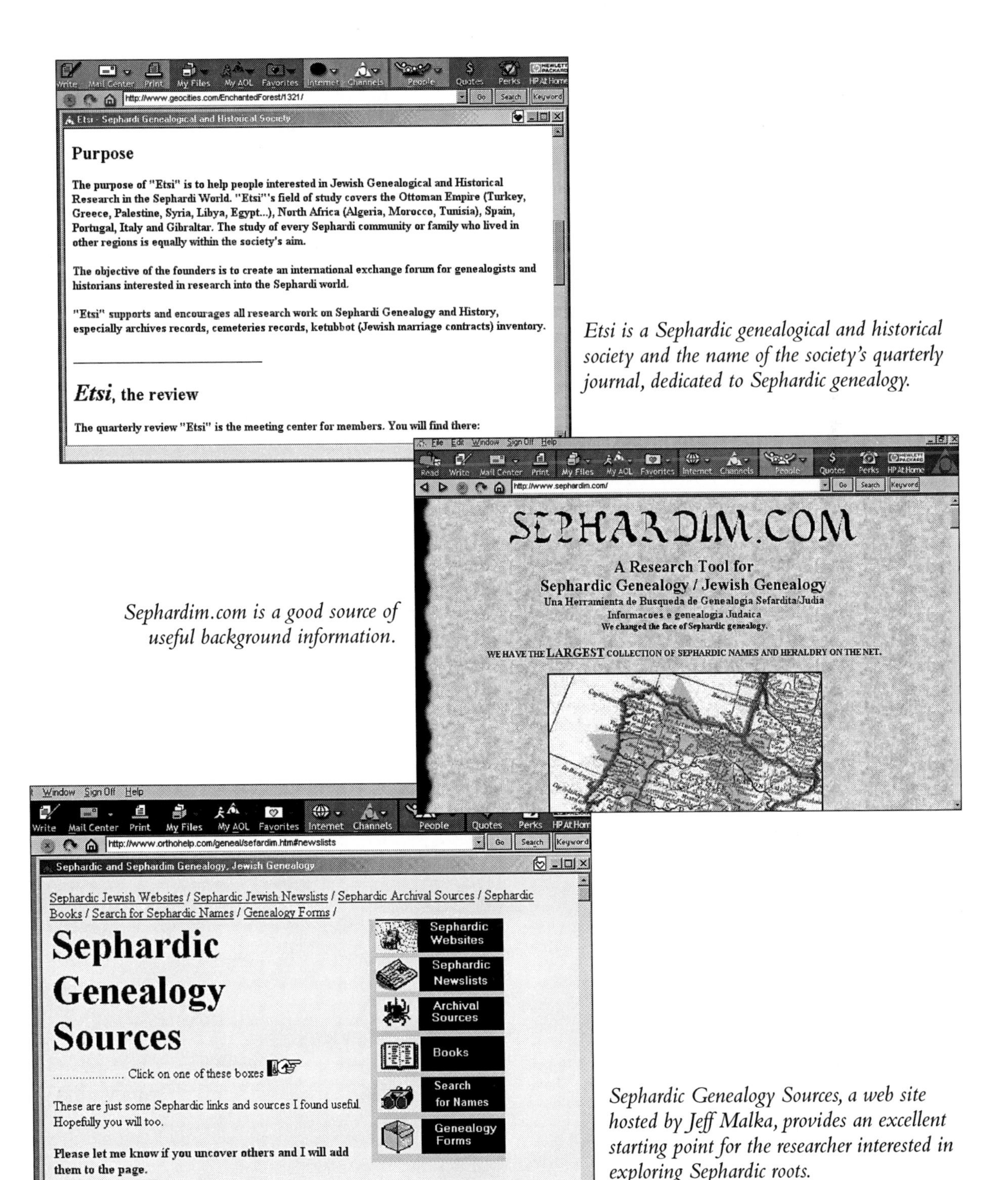
http://www.geocities.com/EnchantedForest/1321/
Etsi - Sephardi Genealogical and Historical Society
Purpose
The purpose of "Etsi" is to help people interested in Jewish Genealogical and Historical Research in the Sephardi World. "Etsi"'s field of study covers the Ottoman Empire (Turkey, Greece, Palestine, Syria, Libya, Egypt...), North Africa (Algeria, Morocco, Tunisia), Spain, Portugal, Italy and Gibraltar. The study of every Sephardi community or family who lived in other regions is equally within the society's aim.
The objective of the founders is to create an international exchange forum for genealogists and historians interested in research into the Sephardi world.
"Etsi" supports and encourages all research work on Sephardi Genealogy and History, especially archives records, cemeteries records, ketubbot (Jewish marriage contracts) inventory.
Etsi, the review
The quarterly review "Etsi" is the meeting center for members. You will find there:
http://www.sephardim.com/
SEPHARDIM.COM
A Research Tool for
Sephardic Genealogy / Jewish Genealogy
Una Herramienta de Busqueda de Genealogia Sefardita/Judia
Informacoes e genealogia Judaica
We changed the face of Sephardic genealogy.
WE HAVE THE LARGEST COLLECTION OF SEPHARDIC NAMES AND HERALDRY ON THE NET.
http://www.orthohelp.com/geneal/sefardim.htm#newslists
Sephardic and Sephardim Genealogy, Jewish Genealogy
Sephardic Jewish Websites / Sephardic Jewish Newslists / Sephardic Archival Sources / Sephardic Books / Search for Sephardic Names / Genealogy Forms /
Sephardic Genealogy Sources
Click on one of these boxes
These are just some Sephardic links and sources I found useful. Hopefully you will too.
Please let me know if you uncover others and I will add them to the page.
Sephardic Websites
Sephardic Newslists
Archival Sources
Books
Search for Names
Genealogy Forms

Etsi is a Sephardic genealogical and historical society and the name of the society's quarterly journal, dedicated to Sephardic genealogy.

Sephardim.com is a good source of useful background information.

Sephardic Genealogy Sources, a web site hosted by Jeff Malka, provides an excellent starting point for the researcher interested in exploring Sephardic roots.

Sephardim.com—A Research Tool for Sephardic Genealogy/Jewish Genealogy

This web site provides good background information, while also featuring music and maps. Seven sections of content address: Sephardic names; a letter from the Catholic Church; Sephardic recipes; Sephardic facts and lore; family heraldry and origins; Sephardic links; and the Forum at Sephardim.com—another Sephardic history and genealogy newsgroup.

Sephardic Genealogy Sources

<www.orthohelp.com/geneal/sefardim.htm#web>

This site is hosted by Dr. Jeff Malka and is an excellent starting point for Sephardic research. The site links to background articles on Sephardic history, newsgroups, archival sources, books, names, and more.

Sephardi Connection

<www.sephardiconnect.com>

You can find on this site some twenty online discussion groups, covering a wide range of geographic origins: Spain, Portugal, Morocco, Tunisia, Algeria, Turkey, Greece, Egypt, Sudan, Syria, Iraq, Israel, Lebanon, France, Italy, England, Ireland, Holland, the Balkans, and other areas.

Sefarad.org

<www.sefarad.org>

This trilingual web site (English, French, and Spanish) is home to the European Sephardic Institute, whose goal is to preserve and provide access to all documents relating to Sephardic Jewry. The Institute publishes the *Los Muestros* ("Sephardic Voice") cultural magazine. The site features a discussion forum as well as subscription to *sephardic-list,* a newsgroup hosted by eGroups.com.

Kahal Sephardim

<www.geocities.com/TheTropics/cabana/5947/main.html>

The Sephardic Community web site contains useful history and travel information. It also provides links to some other Sephardic genealogy sites.

Central Archives for the History of the Jewish People

<http://sites.huji.ac.il/archives>

The Archives is a treasure trove for the genealogist researching Sephardic ancestry. Some of the holdings are listed on the web site and include records from as early as the seventeenth century. Geographic areas covered include France, Italy, South America, Turkey, North Africa, Spain, Portugal, Romania, and more.

Yeshiva University's Mendel Gottesman Library

<www.yu.edu/libraries>
2520 Amsterdam Ave.
New York, NY 10033
(212) 960-5382

The Sephardic Reference Room of the Mendel Gottesman Library at Yeshiva University holds a unique collection of Sephardic books, periodicals, and monographs, donated by Miriam Weiner. Other holdings include manuscripts, letters, and filmed records.

Synagogue records

If such records are available and accessible for the geographic area you're researching, they can provide genealogical data. Often, such records can go back several centuries.

THE AMERICAN SEPHARDI FEDERATION

Founded in 1984, the American Sephardi Federation serves as a coordinating and resource body for all Sephardic communities in the United States. It hosts cultural and educational programs such as "Restoring Glory: The Preservation of Sephardic Heritage Sites around the World" and music and dance of the Bukharian Jewish community of Central Asia.

American Sephardi Federation
Center for Jewish History
15 West 16th St.
New York, NY 10011
(212) 294-8356

SEE ALSO
You can find more detailed information on the Central Archives for the History of the Jewish People in Chapter 7.

Notarial Records

Notarial records—public records of land sales, money lending, etc., dating back to the thirteenth century and sometimes earlier—are believed to be the best genealogical records in Spain. The good news is that the records are abundant. The not-so-good news is that they are not indexed and therefore require a lot of perseverance to get through them. For a given year, there could be as many as 3,000 entries recorded in hard-to-read script. To use these records you need to know timeframe and place and be able to read the handwriting. To test yourself, see Malka's web site for several Spanish script examples.

Marriage Contracts—Ketubot

Says Jane Gerber, author of *The Jews of Spain*, "Even today, Sephardic Jews pride themselves on their noble bearing and illustrious ancestry. Their sense of localism and 'pedigree' is often reflected in meticulously detailed marriage contracts and family trees that trace generations of ancestors back to the medieval cities of Spain."

Sephardic *ketubot*, says Malka, may document several generations of the bride's and groom's families. "Such finds are obviously of wonderful value to the genealogist." He found sixteenth century *ketubot* in a compiled source for a distant branch of his Malka family from Livorna, Italy, who had migrated to the Portuguese community in Tunis. He was able to construct a detailed family tree using the data.

CASE STUDY

Dan Kazez of Springfield, Ohio, began researching his Sephardic roots around the same time as did Malka. Kazez's father was born in Turkey, and Kazez has more than one hundred cousins still living there. Yet, he says, progress has been slow. The name, Kazez says, has been traced to Spain in the 1300s, including a rabbinical family. He has found that letters, e-mail, and faxes do not work as well as the telephone. "As long as language is not a barrier, when I contact relatives by phone, I'm at liberty to learn anything." Working with local archives has been frustrating at best. He has not been able to get his father's birth record. To compensate, Kazez created two web sites, one for his direct family and one for all occurrences of the name Kazez in all its variations.

Nissen Kazez, Istanbul, before 1930. Courtesy of Dan Kazez.

Israel and Rachel Kazez and family, Istanbul, ca. 1928. Courtesy of Dan Kazez.

Kazez family, Istanbul, ca. 1925. Courtesy of Dan Kazez.

Malka's advice to those just starting out to trace Sephardic roots: "Use all the traditional methodologies, like interviewing existing relatives. But you've also got to understand the family's migratory history. It's not unusual in the Sephardic world to have a surname that dates back several centuries. There is a greater likelihood, for some names, that you have a connection to others with your name no matter where they are now. Surname research can help point you in meaningful directions."

He also points out that Sephardic research is not as clearly defined as is Ashkenazic research. Much depends on where the family is from. For instance, if your family came from Holland, you'll find records galore over a long period of time. Not so for certain communities in North Africa and the former Ottoman Empire.

SOME SEPHARDIC SURNAMES

Abenrey, Abitbol, Abrabanel, Abravanel, Abulafia, Aknin, Albaz, Alfassi, Anonios, Aragon, Arapis, Ashkenazi, Assouline, Azulay

Barcilon, Ben Sushan, Botbol

Cabalero, Cardoza, Caro, Carvalho, Castorianos, Castro, Charbit, Cohen, Crespin

Dalyan, Danon, Dayan, De Aragon, De Fez, De Silva, De Soto

Enriquez

Ferreres, Foinquinos, Franco,

Gabbay, Gaguin, Galanos, Guedalia

Hakim, Halfon, Hamu, Hasdai, Hazzan

Kampanaris, Kokkinos

Laredo, Levy, Lombroso, Lugasi

Maimon, Malka, Malqui, Mandil, Marcus, Medina, Mizrahi, Montefiore, Moreno

Nahon, Nahman, Navaro

Obadya, Ohanna, Ohayon, Oiknine

Patish, Perez, Perreira, Pinto, Pisa

Rabi, Rofe, Rosales

Sabah, Santob, Sasson, Sebag, Senor, Serfati, Sevillano, Shalom, Shuraqui, Soberano, Sofer, Soriano, Soto, Susan

Tangier, Turqui,

Uaknin, Uziel,

Valenci, Veniste, Verdugo, Vidal

Zadoq, Zafrani

Source: Sephardic Genealogy Sources *by Jeff Malka*

Summary

The Sephardic genealogical community is growing. As in Ashkenazic and Jewish genealogy in general, networking with other researchers can be key to making major strides. Make use of the web sites to conduct name searches, learn Sephardic history, and join the discussion groups.

What started as a "how could 'Askenazi' possibly be Sephardic?" quest for me has led to a deeper understanding of the rich cultural background of Sephardim. Each day as I research my own Ashkenazic roots, I'm hoping that there's some Sephardic hiding in there somewhere.

Sephardic Jews settled in America as early as 1654, so read on to learn about researching Colonial Jewish roots.

SEE ALSO
If your family came to America in the Colonial Period, turn to Chapter 10.

SOME MAIN SEPHARDIC COMMUNITIES IN THE SECOND DIASPORA

Morocco
Fez

Algeria
Oran
Algiers

Tunisia
Tunis

Egypt
Alexandria
Cairo

Palestine
Jerusalem
Gaza
Tiberias
Safed

Syria
Damascus

Lebanon
Beirut

Greece
Crete
Smyrna
Athens
Arta
Salonika

Turkey
Constantinople
Adrianople

Italy
Messina
Palermo
Naples
Rome
Ancona
Livorna
Pisa
Lucca
Florence
Ferrara
Padua
Venice
Genoa
Milan
Turin

France
Marseilles
Lyons
Biarritz
Bayonne
Tartas
Bordeaux
La Rochelle
Nantes
Paris
Rouen
Nantes
Saint Jean de Luz

Belgium
Brussels
Antwerp

The Netherlands
Rotterdam
The Hague
Amsterdam
Emden

England and Ireland
London
Bristol
Dublin

Germany
Hamburg
Altona
Glueckstadt

Denmark
Copenhagen

Austria
Vienna

Poland
Kraków
Zamość

Hungary
Budapest

Yugoslavia
Belgrade
Split

Bulgaria
Sofia

Source: Encyclopaedia Judaica

10 Jews in Sons of the American Revolution? Colonial Jewish Families

A small cemetery in downtown Manhattan's Chatham Square stands quietly barricaded by locked iron gates. Several years ago, during a walking tour of Jewish New York led by the late, great, Jewish genealogy pioneer, Rabbi Malcolm H. Stern, I came across this protected piece of property: a seventeenth century cemetery of America's first Jewish congregation, Shearith Israel.

The Twenty-three Refugees

Jewish presence in America dates back to 7 September 1654, when twenty-three Jews—four men, six women, and thirteen youngsters—arrived in New Amsterdam from Recife, Brazil. Among them were Abram Israel (de Piza or Dias), David Israel (Faro), Assar Leeven (Asser Levy), Moses Ambrosius (Lumbroso), Judicq de Mereda (Judith Mercado), and Ricke Nunes. These twenty-three were forced to leave their homes when the Portuguese recaptured Brazil from the Dutch.

Tucked away in downtown Manhattan's Chatham Square stands the oldest Sephardic cemetery in America. Courtesy of the American Jewish Historical Society.

Under Dutch rule, a thriving Jewish community in Brazil had been established in the 1630s and 1640s. Jews came from Europe, Asia, and Africa—Poland, Hungary, Germany, Turkey, and particularly, Holland—to form a New World outpost of Old World Jewry. Many originally hailed from Spain and Portugal, escaping the inquisitions of the fifteenth and sixteenth centuries, and found new homes in Holland and in other places that provided a safe haven for religious observance.

When the Portuguese occupied their community, those who had been born Jews chose to leave, fearing they would be subject to another Inquisition. Most of them returned to their former home of Amsterdam. Others found new homes in the West Indies.

But these twenty-three arrived in New Amsterdam—established by the Dutch West India Company—on the ship *Sainte Catherine.* They were met by fellow Jews, Jacob Barsimson and Solomon Pietersen, shareholders of the company. From Amsterdam, Barsimson, who had arrived earlier that year, was the first Jewish settler in New Amsterdam.

New Amsterdam Jews established their congregation, Shearith Israel, in 1655. By the end of the colonial period, congregations were established in New York; Newport, Rhode Island; Philadelphia; Lancaster, Pennsylvania; Richmond, Virginia; Charleston, South Carolina; and Savannah, Georgia.

These immigrants were engaged mostly in mercantile trade, and, like most others coming to this new land, they were looking for economic opportunity and religious freedom.

Jewish Communities and First Families of the Colonial Period

At the time of the first federal census in 1790, the Jewish population was estimated to be between 1,300-1,500 people, about one-thirtieth of one percent of the total population. Though small in number, they had great impact.

New York

By 1655, at least thirteen Jewish males lived in New Amsterdam. The Jewish population rose to about 100 between 1685-

An interior view of the Newport synagogue, dedicated in 1763.
Courtesy of the American Jewish Historical Society.

1695, reached 200 between 1725-1730, and 300 by the middle of the eighteenth century.

One of the first Jewish families in New York was that of Louis Moses Gomez, settling in New York in 1703. His father had fled Spain and lived in France before settling in England in 1696. He and his son, Daniel, developed a flourishing trade business throughout the colony and contributed significantly to communal affairs.

Cantor-minister of the Shearith Israel congregation and the first cantor born in America, Gershom Mendes Seixas, was considered to be an American patriot. When the British took New York, he fled with the synagogue's religious objects in his protection. With the birth of the new republic, he returned and eventually served as a trustee of Columbia College.

Newport

In 1760, the following families were noted: Harts, Moses Levy and his brother, Sarsides (a.k.a. Seixas), Aaron Lopez, Moses Lopez, Jacob Isaacs, Isaac Elizur, old Polloc, Issachar Polloc, Polloc junior, Rodrigues Levarez, Hart, and Lucina. The total number was estimated to be 58 people and ten families.

The Newport synagogue was dedicated on 2 December 1763 in a service performed by Dr. Isaac de Abraham Touro. At this time, there were about 80 Jews in Newport. Touro, born in Holland, himself came to Newport about 1766 from Jamaica. He returned there after the Revolutionary War.

Owning a fleet of whalers, Newport merchant Aaron Lopez became quite the shipping magnate. A former Marrano, he had escaped Portugal and arrived in Newport in 1752, when he changed his first name of Duarte to Aaron. He was considered to be a merchant genius.

Philadelphia and Lancaster

There were about a dozen Jewish families in Philadelphia in 1771, and the Jewish community there organized its synagogue, Mikveh Israel, in 1782. Within a few years, dozens of families left for their former homes in New York, Charleston, Savannah, and elsewhere, having escaped to Philadelphia during the Revolution.

An exterior view of Beth Elohim in Charleston. Courtesy of the American Jewish Historical Society.

Perhaps the most famous Jew of the colonial period was Haym Salomon, a Polish Jew who became well known in the Philadelphia Jewish community. He advanced large amounts of money to the Revolutionary cause.

Brothers Bernard and Michael Gratz from Langendorf, Silesia, armed with an inheritance and careful business training from their British cousin, Solomon Henry, got their start in worldwide trade from Philadelphia between 1750 and 1760. They especially pursued economic interests in areas along the Ohio River.

Outside Philadelphia, the largest number of Jews was in Lancaster. Joseph Simon, who arrived there about 1735, was prominent among them, having made his fortune primarily from Indian trade.

Richmond

A Sephardic Jewish community flourished in western Virginia in the mid-1700s, augmented by the migration of Lancaster Jewish families into Virginia to settle along the Ohio River.

The Richmond Jewish community consisted only of Isaiah Isaacs before the Revolutionary War. It was clearly the youngest community during the colonial period.

Formed shortly after the Revolutionary War, the congregation of Beth Shalom conducted Sephardic services though many of its organizers were of German descent. By 1791, there were 28 members, among them: Jacob Mordechai, Joseph Darmstadt, Isaac Judah, Samuel Alexander, Joseph Marx, Aaron Henry, Manuel Judah, Aaron Cardoza, Benjamin Solomon, Benjamin Myers, and Marcus Elcan.

Charleston

Jews were living in "Charles Town" as early as 1695, but there weren't enough of them to hold a minyan (ten men) for about another thirty years. In 1749, they had sufficient number to organize a congregation, Kahal Kadosh Beth Elohim.

The first president of the congregation was Joseph Tobias, a Sephardic Jew who arrived in Charleston sometime before 1737. He was known as the "linguister" of the Spanish language and was a prosperous merchant, ship owner, and landowner. He married the daughter of Jacob d'Olivera, who had moved with his family to Charleston from Savannah.

By 1791, 53 families—about 200 people—belonged to Beth Elohim.

Savannah

The Board of the Sephardic congregation at Bevis Marks Synagogue in London petitioned Georgia trustees in the early 1730s to permit the immigration of poor Jews to the colony. Forty-two Jews, mostly of Sephardic origin, arrived in Savannah on 11 July 1733, among them: Dr. Samuel Nunes Ribiero and family, Isaac Nunes Henriques and family, Raphael Nunes Bernal and wife, Jacob Lopez d'Olivera and family, Aaron de Pivia, Benjamin Gideon (Abudiente), Jacob Lopez de Crasto, David Lopez de Pass and wife, Isaac da Costa Villareal, Abraham de Molina, David Rodrigues de Miranda, David Cohen Delmonte and family, Benjamin Sheftall and wife, and Abraham de Lyon.

This group became farmers like the rest of the Savannah community. According to Trustee plan, each adult male who came at his own expense received a grant of fifty acres—five for home and garden and forty-five for farming outside of town. As a result, Nunes acquired six farms, Henriques seven, d'Olivera seven, and Delmonte thirty.

Congregation Mikva Israel was established in 1733, though services were discontinued after 1740 when a large piece of the community left for the more flourishing Charleston. By 1791, only about a dozen families constituted the only Jewish congregation in Georgia.

Finding Your Colonial Ancestors

If you have Jewish ancestors from the colonial period, you're in luck. Two books published by Rabbi Malcolm H. Stern detail the first families of America in glorious, painstaking, genealogical detail. *Americans of Jewish Descent* and the more comprehensive *First American Jewish Families* present hundreds of genealogies from 1654-1988. For instance, Haym Salomon—a designated Revolutionary ancestor—was born in 1740 in Lissa, Poland, and married Rachel Franks in New York on 2 January 1777. They had four

CASE STUDY

Dr. Joseph L. (Joel) Andrews of Concord, MA, Surgeon General of the Massachusetts Sons of the American Revolution (SAR), has been studying his family's history for many years, following his father, who did the same. Their Jewish American roots go back more than 300 years to the 1690s with three ancestors active in the American Revolution: Haym Salomon, often called "Financier of the American Revolution," and Isaac Franks and Benjamin Nones, two officers in George Washington's Continental Army.

"I am very proud of my early Jewish heritage," Andrews says. His father was orphaned at the age of 12, but he knew he was the great-great-grandson of Haym Salomon—Salomon's daughter, Sally, had married Joseph Andrews, a teacher from Strassbourg, France.

The family has "all kinds of documentation," mainly because it was required for admittance into the Sons of the American Revolution (SAR). The family joined SAR in the 1890s. "My grandfather was one of the original SAR members—and one of the few Jewish members of this patriotic/genealogical society." Proud of its heritage, the family took a disciplined approach to recordkeeping, which, of course, delights the genealogist in us.

Andrews' family has belonged to the same synagogue, Shearith Israel in New York, for more than 300 years. At the time of the American Revolution, his family, like many at the time, was split between Patriots who supported the Revolution and Loyalists, or Tories, who remained loyal to King George III. After the Revolution, many Loyalists moved to Canada or returned to England, some of the women becoming wives of British officers and mothers of Anglican ministers in England.

This ancestry has inspired Andrews to write a book on Jewish American contributions to colonial and revolutionary America.

Joel Andrews is proud of his colonial American heritage, dating back to Haym Salomon. Courtesy of the American Jewish Historical Society.

PARTIAL LIST OF COLONIAL JEWISH FAMILY NAMES

These names are among the genealogies you'll find in Rabbi Stern's compendia.

Aarons
Abraham
Alexander
Ancker
Arnold
Bach
Barnett
Baruch
Benjamin
Benzaken
Binswanger
Block
Brauer
Cardozo
Cohen
Cromelien
Da Vega
Davies
De Crasto
De Cordova
Delgado
De Leon
De Sola
Elias
Emanuel
Etting
Ezekiel
Fleisher
Fonseca
Franks
Gomez
Gratz
Guggenheimer
Harby
Hart
Hays
Hecht
Heineman
Henriques
Hyman
Isaacs
Jackson
Jacobs
Joseph
Judah
Kraus
Lawrence
Lazarus
Levy
Lewis
Lopez
Louzada
Lyons
Marks
Mendes
Moise
Mordechai
Moses
Myers
Naar
Nathan
Nones
Oppenheimer
Peixotto
Phillips
Pinto
Ritterbrand
Salomon
Samuel
Seixas
Sheftall
Solis
Stern
Stix
Sulzberger
Thorman
Tobias
Wolf
Workum

children: Ezekiel, Sallie, Deborah, and Haym Moses (named for his father who died several months before the birth). Sallie married Joseph Andrews.

Keep in mind that families were not restricted to a single Jewish community. For example, Isaac Henriques from Savannah was naturalized in New York in 1743 and by 1747 was in Lancaster. He died in Philadelphia in 1767. And, intermarriages between Sephardic and Ashkenazic (the medieval Hebrew word for "German") families were not uncommon after the controversial marriage of Sephardic Isaac Mendes Seixas and Ashkenazic Rachel Levy in 1740.

Even if your roots don't take you back to colonial America, it's worth getting familiar with the country's first Jewish families.

QUICK TIP

Beyond the Stern compilations, Andrews suggests contacting the American Jewish Historical Society <www.ajhs.org> and your local Jewish Genealogical Society <www.jewishgen.org)>.

SEE ALSO

To find your nearest Jewish Genealogical Society, see the list in Chapter 15.

11 Holocaust Research

"Zaromb is dead. Parts of our own bodies died a martyr's death along with millions of Jews and Jewish children in every corner of Europe, where thousands were thrown into mass graves and millions of bodies were burned and never given any grave at all.

"If Zaromb would have had palaces, large factories, oil wells, if Zaromb were a large, rich city, the world would sometimes recall it; diplomats would discuss it at their round tables; poets would immortalize it in song; its name would be immortalized in the thick tomes which people would read and perhaps a tear would fall on the Holy Jewish community Zaromb.

"But Zaromb was small and poor. Instead of palaces, there were small wooden houses. Here was the town, here the market place and you were already in green fields outside the shtetl. The small, narrow streets were filled with lovely Jewish children. Poor Jews, exhausted from hard work and long hours, forgotten by G-d, lived poorly and hoped for a visit to America or to Eretz-Israel. Today, Jewish Zaromb lies dead.

"And you, the remaining children of Zaromb, are spread out all over the world. Let your tears fall on this page. This is Zaromb's tombstone, there is no other marker. May your desire for revenge fill your hearts and make you ball your hands into hard fists."

This was a chapter in the *Zaromb Journal*, published in 1947 by the United Zaromber Relief, written by L. Pevka. The *Journal*

ON THE BOOKSHELF
The best and most comprehensive treatment for finding and using Holocaust-related materials for genealogical purposes is Gary Mokotoff's *How to Document Victims and Locate Survivors of the Holocaust.*

was the town of Zaromb's Yizkor book, a memorial book written by *landslayt* to document and remember the town they once knew as home and the family, friends, and neighbors murdered during the Holocaust. This was also the town my grandfather left in 1913 to come to America.

Like many American Jews, I didn't think I had any relatives who died at the hands of the Nazis. My family research led me to believe—and know—otherwise. Using the sources listed on the next few pages, I found that my grandfather's brothers and sisters and their families died, that my paternal grandmother's family—all but her and her youngest brother—died, along with many, many more extended family members.

Yizkor Books

<www.jewishgen.org/Yizkor/>

I used Yizkor Books for the first time when the Jewish Genealogical Society of North Jersey planned a trip in 1991 to the Jewish Theological Seminary in New York. I knew I would be reluctant to go there on my own, because my knowledge of Hebrew is severely limited. I went armed with the surnames I was researching written on a piece of paper in block Hebrew letters so I could check the indices of certain books, that is, providing there was an index.

These memorial books were typically written in Hebrew, Yiddish, or some combination of both by *landsmanshaftn* in the 1950s and 1960s. They describe the history of the town, the Jewish community, notable personalities, and remembrances. Many books contain a necrology, or list of those who perished, and ads from members of the *landsmanshaft* in memory of their loved ones.

At New York's YIVO Institute for Jewish Research, I found a copy of the Zaromb memorial book. I made a photocopy of the entire book. A few years later, there was a posting on JewishGen by someone in Israel looking for the "Zaromb Journal of 1947." I didn't know whether this book was the same one I had, but contacted the inquirer. It turned out that a woman in Israel had an English translation of the book and was looking for a copy of the original because her family's photographs were included. I, on the other hand, had been looking for a translator I could afford. We swapped copies, giving each of us what we wanted. The Yizkor book, for which I created an index of names for anyone interested in the town, gave me an indication of why my grandfather may have left—Zaromb was severely economically depressed. I now also have my grandfather's original copy of the book, donated by my aunt.

Whether or not you think you had family who died in the Holocaust, Yizkor books can provide rich information on your ancestral community. And, thanks to JewishGen's Yizkor Book Special Interest Group and its master database, it's relatively easy to determine whether a book exists for your ancestral town, who else is interested in the town, who has a copy of the book (since many of them are out-of-print and hard-to-find), whether a translation exists, which libraries have the books, and more.

If you don't find your town listed by searching the master database's listing of more than 1,000 books, consider looking in a broader region such as Latvia or Lithuania.

Many libraries have significant Yizkor Book collections, including the following:

California

Los Angeles	Hebrew Union College
Los Angeles	Simon Wiesenthal Center/ Yeshiva University Library
Los Angeles	UCLA Research Library
Los Angeles	University of Judaism
San Francisco	Holocaust Center of Northern California

Florida

Gainesville	Price Library of Judaica, University of Florida

Massachusetts

Boston	Boston Public Library
Brookline	Hebrew College
Cambridge	Harvard University Library
Waltham	Brandeis University Library

Maryland

Baltimore	Joseph Meyerhoff Library

Michigan

Ann Arbor	University of Michigan Harlan Hatcher Graduate Library
West Bloomfield	Holocaust Memorial Center, Morris and Emma Schaver Library-Archives

New York

New York	American Jewish Historical Society
New York	Bund Archives (collection at YIVO)
New York	Hebrew Union College—Jewish Institute of Religion Library
New York	Jewish Theological Seminary Library
New York	New York Public Library, Jewish Division
New York	Yeshiva University Library
New York	YIVO Institute for Jewish Research Library

Oregon

Portland	Congregation Neveh Shalom

Great Britain

Cambridge	Cambridge University Library
Finchley	JGS of Great Britian, Finchley Synagogue
London	University of London, School of Oriental and African Studies
London	Wiener Library

Canada

Montreal	Jewish Public Library
Toronto	University of Toronto John P. Robarts Research Library

Israel

Jerusalem	YadVahsem
Ramat Gan	Bar-Ilan University
Tel Aviv	Ahad Haam Library
Tel Aviv	Hitachdut Yotzei Polin
Tel Aviv	Moadon Ha'Rund
Tel Aviv	Rambam Library

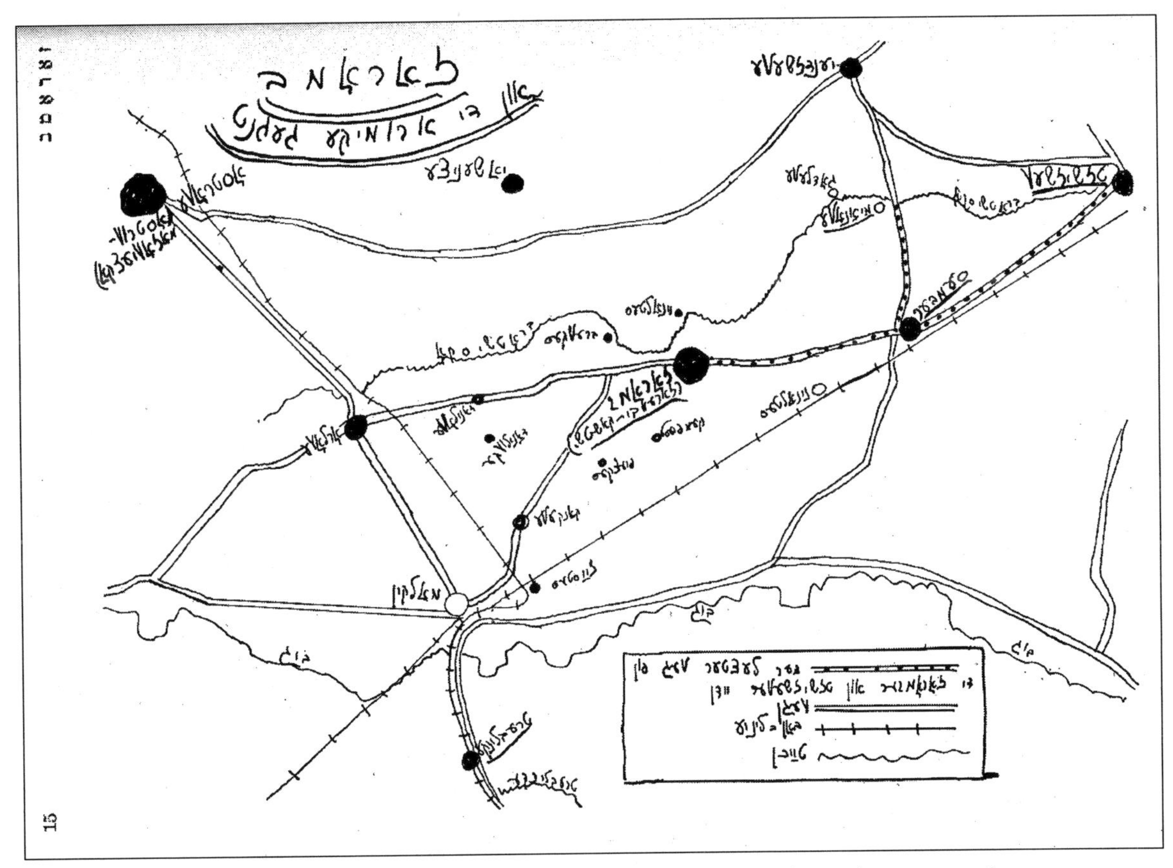

The Zaromb yizkor book includes this hand-drawn map of Zaromb in relation to nearby towns.

648

יזכור!

פלאטאו שלמה און 1 זוהן
פלאטאו־פופקע גישע און קינדער
פלאצקער ישראל, פרוי און קינדער
פלעשער משה, פרוי און קינדער
פלעשער דוד, פרוי און קינדער
פעדערמאן מיכאל, פרוי בריינטשע און
קינדער
פעדער־ליכטענשטיין רבקה און 1 קינד
פעצינער אברהם און קינדער
פעצינער לייבל און פרוי
פעצינער דוד
פעצינער חנה און קינדער
פעצינער איטשע, פרוי רייזל און קינדער
פערלמוטער שלום, פרוי גישע און 1 קינד
פראוודע יוסף, פרוי רחל און קינדער
פראוודע יצחק גרשון
פראוודע נחום, פרוי און קינדער
פראגער איטשע יאדאווער, פרוי און 1 זוהן
פראשקע אברהם, פרוי דבורה און 5 קינדער
פראימאוויטש יוסף, פרוי פרומעט און
2 קינדער
פראווידלע נח, פרוי גרינע און קינדער
פרידמאן אברה םיעקב, פרוי בלומע און
קינדער
פרידמאן אברהם יצחק, פרוי עטקע און
קינדער
פרידמאן אהרן אלי׳, פרוי און קינדער
פרידמאן שמואל, פרוי שרה גיטל און
3 קינדער
פרידמאן אברהם מלמד, פרוי רבקה רחל
און 1 טאכטער
פרידמאן יצחק, פרוי און קינדער
פרידמאן משה, פרוי און קינדער
פרידמאן יוסף, פרוי גאלדע און קינדער
פרידמאן שמערל, פרוי און קינדער
פרידמאן־קראנענבערג חי׳ קיילע און
טאכטער חוה
פרייליך אהרן, פרוי טשיפע און קינדער
פריד זיליג, פרוי און קינדער
פריד גיטל
פריד צירל און מאן

פריזאנט יצחק, פרוי און קינדער
פרענקעל־אלענבערג און קינדער
פרענקל משפחה
פרענקעל ד״ר נחום
פרענקעל לייבל
פריימאן אברהם יצחק און קינדער
פריימאן משה לייב, פרוי רעלטשע און
2 קינדער
פריימאן ישראלקע, פרוי רחל און קינדער
פריימאן חיים בן אברהם יצחק, פרוי אידא
און 2 קינדער
פריימאן משה, פרוי חוה און 7 קינדער
פריימאן אלטער, פרוי און קינדער
פריימאן איטשע משה און קינדער
פריימאן אברהם יעקב, פרוי שרה און קינדער
פריימאן מנדל, פרוי און קינדער
פריימאן יעקב, פרוי און קינדער
פריימאן יצחק, פרוי עלקע און קינדער
פריימאן יוסף, פרוי און קינדער
פריימאן חיים בן בנימין
פריימאן מיכאל, פרוי און קינדער
פריימאן מאריס און פרוי עווא
פרץ יעקב, פרוי טויבא און קינדער
פשיטעק חנה
פשעטיצקי שבתי, פרוי אסתר און קינדער
פשעטיצקי הירשל

צ

צוקראוויטש אברהם, פרוי ליבע און
3 קינדער
צוקראוויטש בן־ציון, פרוי און קינדער
צוקראוויטש חיים מרדכי, פרוי און קינדער
צוקראוויטש יוסף, פרוי צארנע און קינדער
צינאמאן משה, פרוי גיטל און 4 קינדער
צינאמאן באשע און 2 קינדער
צינאמאן הירשל, פרוי און קינדער
צינאמאן יעקב, פרוי און קינדער
צינאמאן רחל
צינאמאן אסתר
צינאמאן נעמה
צינאמאן שלמה

Yitzhok Prizant, my grandfather's oldest brother, perished in the Holocaust. His name, and that of his family members, appears at the top of the second column on this page of Ostrów Mazowiecka's yizkor book necrology.

Says Judie Ostroff-Goldstein of Syosset, New York, who has been graciously donating her time to translate the 653-page Yizkor Book of Ostrów Mazowiecka, "I've seen several Yizkor Books at this point, and some are much better than others. I would have to rank the Ostrów Mazowiecka book among the best. Those who wrote the Ostrów book tried to give the broad view of the town, not just the middle class. It is truly an amazing accomplishment by amateurs, and they accomplished what they set out to do—to leave us a history of our ancestors. The book contains information that goes back to the First World War. The articles take us back in time and present a picture of how our ancestors lived their daily lives—how they earned their living, prayed, married. There is also a large section of Holocaust eyewitness testimony. Translating this book has been an experience that I will always treasure. This book is truly awesome—with a little imagination, you're walking the streets of Ostrova with your ancestors at your side, pumping water at the market place."

Yad Vashem—Martyr's and Hero's Remembrance Authority
Hall of Names
P.O.B. 3477
Jerusalem 91034
ISRAEL
FAX- 972 2 6419534
<www.yad-vashem.org.il>

In 1992, I was at home for a couple of weeks instead of being at work because my son had the chicken pox. During that time, I received a thick packet from Yad Vashem with about 90 Pages of Testimony on Zuckerkandel Holocaust victims across Galicia. The good news was that I received a lot of information. The bad news was that so many Zuckerkandels were murdered.

In 1995, I received a query from a fellow researcher in Atlanta about the Zuckerkandel family. Yes, I had information on the person she was looking for. In return, she sent me the results of an interview she did with a Leo Zuckerkandel in 1980 while visiting her mother in Florida. I opened her reply and screamed. The names of my great-grandparents were staring me in the face, as were the names of six of my grandmother's siblings I didn't know.

My grandmother was the eldest and came to America in 1913. Her baby brother, Leo, came in 1951 after the war from a Displaced Persons Camp in Förenwald, Germany. All the other brothers and sisters and their families were killed.

No one in my immediate family knew that we had such close relatives who died in the Holocaust. I submitted Pages of Testimony on them and that brought us some kind of closure.

So what's to learn from this? First, while you may think no one in your family perished in the Holocaust, that may not be the case. Second, make sure your research information is listed in the JewishGen Family Finder (more on that in Chapter 13). Third, Yad Vashem's Hall of Names is a research must.

Yad Vashem's Hall of Names documents some three million names in a manuscript collection known as Pages of Testimony. Completed and submitted by relatives, friends, and neighbors, these pages record those who perished and give them back their names. Pages, available in several languages, often contain detailed biographical information (last name, first name, father's name, mother's name, birthplace, date of birth, spouse's name, occupation, date and place of death, children's names and ages, along with their dates and places of death). Also very helpful is information on the submitter—name and address and date the form was completed. With the help of telephone books and the Search Bureau for Missing Relatives, you may be able to connect with the informant or his or her descendants.

Yad Vashem began collecting Pages of Testimony in 1955 and has computerized them. The completeness of the forms varies, and information provided by different informants on the same individual may conflict. As mentioned in Chapter 7, Yad Vashem is developing a "List of Lists," a master databank of more than 18 million names and associated information from more than 10,000 lists that it hopes to make available to the public through the Internet.

Be prepared for the eventuality that the name you seek may not be found. Many, many victims have not been registered. In July 1999, JewishGen joined Yad Vashem in its drive to record the missing names. If you find you have names to record, you can download forms from the Yad Vashem web site at <www.yadvashem.org.il/pot>, but it's suggested you use the special, acid-free forms provided by Yad Vashem. You can request these by mail,

QUICK HIT

You can request a search by e-mail at names@yad-vashem.org.il. To do so, you will need to provide certain key information on an individual (wholesale surname searches are not possible when using this service): Last name, first name, permanent place of residence (town and country before the war). Feel free to provide any additional information you have like maiden name, birth or approximate age, birth date and place, victim's mother's, father's, and spouse's name, wartime residence, victim's occupation, and date and place of death.

When requesting the search, state your full name, relationship to the victim, your mailing address, and e-mail address. The first search or name costs $5 to cover expenses for staff time, mailing, photocopying, etc. Any additional search is $2. Payment should be made by check to Yad Vashem.

YAD VASHEM
Martyrs' and Heroes'
Remembrance Authority
P.O.B. 3477 Jerusalem, Israel

דף-עד
עדות-בלאט
A Page of Testimony

אינסטיטוט צום אנדענק
פון אומקום און גבורה

THE MARTYRS' AND HEROES' REMEMBRANCE LAW, 5713–1953
determines in article No. 2 that –

The task of YAD VASHEM is to gather into the homeland material regarding all those members of the Jewish people who laid down their lives, who fought and rebelled against the Nazi enemy and his collaborators, and to perpetuate their NAMES and those of the communities, organisations, and institutions which were destroyed because they were Jewish.

דאס געזעץ אנדענק פון אומקום און גבורה - יד-ושם, תשי״ג 1953
שטעלט פעסט אין פאראגראף נומ׳ 2 :

די אויפגאבע פון יד-ושם איז איינזאמלען אין היימלאנד דעם אנדענק פון אלע יידן, וואס זענען געפאלן, האבן זיך מוסר נפש געווען, געקעמפט און זיך אנטקעגנגעשטעלט דעם נאצישן שונא און זיינע ארויסהעלפער, און זיי אלעמען, די קהילות, די ארגאניזאציעס און אניסטיטוציעס, וועלכע זענען חרוב געווארן צוליב זייער אנגעהעריקייט צום יידישן פאלק — שטעלן א דענקמאל.
(געזעץ-בוך נומ׳ 231, י״ז אלול תשי״ג, 82.8.3591)

דאטען וועגן אומגעקומענעם: יעדן נאמען אויף א באזונדער בלאט, מיט קלארער שריפט
DETAILS OF VICTIM: INSCRIBE EACH VICTIM ON A SEPARATE PAGE, IN BLOCK LETTERS

בילד פון דעם אומגעקומענעם
שרייבט או דעם נאמען אויף דער ריקזייט פון דעם בילד

Victim's photo
write victim's name
on back side please

Family name: — 1. פאמיליע-נאמען:

First name: — 2. פארנאמען:

Previous name: (nee for woman) — 3. פאמיליע-נאמען פאר דער חתונה (פאר א פרוי):

6. פארהייראט? Fam. status — 5. מין Sex — 4. געבורטס-דאטע (ווי אלט) Birth date or appr. age

Birth place and country: — 7. ארט פון געבורט (שטאט, לאנד):

Victim's mother - First name: - Maiden name/nee: — 8. מוטער פון דעם אומגעקומענעם - פארנאמען: - מיידלשע-פאמיליע:

Victim's father - First name: — 9. פאטער פון דעם אומגעקומענעם - פארנאמען:

Victim's spouse - First name: - Maiden name/nee; — 10. מאן/פרוי פון דעם אומגעקומענעם - פארנאמען: - מיידלשע-פאמיליע:

Permanent residence place and country: — 11. סטאבילער וואוינארט (שטאט, לאנד):

Wartime residence place and country: — 12. וואוינערטער בעת דער מלחמה (שטאט, לאנד):

Date/year of death: 14. צייט פון טויט: — Victim's profession: 13. בערוף אדער פאך:

Death place: Circumstances of death: — 15. ארט און אומשטענדן פון טויט:

Reported by: — געשריבן פון:
I, the undersigned ______ איך, דער אונטערגעשריבענער
Residing at (address) ______ וואס וואוינט (אדרעס)
Relationship to victim (family/other) ______ קרובישאפט

דערקלער דערמיט, אז די עדות מיט אלע פרטים איז א ריכטיקע לויט מיין בעסטען וויסן
HEREBY DECLARE THAT THIS TESTIMONY IS CORRECT TO THE BEST OF MY KNOWLEDGE

Place and date ______ ארט און דאטע Signature ______ אונטערשריפט

״...ונתתי להם בביתי ובחומותי יד ושם..אשר לא יכרת״. ישעיהו נו ה
"...even unto them will I give in mine house and within my walls a place and a name...that shall not be cut off." isaiah, lvi,5

Pages of Testimony forms are available in several languages to document the lives of Holocaust victims.

e-mail, from your local synagogue, or Jewish Genealogical Society. There's no charge for the form, and it's available in 12 languages.

If downloading the form, fill in as much information as you can. You must sign the form—it's a legal requirement. Send the form to:

American Society for Yad Vashem
500 Fifth Ave., Suite 1600
New York, NY, 10110-1699

The American Red Cross Holocaust and War Victims Tracing and Information Center

Another helpful source in locating information about specific family members affected by the Holocaust is the American Red Cross and its Holocaust and War Victims Tracing and Information Center. The Center cannot conduct blanket surname searches (i.e., everything on the surname Cohen), and it may take some time before they get back to you with search results. However, the Center states, "A case is never considered closed. Since new documentation is discovered all the time, we may provide information on an inquiry that is 10 to 40 years old."

When requesting research, you'll need to supply the person's given and family names, an approximate year of birth, the country of birth, the country of last known residence (and city if you know it), and the source, date, and place of last communication. Contact the Emergency/Tracing Services Department of your local American Red Cross chapter to get Tracing Inquiry Form 1609 to initiate your search. Your chapter will then forward the completed and reviewed form to the trace coordinator offices in Baltimore.

They will then work with other Red Cross societies, the International Tracing Service of Arolsen, Germany, and Magen David Adom of Israel to best service your request. If you live outside the United States, contact the Red Cross Society in your country as each country's society provides tracing services.

For more information, contact:

Tracing Coordinators
American Red Cross
Holocaust & War Victims Tracing & Information Center
(410) 764-5311

United States Holocaust Memorial Museum

100 Raoul Wallenberg Place, SW
Washington, DC 20024-2126
<www.ushmm.org>

The Benjamin and Vladka Meed Registry of Jewish Holocaust Survivors

In 1981, the American Gathering of Jewish Holocaust Survivors established a national registry to document the lives of survivors—anyone who was displaced, persecuted, and/or discriminated against by the racial, religious, ethnic, and political policies of the Nazis and their allies—who came to the United States after World War II. The Registry was created to help survivors search for relatives and friends and now includes more than 170,000 records related to survivors and their families. Although most of the registered survivors live in North America, the Museum now includes the names of survivors from all backgrounds living all over the world.

In April 1993, the Registry was transferred to the United States Holocaust Memorial Museum. Visitors can access the Registry database on the second floor of the museum.

The Museum now offers access to two new databases. It developed Namesearch to accommodate the public need for digitized access and a single user interface. The database allows you to enter a name while it searches some twenty different sources. GEOFF, says Project Coordinator for the Registry of Survivors Michael Haley Goldman, is the flip side of Namesearch. He says, "Even though you may not know exactly what you are looking for, the database links all terms for each geographic location, so you'll be able to get results. That's particularly useful, given that place names changed before, during, and after the war. For example, if you're looking at Vilna, the database links to Wilno and Vilnius or in other examples, to place names that bear no resemblance to names for the same place."

Collections, Archives, Library

Many helpful documents, photos, personal manuscripts, oral histories, and other sources are housed at the Holocaust Memorial Museum. You can search the collections online. For instance, more than 6,000 oral histories are stored at the museum, mostly in English and on video. There are nearly 30 reels of microfilm on "Extraordinary State Commission to Investigate German-Fascist Crimes Committed on Soviet Territory," that includes information on victims, organized by province or *oblast*.

QUICK HIT
Check out the web site at <www.ushmm.org> where you can search the collections and library catalog online.

Survivors of the Shoah Visual History Foundation

<www.vhf.org>

Steven Spielberg's non-profit project has already filmed more than 50,000 Holocaust survivor oral testimonies. The foundation is working to make the digitized films available to Yad Vashem, the United States Holocaust Memorial Museum, the Simon Wiesenthal Center at the Museum of Tolerance in Los Angeles, the Fortunoff Video Archive for Holocaust Testimony at Yale University in New Haven, Connecticut, and the Museum of Jewish Heritage in New York. While this source may not be directly useful in tracing individual members of your family, it can provide some profound insights into the fate of your ancestral Eastern European towns.

Camp Records

Miriam Weiner's July 2000, "Concentration Camp Records May Fill in Gaps on Family Tree," appeared on the SierraHome Network. Here she notes, "Although numerous published and computerized sources exist for documenting both victims and survivors, the actual records maintained in the various concentration camps, ghettos, and annihilation centers are a seldom-used source for the average genealogist. These records consist of documents, photographs, and detailed lists compiled from transport data."

Majdanek. The Majdanek camp documents more than 350,000 people who perished there. To research family who perished at Majdanek, you can request a search by contacting Archiwum Państwowego Muzeum na Majdanku, ul. Droga Męczenników Majdanka 67, 20-325 Lublin, Poland.

Auschwitz-Birkenau. At Auschwitz-Birkenau, Weiner saw rows of filing cabinets that contained more than 1.5 million index cards, each representing just one document in the Auschwitz archives. You can request a search by completing an inquiry form. The Auschwitz archives personnel will conduct the search and send copies of any documents found at no charge. Contact Archiwum Państwowego Muzeum w Oświęcimiu-Brzezince, ul. Więznów, 32-603 Oświęcim, Poland.

In addition, some 3,000 family photographs were glued into ledger books originally intended for accounting purposes.

ON THE BOOKSHELF
For much more detailed coverage of concentration camp records, see Chapter Six in Miriam Weiner's *Jewish Roots in Poland,* written by archivists at Majdanek and Auschwitz. The chapter describes archive holdings, includes samples, and instructs how to access materials.

FINDING FAMILIES OF HOLOCAUST VICTIMS

Jewish Agency Search Bureau for Missing Relatives
P.O. Box 92
91920 Jerusalem
ISRAEL

I had one Page of Testimony on Simcha Pryzant from the town of Zaromb. Since my grandfather, Avram Mendel Pryzant, was also from Zaromb, I was anxious to find the connection. The informant was Tova Rubinstein, Simcha's sister. I wrote a letter in late 1995 to Batya Unterschatz at the Search Bureau for Missing Relatives asking for the whereabouts of Tova. She responded with contact information and noted I should contact Tova quickly, because she was quite old. I quickly wrote a letter. In January 1996, I received an e-mail from Tammy Goldstein, Tova's granddaughter. Tova had already passed away. It turned out that Tova's and Simcha's father was Jankel David, one of my grandfather's older brothers. Jankel David survived the war and eventually settled in Israel. I will always wonder if my grandfather knew this. None of the current family in Israel knew of my grandfather, presumably because he left for America when Jankel David's children were very young and because my grandfather was disowned by his father. The Page of Testimony led me to relatives who had not had a connection with us in about 80 years.

Weiner also discussed the Auschwitz-Birkenau "death books," detailing the deaths of more than 74,000 people in 46 volumes. Data included names, birth dates, and names of parents.

Theresienstadt. Terezin, known in German as Theresienstadt, was the "model ghetto" established in Czechoslovakia. Nearly 140,000 Jews from Bohemia and Moravia, Germany, Austria, Holland, Denmark, Slovakia, and Hungary were deported to the Terezin Ghetto. More than 30,000 died there while the remainder moved eastward to the death camps of Treblinka, Maly Trostinec, and Auschwitz-Birkenau.

An almost complete list of people and their transport numbers exists. There is also a complete list of transports into and out of the Terezin Ghetto in two volumes, including a name index, date of birth, date of arrival at Terezin, the date and code of the person's next transport, and date and place of death. The Museum History Department in Terezin can help identify pre-war addresses from the transport records.

Terezín Memorial
Památník Terezín
411 55 Terezín
CZECH REPUBLIC
Tel: +42–416–782-225, 782 442, 782 131
Fax: +42-416-782-245 , 782 300
E-mail: archiv@pamatnik-terezin.cz

Summary

Resources do exist to help you identify and locate information on family members who perished in the Holocaust. Researching our family history during this period allows us to renew connections and to give names back to the victims.

יד ושם

דף-עד

Prizant פריזנט

Simcha שמחה

BORN OSTROW – MAZ WARSAW

[illegible]

This Page of Testimony on Simcha Prizant from Yad Vashem's Hall of Names led to the discovery of living relatives in Israel and the United States.

THE JEWISH AGENCY הסוכנות היהודית לארץ-ישראל

Search Bureau for Missing Relatives המדור לחיפוש קרובים

P.O.B. 92, Jerusalem Phone (02) 231606/247770 טל׳ ת.ד. 92, ירושלים

Jerusalem 29.10.96 ירושלים

Your Ref. No. ______ מספרכם

Our Ref. No. 0621 ______ מספרנו

Barbara D. Krasner-Khait
189 Matlock Pl
Somerset N.J. 08873-6410

Dear Sir (Modam) א. (ג.) נ.

In reply to your communication dated 10.10.96 בתשובה לפניתך מיום

which has been addressed to me שנשלחה על שם

I have pleasure in notifying you the הרינו להודיעך את

following addresses : הכתובות הבאות :

1) Joseph Etzioni's widow Rina Etzioni (1
2) Kibbutz Dan 12245 (2
ph. 6-953030
3) Chana Aloni left the country in 1964. I don't know where to
4) Israel Entel (the informant on Ruchel) died in 1977. His

your address and message have been transmitted to the enquirer. העברנו לנ״ל את הידיעה ממך וכן את כתובתך.

Further Information about the other persons sought will be forwarded to you only when received by us הודעה נוספת בדבר שאר המבוקשים תשלח לך אחרי שיעלה בידנו למצאם

your faithfully, בכבוד רב,

Search Bureau for Missing Relatives המדור לחיפוש קרובים

טופס 12 ב- 2500 - (7.92)

Batya Unterschatz of the Jewish Agency's Search Bureau for Missing Relatives provides comprehensive response.

CASE STUDY: VILNA

Judy Baston of San Francisco wrote an article in Zichron Note, *the publication of the San Francisco Bay Area Jewish Genealogy Society, about the role of Holocaust sources in her research. It is reprinted here with her permission.*

As I stood by the mass graves in Eishishok and in Ponar (near Vilna) during my trip to Lithuania in September, I felt strongly the need to call by name the ghosts of my murdered family members.

Not difficult in Eishishok—from family and *landslayt* I knew the names of my grandparents Eli and Ethel Bastunski, my aunts and uncles Altke and Abram, Rivka and Shmuel, my cousins Sorele, Leib, Maishke, Rochele and Maishke, and my half-sister Rifka. But two of my father's brothers had moved to Vilna. And because of the size of the city and what appeared to be the absence of documentation about ghetto residents, getting information about them was far more difficult.

My older uncle, Motl (Mordechai), had married a woman named Rachel, and had three children, Meir, Maishke and Chasia. I had found their names in 1995 at the Holocaust Research Institute in Washington, DC in the microfilms of the Extraordinary Commission to Investigate German-Fascist Crimes Committed on Soviet Territory. Almost miraculously, their names had been listed in a few dozen pages typewritten in Lithuanian—and easy for me to read—sandwiched among hundreds of pages in handwritten Cyrillic.

But the names of my Uncle Yankel's wife, or any children he had, remained a mystery to me. A letter from my uncle to my father in 1934 had given a wedding date: August 21, 1934; I hoped this would help me find a record of the marriage at the archives in Vilnius that kept post-1916 documents.

I had gone to Lithuania along with a group of *landslayt* from Eishishok, where my father had been born. Some were survivors of the Holocaust who had fought with the partisans or been in family camps in the forest; some had gone to the U.S. or Israel before the war; some were their children, nieces or nephews; a few had only learned of their connection to the town through the Tower of Faces at the United States Holocaust Memorial Museum, a collection of 1,100 photos from Eishishok. Knowing how difficult it is to do archival research as part of a group, I had arranged to stay in Vilnius two days after the group had left.

The Bastunski family. Courtesy of Julie Brown.

ŽYDŲ MUZIEJUS 267

Eil.Nr.	Pavardė, vardas	Gimimo metai	Amatas	Adresas
170	Pick Benjomin	1910	šaltkalvis	Rūdninkų g. 23 - 8
171	Pick Mira	1912	tekstilės fab. darbininkė	Rūdninkų g. 23 - 8
172	Pick Lejser	1937	-	Rūdninkų g. 23 - 8
173	Pick Josel	1936	-	Rūdninkų g. 23 - 8
174	Grinberg Chaim	1888	mechanikas	Rūdninkų g. 25 - 1
175	Grinberg Rachela	1896	dipl. virėja	Rūdninkų g. 25 - 1
176	Grinberg Estera	1928	-	Rūdninkų g. 25 - 1
177	Klainplacas Abram	1908	stalius	Rūdninkų g. 25 - 1
178	Klainplacas Fruma	1918	siuvėja	Rūdninkų g. 25 - 1
179	Klainplacas Chilelis	1901	stalius	Rūdninkų g. 25 - 1
180	Klainplacas Frieda	1912	-	Rūdninkų g. 25 - 1
181	Icchokin Šymon	1885	fotografas	Rūdninkų g. 25 - 1
182	Icchokin Pesia	1887	fotografė	Rūdninkų g. 25 - 1
183	Sygall Šmuelis	1903	technikas	Rūdninkų g. 25 - 1
184	Sygall Anna	1911	-	Rūdninkų g. 25 - 1
185	Sygall Lina	1937	-	Rūdninkų g. 25 - 1
186	Schelupski Israel	1904	sandėlininkas	Rūdninkų g. 25 - 1
187	Schelupski Dveira	1907	-	Rūdninkų g. 25 - 1
188	Schelupski Josel	1925	šaltkalvio pad.	Rūdninkų g. 25 - 1
189	Merlis Isaak	1885	maš. inž.	Rūdninkų g. 25 - 1
190	Merlis Scheina	1889	daktarė	Rūdninkų g. 25 - 1
191	Globus Anna	1889	daktarė	Rūdninkų g. 25 - 1
192	Globus Rosa	1906	siuvėja	Rūdninkų g. 25 - 1
193	Globus Dawid	1934	-	Rūdninkų g. 25 - 1
194	Zylberschlag Jadwiga	1909	dekoratorė	Rūdninkų g. 25 - 2
195	Zylberschlag Seweryn	1941	-	Rūdninkų g. 25 - 2
196	Distel Lejba	1922	elektromechanikas	Rūdninkų g. 25 - 2
197	Distel Chasia	1922	-	Rūdninkų g. 25 - 2
198	Fischer Tschernia	1899	-	Rūdninkų g. 25 - 2
199	Friedman Šymon	1909	policininkas	Rūdninkų g. 25 - 2
200	Tabakowitsch Chasia	1901	chem. skalbėja	Rūdninkų g. 25 - 2
201	Goldeweig Mosel	1886	automechanikas	Rūdninkų g. 25 - 2
202	Goldeweig Scheindel	1895	-	Rūdninkų g. 25 - 2
203	Taubes Israel	1922	skardininkas	Rūdninkų g. 25 - 2
204	Golumb Chaja	1897	siuvėja	Rūdninkų g. 25 - 4
205	Bokscha Rachela	1897	siuvėja	Rūdninkų g. 25 - 4
206	Bokscha Guta	1927	-	Rūdninkų g. 25 - 4
207	Schneider Dawid	1896	stalius	Rūdninkų g. 25 - 4
208	Schneider Kuna	1888	-	Rūdninkų g. 25 - 4
209	Schneider Aba	1929	-	Rūdninkų g. 25 - 4
210	Schneider Golda	1930	-	Rūdninkų g. 25 - 4
211	Urbach Johan	1897	chromo odos išdirb.	Rūdninkų g. 25 - 4
212	Urbach Sara	1902	siuvėja	Rūdninkų g. 25 - 4
213	Bastumski* Jakob	1908	stalius	Rūdninkų g. 25 - 4
214	Bastunski Teiba	1909	siuvėja	Rūdninkų g. 25 - 4
215	Bastunski Chana	1935	-	Rūdninkų g. 25 - 4
216	Bastunski Morduch	1896	stalius	Rūdninkų g. 25 - 4
217	Bastunski Rachela	1898	-	Rūdninkų g. 25 - 4
218	Bastunski Mejer	1926	-	Rūdninkų g. 25 - 4
219	Bastunski Moises	1927	-	Rūdninkų g. 25 - 4
220	Klatschko Selman-Israel	1893	maleris[1]	Rūdninkų g. 25 - 4

[1] Vokiškai "Maler" - dažytojas.

The Vilna Ghetto Prisoner List identified members of the Bastunski family. Courtesy of Judy Baston.

Two years ago, I had learned from Jewish genealogist Howard Margol of Atlanta about a list of Vilna Ghetto residents at the Jewish State Historical Museum in Vilnius. I might not have remembered this had not several references to this list been made in the Internet discussion group of the newly resuscitated Litvak Special Interest Group (Litvak SIG).

On my next to the last day in Vilnius, I went to the Jewish Museum and obtained a copy of the list. Without knowing about it in advance, I'm not certain I would have found it; the list, now published in book form, is in a display case, with the front title saying only *Zydu muziejus* and the spine bearing the title *Vilnius Ghetto* in Lithuanian, Cyrillic, and English.

This volume lists, by their addresses in the Ghetto, the 15,000 Jews who were still left in the Ghetto on May 26, 1942, when a general population census of Lithuania was conducted. By then, more than 50,000 Vilna Jews had already been slaughtered at Ponar. The census was discovered in the Lithuanian State Central Archive in1993 by former Vilna Ghetto resident Rachel Margolis.

Volume 1 has no index and several respondents to the Litvak SIG discussion had, for that reason, decided it would be too difficult to search, opting to wait for Volume 2, currently in production, which is supposed to provide an index to Volume 1 as well as to contain lists of prisoners in labor camps such as HKP and Kailis, located just outside the ghetto.

But even without an index, reading this list was for me like a walk through the Ghetto. Evsey Tseitlin's comments in the volume itself reflected my feeling as I began to read through the list: "It seems that together with the census scribes we enter the houses on the territory of the ghetto. We visit people who are sometimes in dozens squatting in one tiniest room."

It was indeed with such a feeling that I thumbed through the pages, feeling almost privileged to have these names of Vilna Ghetto residents imprinted on my memory for even a fraction of a second—something that indexed research often prevents. And then, after about 45 minutes, I came to Page 267, the listing of residents at Number 25-4 Rudnicka St.:

Bastunski Jakob	1908	stalius
Bastunski Teiba	1909	siuveja
Bastunski Chana	1935	----
Bastunski Morduch	1896	stalius

Bastunski Rachela	1898	----
Bastunski Mejer	1926	----
Bastunski Moises	1927	----

I had not expected to find them; with the majority of Ghetto residents massacred by the end of 1941, the odds were clearly against it. What I had found: The first names and birth dates of Yankel's wife and daughter, which I had not known; that my two uncles and their families were together in the Ghetto during their last days; that they were among the minority that had survived beyond 1941; that my two uncles, who had a lumber and forest products business, worked as carpenters in the ghetto, probably in the furniture workshop that was located on Rudnicka St., and that my Aunt Taibe worked as a tailor, probably in a workshop making uniforms for the German Army.

There was, of course, a name missing from the list, Motl and Rachela's daughter Chasia. Ghetto work permits covered two adults and two children, although occasionally children were shifted around to childless families under whose *shain* they could continue to survive. Was this Chasia's lot? Or had she already perished?

On the next day, my last in Vilnius, I went to the Lithuanian Vital Statistics Records Archives (at Kalinausko 21, Vilnius 2600 Lithuania). With me was Rita Petrikiene, the Lithuanian guide who had so expertly worked with me during a short foray to Sokoly, Bastuny and Voronovo in Belarus. We first applied for the wedding record of Yankel and Taibe. The clerk consulted the written indices to Vilna Jewish marriages, not only for 1934, but also for 1933 and 1935, and could find no listing.

But because I now knew their child's name and birth year, we then applied for the birth record of Chana. She checked the birth index, and I could see her eyes moving down each page. "Bastatski," she said. "No, Bastunski," I answered. Then she stopped again. "Bastunski... Chana... Yankel," she said. Tears came to my eyes with the realization that my first cousin, whose name I hadn't even known 24 hours before, was listed in a book in a contemporary archive, one where people living today in Vilnius go to get documents for a passport, a marriage, all the matters of ordinary life that continue in the city more than a half-century after the Jews of Vilna were murdered.

Rita explained that I was leaving the next day for America, and the clerk said she would try to have an extract of the record available by the end of the workday. We returned at 4:30 to get the extract, which provided a birth date but made no mention of the mother's maiden name. Although the clerk said such information is customarily not provided on extracts, we persuaded her to get it for us. Reading from the record itself, she informed us that Taibe's family name had been Alperowicz. "Ask her if I could just look at the record for a moment," I told Rita. She asked, and the clerk then turned the record around to me. The short record, in Polish and Hebrew, listed Taibe's parents' names as well, and I wrote them down.

As I held that paper in my hands, the past and the present seemed to come together, and for the first time during my trip, Vilnius had turned into Vilna for me.

12 Cemetery Research

Each fall I anxiously search through the *New Jersey Jewish News* just prior to the High Holy Days, looking for the announcement of the one day during the entire year when the Grove Street Cemeteries in Newark are open to the public.

It would seem odd that the cemetery is only open one day. But the dozen or so Jewish cemeteries along South Orange Avenue and Grove Street that comprise the Grove Street Cemeteries are located in an area of the city that is no longer safe. On this one day, typically sandwiched between Rosh Hashonah and Yom Kippur, the city's finest patrol these streets. On this one day the descendants of those buried here make their annual pilgrimage. On this one day several years ago, I discovered the burial sites of my great-grandparents, Mordechai and Breina Dvorkin Krasner.

At some point in your research, you will undoubtedly need to visit one or more cemeteries. The information inscribed on the gravestone and the information held in the cemetery office can increase your knowledge about your family.

Where They Are Buried

The following sources can help you determine where your ancestors were interred:

Death certificates. Typically an informant would supply burial place on the decedent's death certificate, including both cemetery name, city, and state. If the cemetery office is computerized, it will be relatively easy to find the grave's exact location. If not, it is very helpful to know whether your ancestor belonged to a particular synagogue, *landsmanshaft* society (for example, the Ostrover Verein, or Ostrover Society), or family circle plots.

Obituaries. Newspaper obituaries in both secular and non-secular papers can also identify the final resting place. They may also name the funeral home that may have additional information.

Perpetual care payments and papers. Though my father had never visited his grandparents' gravesite, he remembered that he and his father made payments to "Ain Yankiff"—and that helped me identify in which plot my great-grandparents were interred. That proved to be a good thing since this particular cemetery does not have computerized data. On my mother's side of the family, my aunt came across receipts and other papers relating to the burial of my great-grandparents, Chaim Joseph and Esther Drewno Entel, in Staten Island.

Oral traditions. When I asked my father's cousin where her grandparents were buried, she answered: turn right at the mausoleum for Rabbi Cohen, go up ten rows, and turn right again. Her recollection enabled me to find them without bothering the office staff on that one extraordinarily busy day the cemetery is open. Ask your family members for information on burial locations.

QUICK HIT

The International Cemetery Project

Soon you'll be able to query a database to find out exactly where your Jewish ancestors are buried without slathering on insect repellent and sunblock. The International Association of Jewish Genealogical Societies began a three-phased International Jewish Cemetery Project in 1994 to determine where Jews are buried, identify the names of the people buried, and make this information accessible to researchers in a database. The first phase of the project has gathered information on more than 21,000 cemeteries and so far, the second phase has identified more than 400,000 names across the globe from more than 875 cemeteries. This resource is particularly useful in areas you just can't get to from where you live.

For more information, go to <www.jewishgen.org/cemetery/>.

What You'll Find

A quick stop at the cemetery office may help you find what you're looking for. Ask the staff for the exact location of the grave and a map.

Once at the site, you'll typically find the deceased person's first and last name, Hebrew name and name of father, indication of whether he was a Kohen or Levite, birth date, and death date. Often, much of the information can be in Hebrew. You don't have to be a Hebrew expert to be able to read the stones, but some familiarity will help.

The Decedent's Name. If a Hebrew name is given, it can often provide a clue to the person for whom the deceased was named. In some cases, you may find the American given name has no resemblance whatsoever to the Hebrew name. For instance, my mother knew one of her cousins only as Philip. Imagine her surprise to see that his given name inscribed on the tombstone was Isidore Philip, in Hebrew Yitzhak Shraga.

Symbols. When you see a pair of hands joined at the thumbs with fingers spread like a fan, you will likely find Hacohen (הכהן) in the inscription, for here lies a Kohen, a descendant of Aaron and member of the priestly class. The finger display, resembling the Hebrew letter "shin" (ש), represents the manner in which Kohanim performed the priestly blessing. It was only when I saw Hacohen on my mother's cousin's stone in one of the Zaromber plots at Montefiore Cemetery in Queens that I understood her maiden name of Cohen may have just been a reflection of her father's Kohen descent. Her father's name was given as Alexander Ziskind Hacohen. Cohen was just the name she used in America; she arrived in America under the name of Kruk.

When you see the image of a pitcher on the stone, it means the deceased was a Levite, descended from the Levi tribe, reminiscent of their duty to wash the hands of the priest. You will likely see Halevi (הלוי) in the inscription.

Typically, a menorah signifies a woman and a Star of David signifies a man. A broken branch means the person buried there died young.

Family Relationships. Look carefully at the words about family relationships on the stone. If, for instance, the inscription reads, "Beloved Son and Brother," you'll know that one or both parents survived the deceased and that there was at least one sibling.

Perpetual Care. Sometimes you may see a "PC" sticker on the gravestone, indicating someone paid for the perpetual care of the grave site. Check with the cemetery office to determine who this person is. You may discover an unknown relative!

Photographs. Some stones bear photographs of the deceased. Consider this a lucky find, especially if you have no other photos.

Proximity. Take a look around at the surrounding graves. Often, relatives may be buried nearby.

Capturing the Image

It is an extremely depressing sight to enter a cemetery to find broken or overturned stones. The ravages of weather and time

The pitcher symbol above the inscription for Salomon Teich, Kozlover society plot, Mt. Hebron, Flushing, New York, indicates he was a Levite.

The tree branches on the stone of 23-year-old Irwin Zahnstecher, Kozlover society plot, Mt. Hebron, Flushing, New York, signifies his youth at the time of death.

The hands symbol that adorns the grave of Samuel Sass, Kozlover society plot, Mt. Hebron, Flushing, New York, indicates he was a Kohen.

wreak havoc on the stones, sometimes making it very difficult to read the inscriptions. When you visit an ancestor's grave, it's a good idea to make the effort to capture the image on film for yourself and future generations. You may need to have some tools with you like garden shears to clear away the brush, a soft-bristled brush like a vegetable brush to remove dirt from the stone, a camera, a notebook and pencil, a rubbing kit, a carpenter's apron with pockets to hold all of this stuff, and a pair of gardening gloves.

If the inscription is legible, be sure to take several photos and jot down the location of the grave and the stone's full inscription. Photos are best taken in bright sunlight; other conditions may result in inferior images.

If the inscription is not very legible, you may need to immerse yourself in the art of tombstones rubbing. Apply paper or fabric (many experts suggest interfacing material like Pellon) to the stone with masking tape and literally rub a piece of large sidewalk chalk across the lettering to capture the image, preferably in long strokes. No harm will come to the stone and you'll end up with a full-size rendition of the inscription. Oldstone Enterprises of Bedford, Massachusetts, has special paper and crayons for this purpose.

QUICK TIP
Take a photo of the epitaph so you can decipher it at home. Depending on the time of year you visit, it can get very hot in the cemetery.

Maps to the Buried Treasure

Cemetery and plot maps can help you navigate through the maze of graves. Depending on the cemetery, it can be very easy to wander into the plot of another group and not realize it. These maps can also be useful tools for your descendants to find the graves. For more than thirty years, my mother and her siblings have been making their annual pilgrimage to Montefiore Cemetery in St. Albans, New York, to visit their parents' graves in the Zaromber society plot. It wasn't until I joined them just a couple of years ago that they discovered the society actually had two plots. Their uncle and cousins were buried in that second plot, revealed by the cemetery office's map.

Stanley Diamond of Montreal put a new twist on cemetery research when a map to Chicago's Waldheim Cemetery helped him identify carriers of the Beta-Thalassemia trait he also carries. Through the generous help of a cemetery office staffer, Diamond

SEE ALSO
See Chapter 18 for the case study on Stanley Diamond's search for the source of his Beta-Thalassemia trait.

was able to link the people he knew as Dawid and Frajde, born in Poland, to David and Fanny, shown on the Ostrover society plot map. What makes the cemetery records so valuable is that they provide much more current information than the records accessible from Polish archives. They provide the link between living families and immigrant ancestors. As Diamond asserts, "That is why Waldheim's Ostrover Section was so important to me and why burials in all Jewish cemeteries are of potential importance for scientific research as well as conventional genealogical study and family reunification."

Caveats

As with any genealogical information, be prepared for misstatements and inaccuracies. For instance, my great-uncle's stone says he was a Levite. He wasn't, but his wife's family was. Sometimes ages of the deceased are rounded to the nearest five. You may also notice that birth dates seem to conveniently fall on the first or fifteenth of the month, particularly for immigrants.

Also note that the time around holidays is extremely busy for the office staff. They may not be able to answer all your questions when the hordes are descending upon them. If you can, visit on an "off" day. Irwin Lapping of the Waldheim Cemetery says, "We certainly want to accommodate everyone. We just need the requests to be reasonable—one or two names, not whole projects—and a reasonable time to look them up. We have more time in the winter than during the visiting season." Naturally, it's harder to find the right person if the name was common. Spelling variations can also cause delays.

A Word on European Jewish Cemeteries

There is the popular belief that most, if not all, eastern European Jewish cemeteries were destroyed during the Holocaust. To a large extent that is unfortunately true. Stones have been known to be reused in roads and other civic projects. However, cemeteries do exist in certain places. In *Jewish Roots in Poland* and *Jewish Roots in Ukraine and Moldova*, professional genealogist and author Miriam Weiner describes cemeteries in more than 100

The person who sent this postcard of the Prague Jewish Cemetery in 1910 wrote that the oldest grave in the cemetery dates to 1497 and the cemetery had not been used since 1787. He also wrote that the stones showed Kohen, Levite, and tribal assignations.

Gathering of the Pryzant family, Czerwińsk, Poland at the grave of Devora Pryzant (died 1904) and her daughter-in-law, Chava (died 1902).

Gathering of the Przestrzeleniec family at the grave of Frejde Jente, Ostrów Mazowiecka, Poland, 1932.

towns and cities, providing current and pre-Holocaust photos, addresses, and information on the cemetery condition.

Final Note

Tombstones were meant to be read. Their inscriptions have been crafted with loving care. It's up to you to capture the information and record it for posterity.

Pursuing family research as part of a group eases the search while also providing great networking opportunities. The next part of this book shows how you can take advantage of group activities by surfing the web, participating in town-based research groups, and joining your local Jewish Genealogical Society and Special Interest Groups based on the geographic roots of your ancestors.

QUICK HIT

A real boon for anyone with ancestors from Warsaw is the Internet-based index of a quarter of a million graves in the Warsaw Jewish Cemetery, undertaken in conjunction with the Jewish Records Indexing – Poland Project. Just use the search capabilities at <www.jewishgen.org/jri-poland>. And, if you're interested in eastern Galicia, check out <www.geocities.com/pikholz/trip/cems.htm>.

FOR MORE INFORMATION

Jewish Heritage Council
World Monuments Fund
949 Park Avenue
New York, NY 10028

Oldstone Enterprises
1 DeAngelo Drive
Bedford, MA 01730
(781) 271-0480

DECIPHERING HEBREW TOMBSTONES

"Don't be intimidated by the foreign alphabet. The Hebrew inscription on most tombstones follow a set pattern which can be easily interpreted with a little guidance and practice," says Warren Blatt, author of an excellent JewishGen infofile, "How to Read a Hebrew Tombstone."

By familiarizing yourself with the alphabet, numerical values, months, and a few key phrases, you'll be reading tombstones like a pro in no time!

The Year of Death

The tombstone of Mordechai, son of Yitzhak, Krasner features the letters **תרעו** that represent the Jewish calendar year. Here's how to use the letters to determine the year:

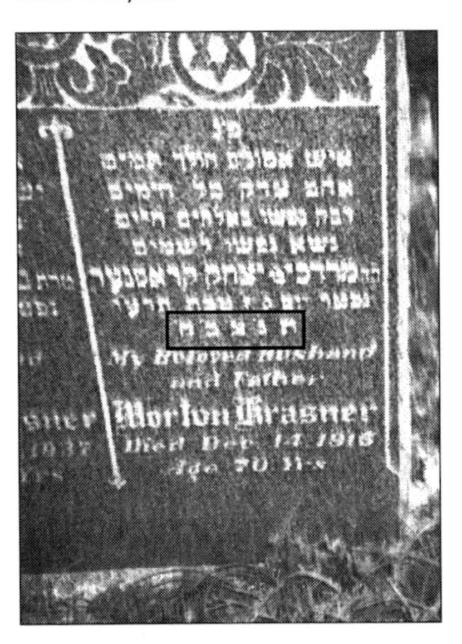

Mordechai Krasner's burial site in the Ain Yankiff section, Grove Street Cemeteries, Newark, New Jersey.

1. Look up the numerical value of each letter according to the table of numbers. This example will give us "400, 200, 70, 6."
2. Add the numbers together: 400+200+70+6 = 676. The "5000" is usually left off, so the Jewish calendar year of the death of Mordechai was 5676.
3. As a general rule of thumb, you can add 1240 to 676 to calculate our Gregorian calendar year. However, when using this for Mordechai, we come up with 1916, which is off by one year.
4. When I entered the death date of 14 Dec 1915 into JewishGen's Calendar Conversion program at <www.jewishgen.org/jos/josdates.htm> I got the date of 7 Tevet 5676, which is the date on the tombstone.

Abbreviations

Abbreviations frequently appear on tombstones, so some of the words you find may never show up in a Hebrew-English dictionary.

One commonly used abbreviation begins the inscription: **פ'נ**. It stands for *po-nikbar* or *po-nitman,* "Here lies."

Another commonly used term ends the inscription. At the bottom of Mordechai's inscription you'll see the abbreviation **תנצבה**. It comes from Samuel 25:29, "May his soul be bound up in the bond of eternal life."

NUMBERS

1	א	30	ל
2	ב	40	מ
3	ג	50	נ
4	ד	60	ס
5	ה	70	ע
6	ו	80	פ
7	ז	90	צ
8	ח	100	ק
9	ט	200	ר
10	י	300	ש
20	כ	400	ת

MONTHS

תשרי	Tishri	September/October
חשון	Heshvan	October/November
כסלו	Kislev	November/December
טבת	Tevet	December/January
שבט	Shevat	January/February
אדר	Adar, Adar I	February/March
אדר ב׳	Adar II	March
ניסן	Nisan	March/April
אייר	Iyar	April/May
סיון	Sivan	May/June
תמוז	Tamuz	June/July
אב	Av	July/August
אלול	Elul	August/September

KEY PHRASES

ENGLISH	PRONUNCIATION	HEBREW
Here lies	po nikbar	פ״נ
Son of	ben	ב
Daughter of	bat	בת
"Mr."	reb, rav	רבר׳
Son/daughter of the honored	ben/bat reb	ב״ר
The Levite	ha-levi	הלוי
The Cohen	ha-kohen	הכהן
The Rabbi	ha-rav	הרב
Dear, beloved (masc.)	ha-yakar	היקר
Dear, beloved (fem.)	ha-y'karah	היקרה
Father	av	אב
My father	avi	אבי
Our father	avinu	אבינו
Mother	eem	אמ
My mother	eemi	אמי
Our mother	emanu	אמנו
My husband	baali	בעלי
My wife	ishti	אשתי
Brother	akh	אח
My brother	akhi	אחי
Our brother	akhinu	אחינו
Sister	akhot	אחות
Aunt	dodah	דודה
Uncle	dod	דוד
Man	ish	איש
Woman	ishah	אשה
Woman (unmarried)	b'tulah	בתולה
Woman "Mrs."	marat	מרת
Old (masc., fem.)	zakain, z'kaina	זקן זקנה
Child (masc., fem.)	yeled, yaldah	ילד ילדה
Young man/woman	bakhur, bakhurah	בחור בחורה
Died (masc., fem.)	niftar, nifterah	נפטר נפטרה
Born (masc., fem.)	nolad, noldah	נולד נולדה
Year, years	shanah, shanim	שנה שנים
Day, days	yom, yamim	יום ימים
Month	khodesh	חדש
First of the month	rosh khodesh	ראש חדש

PART IV

Birds of a Feather Research Together

13 Surf's Up! Researching Your Jewish Ancestry on the Internet

Want to jump start your research? Get your mouse ready, because you can search dozens of databases with a simple click. Whether the surnames you're researching are unique or common, you'll find instant gratification on the Web.

There are two major sites for Jewish surname surfing, JewishGen and Avotaynu. Let's take a look at what each one offers.

JewishGen

<www.jewishgen.org/databases>

General Databases

JewishGen Family Finder (JGFF) <www.jewishgen.org/jgff>

Perhaps the easiest and best way to start out using the site's nearly 40 surname-queryable databases is with the "JewishGen Family Finder" or JGFF, probably the most heavily visited of all the JewishGen searchable databases. You can search by surname or place among more than 200,000 surnames and towns. Using this research tool, you can find others who are researching your name or your town. If you find someone researching the surname you're interested in, simply click on his or her e-mail address and your e-mail screen will pop up, so you can send a message.

Whether you find a match or not, it's important to enter your own information so others can find you. Numerous lost relatives "found" me through my Family Finder entries. To enter the

QUICK HIT
Just use the address of <www.jewishgen.org/databases> to access all the databases mentioned in this section.

names and towns you research, go to the web site and click on "Enter." Then you'll follow a step-by-step process where you create and password and receive a computer-generated researcher code. Make certain you write these down, because you'll need them if you ever want to modify your JGFF information in any way—surnames, names of towns, your e-mail, or your postal mail address. When you keep this information up to date, others can find you.

Family Tree of the Jewish People

<www.jewishgen.org/gedcom>

Using the JewishGen Family Finder researcher code and password is the only way you gain access to "Family Tree of the Jewish People," where you can view individual pedigrees and send e-mail that will be forwarded to the contributor. This database contains information on more than two million people. On 24 October 1999, an historic document was signed by JewishGen, Inc., the International Association of Jewish Genealogical Societies (IAJGS) and The Nahum Goldmann Museum of the Jewish Diaspora (Beth Hatefutsoth) that established a process by which the three agencies will cooperatively create a "Family Tree of the Jewish People" that will be accessible through the web, on CD, and onsite at the Museum. The project is aimed at enhancing our ability to connect and re-connect with our families, to increase interest in Jewish genealogy, to allow for historical research, and to preserve our Jewish history for future generations. Using this database, I found second cousins living in Israel, never before knowing they survived the Holocaust.

Online Discussion Groups

<www.jewishgen.org/JewishGen/DiscussionGroup.htm>

JewishGen also offers close to 30 online discussion groups, freely available to anyone who is interested. You can search the discussion group archives that contain all messages posted to the JewishGen Discussion Group since September 1993. Additional JewishGen mailing lists for the Special Interest Groups (SIGs), such as Belarus, Bohemia-Moravia, Denmark, Galicia, Hungary, Latvia, Lithuania, Romania, South Africa, and Ukraine are also archived

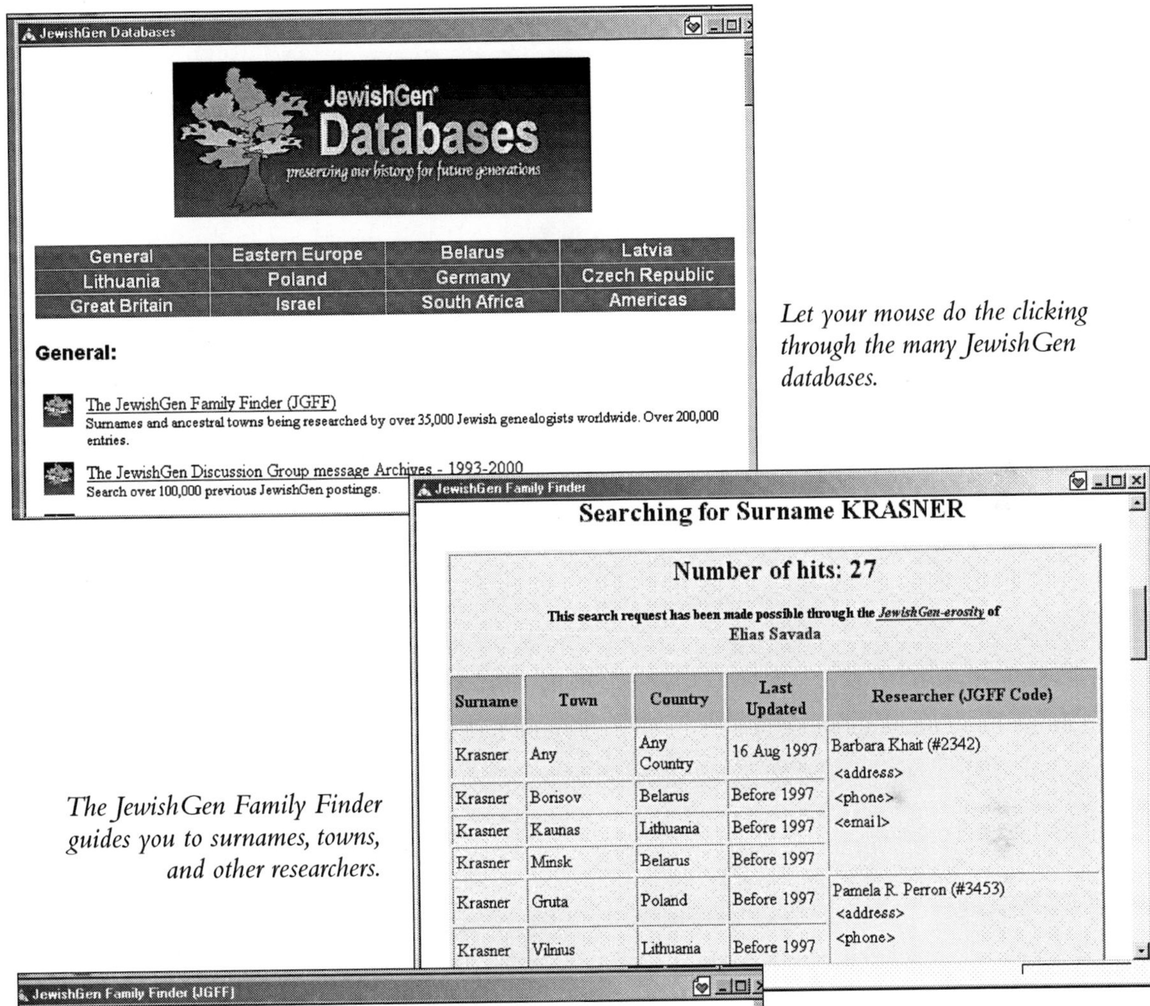

Let your mouse do the clicking through the many JewishGen databases.

The JewishGen Family Finder guides you to surnames, towns, and other researchers.

JewishGen Family Finder (JGFF)

The JewishGen Family Finder (JGFF)

The *JewishGen Family Finder* (JGFF) is a database of ancestral towns and surnames currently being researched by Jewish genealogists worldwide.

By using the JGFF, you can learn whether others are seeking ancestors of the same surname or town of origin.

Search	Enter	List	Modify
Search the database	Register your own surnames and towns	View your existing entries	Update your existing entries

Search, Enter, or Modify functions on the JewishGen Family Finder screen help you get the most from the database's capabilities. Don't forget that entering your own information into the database is an important step!

from their very first postings. Subscribe to one or more of these SIG mailing lists at <www.jewishgen.org/listserv/sigs.htm>.

Eastern Europe

After the Holocaust, many *landsmanshaftn* wrote memorial books, largely in Hebrew and/or Yiddish called Yizkor books to remember those who perished. These books are rich sources of information as they often contain town histories as well as names and photos of the deceased. The "Yizkor Book Project" has put 200 of these books online in some shape or form, most often the necrologies (lists of those who perished). You can search here for your town or your name.

If your family was from the Ukrainian *gubernias* of Kiev, Poltava, or Chernigov, check out the "*Vsia Rossia* 1895 Database." *Vsia Rossia* was a business directory covering the Russian Empire.

Review the list of more than 4,000 "Jewish Religious Personnel in Russia, 1853-54" in more than 900 communities. Culled from Professor Genrich M. Deych's book on synagogues, prayer houses, and their employees in the Pale of Settlement, and the Russian provinces of Courland and Livonia, this index allows you to query by name either in standard format or by using the Daitch-Mokotoff Soundex system.

Specific Geographic Areas

Belarus

<www.jewishgen.org/databases/Belarus>

The databases for Belarus are fairly new to this site, being uploaded since the Belarus Special Interest Group formed at the 1998 Annual Summer Seminar on Jewish Genealogy in Los Angeles. You can access the 1903 *Vsia Rossia* set of business directory entries for Minsk Gubernia and the 1911 set for Mogilev Gubernia. A tremendous time-saving finding aid to Minsk Jewish vital records filmed by the Church of Jesus Christ of Latter-day Saints, the database of "Minsk Surnames" will help you find the surname you seek, identifying which specific years carry that name. The "Mogilev Birth Index of Boys, 1864-1894" identifies surnames by year so you can easily find what you need when you use the Mogilev Jewish vital record films at your Family History Center.

In addition to these, the "Grodno Gubernia 1912 Voters List" holds names of more than 26,000 men of this province who were eligible to vote in the Russian parliamentary elections of 1912.

There is also a database for Belarus that includes names and basic demographics of more than 12,000 people in the "Brest Ghetto," the first phase of a project to name Holocaust victims drawn from Soviet Archives. The "Rechitsa Uezd 1906 Voters List" contains the names of nearly 3,000 men of this district within Minsk Gubernia who were eligible to vote in the Duma election of 1906. The Belarus SIG is now working on developing additional listings of these voter lists for other districts within Belarus. Perhaps an unusual source for Belarus is the 1929 Polish Business Directory for Nowogrodek Province that lists more than 15,000 names.

The Belarus SIG developed an "All Belarus" database of more than 100,000 records, which provides links to smaller databases. You can find more databases organized by town through the "ShtetLinks" link from the JewishGen Home Page. As an example, I found several lists on the Borisov ShtetLinks page, including ghetto, army personnel, and factory employee lists. Shtetlinks represents more than 200 communities.

SEE ALSO

See Chapter 14 for more on Shtetlinks.

Latvia

<www.jewishgen.org/databases/Latvia>

The "All Latvia" database contains nearly 25,000 records—voter lists, tax records, newspaper notices, permits, and military records—covering Courland and Livland *gubernias*.

Lithuania

<www.jewishgen.org/Litvak/all.htm>

The Litvak SIG developed an award-winning "All Lithuania" database of more than 200,000 records that serves as a search engine to many smaller databases. These may be queried with a single search. The first Search Results page gives you a table, indicating the source of the information, how many "hits" the search located in each database, and links you to the sub-database.

Two sources are lists of donors that appeared in Hebrew periodicals. The first contains names of 5,000 donors to the Per-

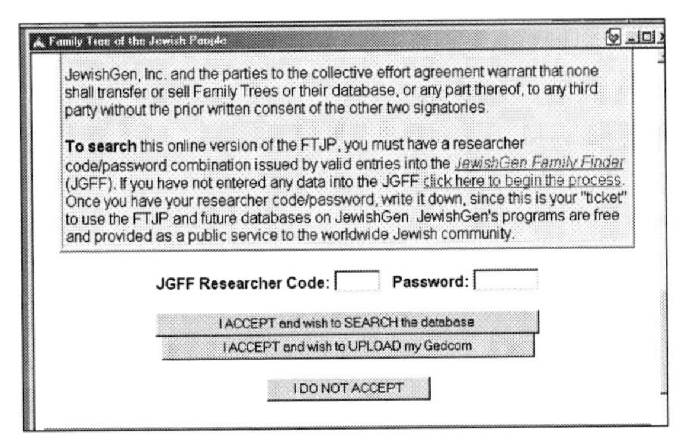

Family Tree of the Jewish People

JewishGen, Inc. and the parties to the collective effort agreement warrant that none shall transfer or sell Family Trees or their database, or any part thereof, to any third party without the prior written consent of the other two signatories.

To search this online version of the FTJP, you must have a researcher code/password combination issued by valid entries into the *JewishGen Family Finder* (JGFF). If you have not entered any data into the JGFF click here to begin the process. Once you have your researcher code/password, write it down, since this is your "ticket" to use the FTJP and future databases on JewishGen. JewishGen's programs are free and provided as a public service to the worldwide Jewish community.

JGFF Researcher Code: **Password:**

I ACCEPT and wish to SEARCH the database

I ACCEPT and wish to UPLOAD my Gedcom

I DO NOT ACCEPT

Your JewishGen Family Finder researcher code and password allow you to search the Family Tree of the Jewish People.

The All Belarus Database

The All Belarus Database

Searching for Surname KRASNER
Run on Saturday 14 October 2000 at 22:40:59

Description	Press the Button to view the matches
Minsk Surnames Database	List 1 records
Mogilev Birth Index of boys, 1864-1894	List 1 records

The All Belarus Database search engine found the surname Krasner in two of its databases.

LitvakSIG - Search the AWARD WINNING All Lithuania Database

Search the Award-winning ALD

© 1999/2000 LitvakSIG, Inc. All Rights Reserved.

[Home] [Up] [FAQ's] [Research Groups] [Membership Form] [Donor Form]
[Goals & Objectives] [LitvakSIG Honored] [LitvakSIG Digest]
[Publications, Books, Video, etc] [Online Journal] [Kaunas Regional Archives Catalog]
[Interest Links] [Holocaust Names Project] [Picture Library] [What's New]
[Board of Directors] [Contacts]

Enter **text** to search for in the *All Lithuania Database*.
and choose the **type** of search Surname - Daitch-Mokotoff Soundex

For Global Text Searches you can search for single words or you can search for word combinations using 'AND' and 'OR'. For example:

"TOKAR and Nissel" or

The All Litvak Database allows you to search several databases at once.

The Galicia 1891 Business Directory Database

Searching for Surname ZUCKERKANDEL
(D-M code 459563 or 445956)
Number of hits: 7
Run on Saturday 14 October 2000 at 22:45:40

This search request has been made possible through the *JewishGen-erosity* of
JGS, Inc. New York

Surname	Givenname	Town	Near Town (s)	Occupation	Occupation (English)
ZUCKERKANDEL	Nachman	Gologory		Schneider	Tailor
ZUCKERKANDEL	O & Sohn	Zloczow		Lithographische Anstaiten	Lithographic Printer
ZUCKERKANDEL	Salom	Gologory		Muhlen	Mill
ZUCKERKANDEL	O	Zloczow		Buchdruckereien	Book Printer
ZUCKERKANDEL	O & Sohn	Zloczow		Buch,kunst,und Musikalienhandler	Book Art & Music Store

The 1891 Galicia Business Directory provides information on surname, given name, town, and occupation in German and English.

sian famine relief listed in "*HaMagid*" for 1871-1872. The second lists names of nearly 20,000 Lithuanian and Latvian charity donors from "*HaMelitz*" from 1893-1903. Two Lithuanian medical directories from 1923 and 1925, respectively provide names on 874 "Jewish Medical Personnel" in yet another database. The "Sugihara" database contains names and visa dates of 2,139 Lithuanian, Polish, German, and Russian Jews, all of whom were saved by passports from the Japanese diplomat, Chiune Sugihara, in 1940.

Two town-specific databases provide indices to various archival and published records about the town of Kelme from 1816-1944 and tombstone inscriptions from seven cemeteries for members of the Keidan community in Lithuania, New York, and Chicago. Finally, this site also includes transcripts of nearly 900 burials from the register of the Chevra Kadisha (burial society) of Viliampole Slobodka from 1941 to 1943 in the Kovno Ghetto.

Poland

The award-winning Jewish Records Indexing - Poland Project (see sidebar) houses indices to more than 800,000 birth, marriage, and death records for more than 150 Polish towns and is growing every day. This project has also entered into a milestone agreement with the Polish State Archives to create inventories and indexes for town records not filmed by the Mormons, handled on an archive-by-archive basis.

QUICK HIT
Consult "LDS Microfilm Master for Poland" at <www.jewishgen.org/jri-pl> to see if vital records for your town have been filmed.

The "1891 Galicia Business Directory" is a comprehensive listing covering the part of southeastern Poland formerly known as Galicia and serves as a real boon to those researching this area. Just enter your surname and see what comes up from this database listing more than 12,000 names from more than 1,000 towns, complete with occupation description in German and English.

Two Holocaust-related databases also cover Galicia: names of more than 10,000 Jews in the Lwow Ghetto from 1942-1945 and more than 18,000 Jews in the Kraków Ghetto from 1940.

And finally, the 1890 New York Immigrants from Poland, Austria, and Galicia index to more than 44,000 arrivals is accessible from this site.

Germany

Two databases covering Germany list names of Holocaust victims. The first, "Germans, Swiss and Austrians Deported from France," provides information on about 825 people and the second, "Westphalian Jews and the Holocaust," provides information for more than 8,000 Jews from the area. If you suspect you had family members at the Stutthof Concentration Camp near Gdansk, you can access names of nearly 3,000 German Jews in the "German Jews at Stutthof Concentration Camp" database.

The "Jewish Families of Northern Germany" database cites 3,000 families from Lower Saxony, North-Rhine-Westphalia, Hamburg, Bremen, and Hessen. And the names of 2,400 Jews in 50 towns in West Prussia who were granted citizenship in 1812 are also included in the "West Prussia 1812 Citizenship" database.

Czech Republic

The register of the Nikolsburg (now Mikulov) graveyard with more than 4,500 burials is the only database on the JewishGen site covering the Czech Republic so far.

Great Britain

From London trade directories, "The Jews of London (pre-1850)" database lists names and addresses for London's Jews. If your family lived in South Wales, you may find them enumerated in the "Welsh Census Returns—1851, 1891" database. For Bristol, you'll be able to access the index and tombstone photographs of three cemeteries in the "Bristol Cemetery Database."

Israel

The "U.S. Department of State Consular Post Records" database indexes more than 9,000 records of U.S. consulates in Jerusalem, Jaffa, and Haifa between 1857-1935.

South Africa

Many eastern European Jews immigrated to South Africa, particularly Lithuanian Jews. You can quickly check the "1929

South African Jewish Year Book Database" that indexes biographies of South African Jews.

America

JewishGen currently provides access to nine databases of American sources, including more than 50,000 obituaries from the *Boston Jewish Advocate*, *Cleveland Jewish News*, *Chicago Tribune*, and *American Jewish Year Book*. If your family had members fighting in the Civil War, you may find the "Jewish-American Civil War Veterans" database helpful—it cites more than 7,000 Jewish-American Union and Confederate veterans. In addition, three databases refer to marriages: "Chicago Marriages—Sinai Congregation," "The *Boston Jewish Advocate* Wedding Announcements Database," and "Boston Marriages—Rabbi Aaron Gorovitz."

Avotaynu

<www.avotaynu.com>

This publisher, well known in Jewish genealogical circles, has made the Consolidated Jewish Surname Index (CJSI) available on its web site. Previously available only on microfiche to Jewish Genealogical Societies and then to interested individuals, this index brings together some 230,000 Jewish surnames from 28 different database sources. Using the search capability, I was sur-

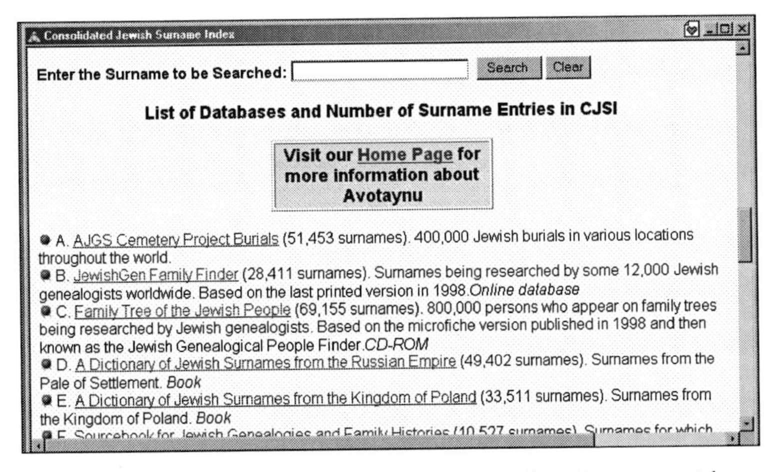

Avotaynu's Consolidated Jewish Surname Index gives you quick access to 28 databases with a single search.

QUICK TIP
Avotaynu, Inc. <www.avotaynu.com> is a prominent publisher in the field of Jewish genealogy. It develops and issues a quarterly journal, *Avotaynu: The International Review of Jewish Genealogy,* many important reference works in both print and fiche, and an email newsletter. Subscribing to the journal and the e-mail newsletter should be among the first things to do as you begin to research your family's history.

prised to see that one of my surnames, Zuckerkandel, which I thought was restricted to Galicia, appears to have been cited in the *Dictionary of Jewish Surnames from the Kingdom of Poland* under a different spelling, uncovered in the CJSI through the Daitch-Mokotoff Soundex system. Some of the 28 databases are duplicated on the JewishGen web site; the beauty of it is that you need enter your surname only once, and then you can refer back to the individual sources, whether they are databases, fiche, or books.

The number of people involved in Jewish genealogy has grown dramatically as a result of a large web presence. You'll get faster results, easier ways to communicate and share, and satisfaction from searching yourself, free to explore all possible name variations. So go ahead, surf your surname on the Web for a thrilling ride!

JEWISH RECORDS INDEXING – POLAND PROJECT

Finding Your Jewish Ancestors in Nineteenth-century Poland

For months, I religiously trekked to the nearest LDS stake's Family History Center to research my Zarember family from the Polish town of Zaręby Koscielne. I didn't have to comb indices, if they existed, in the LDS civil registration films of Jewish births, marriages, and deaths for the town. Instead, I printed search results of more than 200 occurrences of the Zarember name from the Jewish Records Indexing – Poland Project (JRI Poland) web site at <www.jewishgen. org/jri-pl>. Using my printout, I knew, for instance, that I would find the 1826 birth record for Abram Zarember, record number 46, on LDS film number 0810589. No frustration. No guesswork. No hassle.

The JRI-Poland database contains English-language references to over 1,000,000 records from more than 170 Polish towns with more being added each month.

Creation of the Database

The archives of Poland contain a remarkable collection of Jewish vital record registers that have survived the ravages of time and upheavals of history. The majority—generally from 1810 to 1865 and, in some cases, beyond—have been microfilmed by The Church of Latter-day Saints, resulting in some 2,000 reels of microfilm covering more than 500 cities and towns. A growing number of volunteers photocopy the index pages from the films for the towns they are researching and enter the data from the indices (or in some cases, the records themselves where no indices exist) onto a spreadsheet that will get loaded into the database. These volunteers conduct most of the work using the Polish language, pre-1867 Russian era registers. Professionals, whose work is funded by individuals and groups of Jewish genealogists, are typically called upon to transliterate Cyrillic script entries from the post-1867 Russian era registers. Also, volunteers at The Douglas E. Goldman Jewish Genealogy Center in Tel Aviv have been instrumental in extracting records for Bialystok, Warsaw, and other important meccas of Jewish life. This is a global effort, facilitated by a Board of Directors that spans the globe itself—Canada, Israel, Scotland, and the United States.

Using the JRI - Poland Database

From among the millions of Jewish vital records for hundreds of Polish towns and villages, the JRI - Poland database provides quick insights into the locations where family records may exist. The database offers search capability using the Daitch-Mokotoff Soundex system.

While the database does not contain actual vital records, successful searches will give an index entry with the name, record number, the year the event was recorded (but not necessarily when it actually occurred), and the LDS microfilm number so you can order the film and review the actual record at your local Family History Center. Of particular note is the ability to query the database for a particular surname irrespective of town—this allows you to identify other towns where your family lived. For instance, I found my grandmother's Entel family (as well as her Szumowicz, Przestrzeleniec, and Mularzewicz relatives) records in Zaręby Koscielne—not their main town of residence.

A Typical JRI - Poland Search

1. Access <www.jewishgen.org/jri-pl>.

SEE ALSO

See the sidebar on the Daitch-Mokotoff Soundex system in Chapter 5.

2. Click on the "Search the Database" button.
3. Enter the surname you seek, select Soundex system, and then enter any specific *gubernia,* province (a geographic classification system used in Poland between 1945-1975), or town. Click on "start search."
4. Receive search results.
5. Note the LDS microfilm number.
6. Order the LDS film.
7. Access actual entry and record information.
8. Input to your family tree.

Though I had written the local civil records office in Zaręby Koscielne many times, I could not locate the 1891 birth record of my grandfather, Avram Mendel Pryzant. I found the record number immediately when I used the JRI-Poland database. The database guided me to the source—the Jewish Historical Institute in Warsaw. I wrote for and received nearly 200 family records. Without the database, this would have been impossible.

Just the Beginning

The current database is just the beginning. The major work to index all the nineteenth- century Jewish vital records of Poland lies ahead. Launched in 1997 to speed up the indexing, the *shtetl* (the Yiddish word for "little town") Co-op initiative organized groups of volunteers with a common interest in an ancestral town or area. These volunteers share the work and cost of copying index pages in the LDS films for their town(s) and entering these indices into a spreadsheet. Files are checked for quality and then added to the database.

Shtetl co-ops emphasize cooperative research and sharing. While towns with one or two microfilm reels have been indexed by a single dedicated volunteer, the team approach is valuable for cities and towns that had large Jewish populations and for which there are many microfilms. What I find particularly remarkable is that the database has been built and is maintained by devoted volunteers. Where paid help is required, shtetl co-op leaders pursue fund-raising efforts among other researchers interested in the town's records.

Finding Your Town in the Database

Indices to birth, marriage, and death records from the following towns are already in the JRI - Poland database.

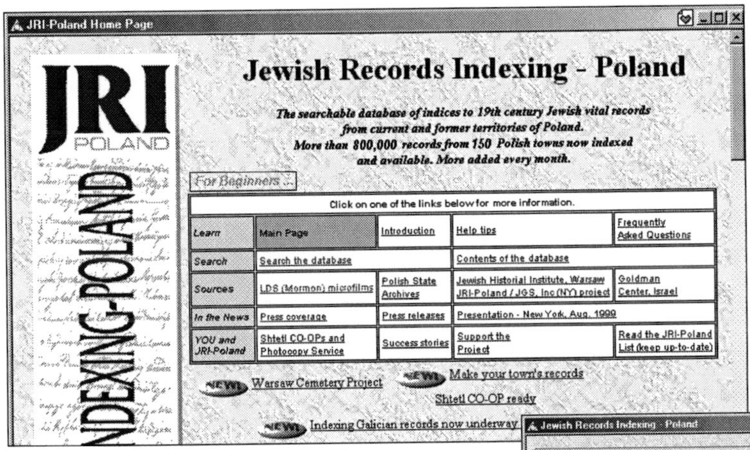

JRI-Poland Home Page

Jewish Records Indexing - Poland

The searchable database of indices to 19th century Jewish vital records from current and former territories of Poland. More than 800,000 records from 150 Polish towns now indexed and available. More added every month.

For Beginners

Click on one of the links below for more information.

Learn	Main Page	Introduction	Help tips	Frequently Asked Questions
Search	Search the database		Contents of the database	
Sources	LDS (Mormon) microfilms	Polish State Archives	Jewish Historial Institute, Warsaw JRI-Poland / JGS, Inc (NY) project	Goldman Center, Israel
In the News	Press coverage	Press releases	Presentation - New York, Aug. 1999	
YOU and JRI-Poland	Shtetl CO-OPs and Photocopy Service	Success stories	Support the Project	Read the JRI-Poland List (keep up-to-date)

NEW! Warsaw Cemetery Project NEW! Make your town's records Shtetl CO-OP ready

NEW! Indexing Galician records now underway

Click on "Search the Database" to begin.

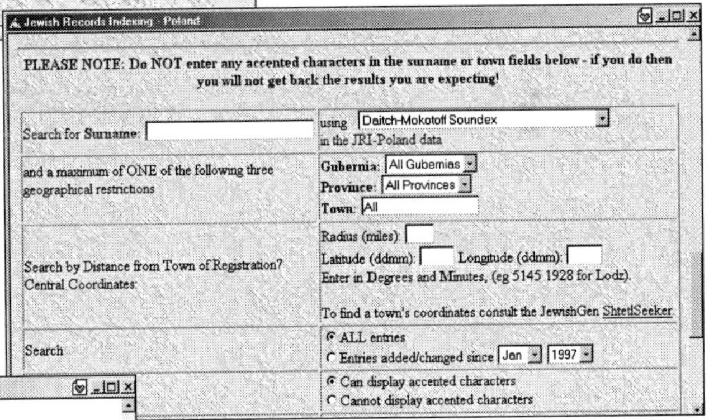

Jewish Records Indexing - Poland

PLEASE NOTE: Do NOT enter any accented characters in the surname or town fields below - if you do then you will not get back the results you are expecting!

Search for Surname:	using Daitch-Mokotoff Soundex in the JRI-Poland data
and a maximum of ONE of the following three geographical restrictions	Gubernia: All Gubernias Province: All Provinces Town: All
Search by Distance from Town of Registration? Central Coordinates:	Radius (miles): Latitude (ddmm): Longitude (ddmm): Enter in Degrees and Minutes, (eg 5145 1928 for Lodz). To find a town's coordinates consult the JewishGen ShtetlSeeker.
Search	ALL entries Entries added/changed since Jan 1997
	Can display accented characters Cannot display accented characters

Use surname, Soundex system, gubernia, province, town to execute the search.

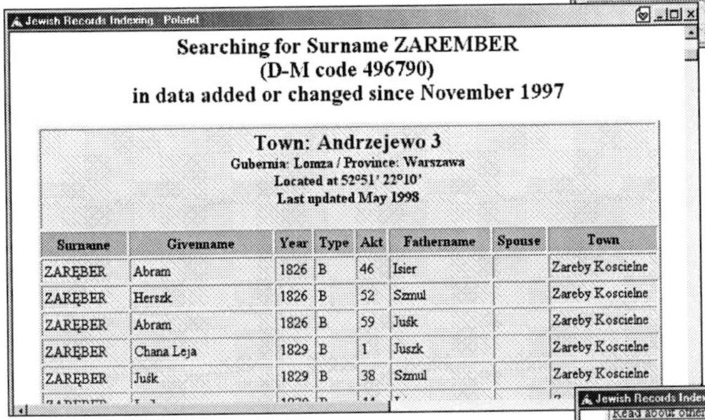

Jewish Records Indexing - Poland

Searching for Surname ZAREMBER (D-M code 496790) in data added or changed since November 1997

Town: Andrzejewo 3
Gubernia: Lomza / Province: Warszawa
Located at 52°51' 22°10'
Last updated May 1998

Surname	Givenname	Year	Type	Akt	Fathername	Spouse	Town
ZARĘBER	Abram	1826	B	46	Isier		Zareby Koscielne
ZARĘBER	Herszk	1826	B	52	Szmul		Zareby Koscielne
ZARĘBER	Abram	1826	B	59	Juśk		Zareby Koscielne
ZARĘBER	Chana Leja	1829	B	1	Juszk		Zareby Koscielne
ZARĘBER	Juśk	1829	B	38	Szmul		Zareby Koscielne

A typical JRI-Poland research results report.

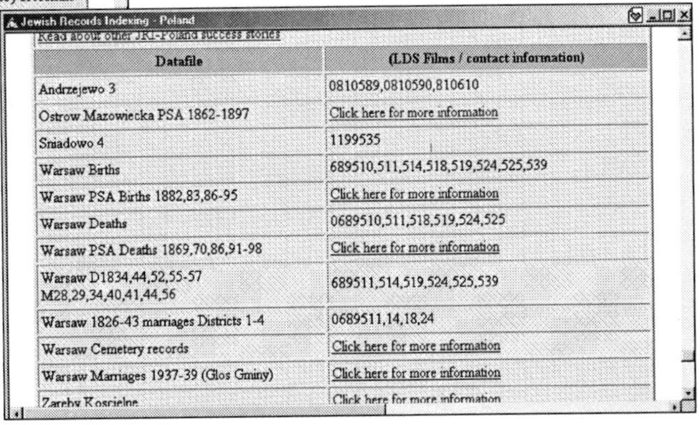

Jewish Records Indexing - Poland

Read about other JRI-Poland success stories

Datafile	(LDS Films / contact information)
Andrzejewo 3	0810589,0810590,810610
Ostrow Mazowiecka PSA 1862-1897	Click here for more information
Sniadowo 4	1199535
Warsaw Births	689510,511,514,518,519,524,525,539
Warsaw PSA Births 1882,83,86-95	Click here for more information
Warsaw Deaths	0689510,511,518,519,524,525
Warsaw PSA Deaths 1869,70,86,91-98	Click here for more information
Warsaw D1834,44,52,55-57 M28,29,34,40,41,44,56	689511,514,519,524,525,539
Warsaw 1826-43 marriages Districts 1-4	0689511,14,18,24
Warsaw Cemetery records	Click here for more information
Warsaw Marriages 1937-39 (Glos Gminy)	Click here for more information
Zareby Koscielne	Click here for more information

Individual databases reference LDS microfilms.

Посадъ
Гмина
Зарамба
Костельне
№ 63.

Г зачеркнутое слово [illegible] почитать поправку [illegible] Призантъ Свидѣтели [illegible] Жбиковскій

Состоялось въ Посадѣ Зарамбы Костельне
Дня девятаго двадцать перваго Іюня
тысяча восемьсотъ девяносто перваго года
въ три часа пополудни, Явился [illegible]
Іоско Мошковичъ Призантъ владѣлецъ
дома [illegible] житель посада
Зарамбы Костельне имѣющій отъ роду
тридцать шесть лѣтъ, въ присутствіи
свидѣтелей Мордки [illegible] Сапожника
имѣющаго отъ роду сорокъ лѣтъ и Герша
[illegible] владѣльца дома имѣющаго
отъ роду пятьдесятъ девять лѣтъ
постоянно жительствующихъ въ Посадѣ Зарамбы Костельне и предъявилъ намъ
младенца мужескаго пола объявляя
что таковый родился въ Посадѣ Зарамбы
Костельне Дня второго четырнадцатаго
Іюля [illegible] года въ девять ча-
совъ утра отъ законной его жены
Хаи урожденной [illegible] имѣющей
отъ роду тридцать [illegible] лѣтъ. Младенцу
этому дано имя Абрамъ
[illegible]. Актъ сей прочитанъ явившимся
нами только подписанъ. Отецъ и Свидѣтели
неграмотные.
Содержащій Акты Гражданскаго Состоянія Жбиковскій

JRI-Poland was the only way I found my grandfather's birth record.

More are added each month, so keep checking the web site at <www.jewishgen.org/jri-pl>.

Andrzejewo
Bakałarzewo
Będzin
Bełchatów
Berżniki
Białystok
Bielawy
Bieżuń
Błaszki
Bodzentyn
Bogoria
Brok
Brzeziny
Brzeźnica
Bychawa
Bytom
Chęciny
Chmielnik
Choroszcz
Chorzele
Ciechanów
Ciechanowiec
Czemiemicki
Czerwińsk
Czyżewo
Dąbie
Daleszyce
Drobin
Dzyatlava
Filipów
Gąbin
Golina
Grajewo
Hrubieszów
Iłża
Izbica
Jabłonka
Jasienica
Jedwabne
Jędrzejów
Jeleniewo
Józefów nad Wislą
Kaletniki
Kalisz
Kazimierz Dolny
Kielce
Kleczew
Klimontów
Kodeń
Kolno
Koło
Komarów
Konin
Końskie
Kosów Lacki
Kozienice
Kraków
Kraśniczyn
Kraśnik
Krasnopol
Krasnystaw
Krotoszyn
Krzeszów
Kuczbork
Kurów
Łódż
Łomża
Łosice
Łowicz
Lozdieje
Lublin
Małogoszcz
Mariampol
Metele
Mława
Nasielsk
Nowe Miasto
Nowogród
Nowy Dwór
Nur
Okuniew
Olita
Olkusz
Opatów

Opoczno
Opole Lubelskie
Ostrołęka
Ostrów Mazowiecka
Ożarów
Pajęczno
Piątnica
Pińczów
Piotrków Trybunalski
Pławno
Płock
Płońsk
Przasnysz
Przedbórz
Przerośl
Przytyk
Puławy
Pułtusk
Puńsk
Raciąż
Radom
Radomsko
Radoszyce
Radzanów
Radziłów
Radzymin
Rajgród
Rozprza
Rutki
Rzeszów
Samaki
Sejny
Sereje
Serock
Skulsk
Ślesin
Słupca
Śniadowo
Sobków
Sochocin
Sokołów Podlaski
Sokoły
Sompolno
Staszów
Stawiski
Suwałki
Szaki
Szczebrzeszyn
Szczekociny
Szczuczyn
Szreńsk
Tamów
Tomaszów Lubelski
Tomaszów Mazowiecki
Trzcianne
Turobin
Tuszyn
Tyczyn
Tykocin
Ujazd
Warka
Warszawa
Wąsosz
Wąwolnica
Weisieje
Widawa
Wieluń
Wieniawa
Wierzbicz
Wilczyn
Wiślica
Wiżajny
Wizna
Włoszczowa
Wolanów
Wolbrom
Wysokie Mazowieckie
Wyszków
Wyszogród
Zakroczym
Zambrów
Zamość
Zaręby Koscielne
Zawichost
Zduńska Wola
Zgierz
Żuromin
Żychlin

Borisov, Belarus was the ancestral home of dozens of researchers.
Courtesy of Boris Feldblyum Collection © 1983.

14 Shtetl-Based Research Groups

Many immigrants joined *landsmanshaftn* upon their arrival in America. They sought the comfort of home among people they knew. During and after World War II, they coordinated efforts to send relief packages to Europe and developed memorial books to remember their brethren and their communities that no longer existed.

In the past few years, town-based research groups have formed for genealogical purposes. Researchers who have ancestors from the same town come together, usually with a coordinator to guide their communication and initiatives, to share information on the town and its Jewish community.

In the early years of my genealogical pursuit, I used the Family Finder (now the JewishGen Family Finder) to contact everyone listed with roots in Borisov, located in Minsk Gubernia, Belarus. I wrote letters to them and included information on my family. A small group of people emerged, and we found several of us were actually researching the same names, like Elkind and Gurevich.

The explosion of the Internet has taken these grass-roots efforts to a new level. Broadcast messages to landsmen give us instant gratification. You can send an e-mail to a fellow researcher right from the JewishGen Family Finder and Family Tree of the Jewish People.

At the 1996 Summer Seminar on Jewish genealogy, I founded the Borisov Research Family. We created a newsletter so

$2,040,000

1938 GREATER NEW YORK J.D.C. Campaign

AMERICAN JEWISH JOINT DISTRIBUTION COMMITTEE

June 28, 1938

100 EAST 42nd ST.
NEW YORK, N. Y.
Phone: LEXINGTON 2-5200

CAMPAIGN OFFICERS

PAUL BAERWALD
HENRY ITTLESON
HERBERT H. LEHMAN
Honorary Chairmen

EDWARD M. M. WARBURG
Chairman

CARL J. AUSTRIAN
GEORGE BACKER
I. EDWIN GOLDWASSER
HAROLD K. GUINZBURG
SANFORD JACOBI
EDWARD A. NORMAN
JONAH B. WISE
Co-Chairmen

MORRIS C. TROPER
Executive Vice-Chairman

MAURICE WERTHEIM
Treasurer

ABNER BREGMAN
Associate Treasurer

JOSEPH C. HYMAN
Secretary

EXECUTIVE COMMITTEE

JAMES N. ROSENBERG
Chairman

I have learned with a great deal of satisfaction of the campaign which is being carried on among the Zarombor Landsmanschaft in behalf of the unfortunate people in your hometown, Zaremby, Poland, especially for constructive aid in cooperation with the Joint Distribution Committee.

Zaremby-Koscielne, as you know, is one of the towns in Poland which has suffered severely from the recent anti-Jewish disturbances; an uninterrupted terror and boycott are continuously being exerted against the Jewish population.

The following excerpts from a letter received by the Warsaw office of the Joint Distribution Committee from Zaremby speak for themselves:

"The general situation in our town is most critical. Pickets watch continually the Jewish shops and the boycott is very strong. Jews are beaten, window-panes smashed. Last night, twenty Jewish tombs were desecrated for the third time by wild ruffians. They have the audacity to prevent any customer from entering a Jewish shop".

"The situation is very alarming and becomes from day to day more critical. Never has the population been so poor, and the boycott stronger. The pickets which used to watch the Jewish shops on market days, do it now continuously. We do not know how to face the situation. It is so distressing to see all these people compelled to sell their shops to Christians and move on to larger towns. All our efforts to prevent this are useless. Every week, we must face new cases of members of our kassa who ask for help".

In addition to this, a fire which took place on May 15th, 1938, destroyed many houses and work shops and 69 persons lost everything and are without food and clothing. The Joint Distribution Committee sent immediate help, and substantial amounts were granted to aid the victimized Jews in rebuilding their lives. But the Joint Distribution Committee is not in a position to meet all these requirements and needs without the assistance of the Landsleit here. According to an agreement made with the Zarombor Relief Committee, the Joint Distribution Committee will match, for constructive and rehabilitation work in Zaremby, the amount raised by your Landsmanschaft-Group here.

I feel confident that you, who are so closely related to these sufferers, will want to make your contribution as generous as the need requires, when called upon by the Zarombor Relief Committee.

Sincerely yours,

Edward M. M. Warburg

Edward M. M. Warburg
Chairman

EMMW:MO

ACT NOW

A 1938 fund-raising letter from the American Jewish Joint Distribution Committee (The "Joint") on behalf of the Zarombor landsmanshaft's *Zarombor Relief Committee.*

we could share information and banded together to fund the transliteration of the 1874–1875 Revision list for Borisov. Though we quickly grew to nearly 40 members, it only took the financial contributions of about ten people to fund the research. Other members chose to contribute their time to data entry. Another member created a web-based database that's searchable by name. One member traveled to Borisov and took pictures of the cemetery. I created a list of factory workers that I had received years earlier from someone in the town. Other members shared information on a cemetery plot in New York and background information on the town.

By joining with people with like interests, we were able to advance our research cooperatively in a way we could not individually. You can do the same.

JewishGen Shtetlinks

<www.jewishgen.org/shtetlinks>

The fastest way to link up with your *Landsmen* is to check out JewishGen's Shtetlinks web site. Hundreds of town-based groups have created their own web sites with the help of JewishGen. Check out the list below (and visit the web site as well, because this list is growing every nanosecond) to see if a group already exists for your town. In some cases there's more of a regional approach than an individual town, so be sure you know

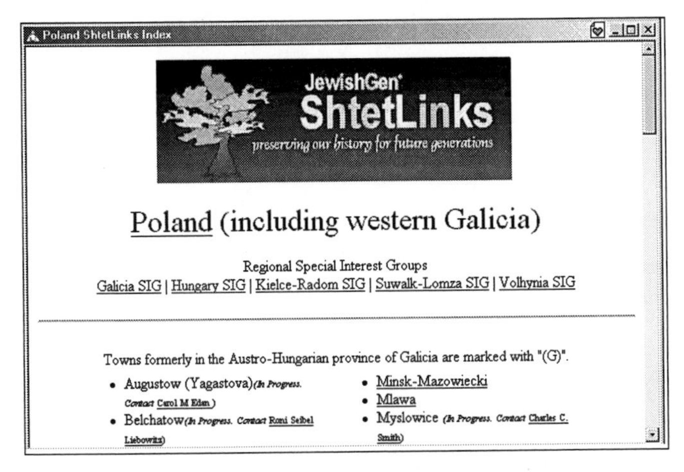

Shtetlink pages create new communities of landslayt.

SEE ALSO
In many cases, researchers have chosen to form more formal Special Interest Groups. You can find out more about those in Chapter 15.

your town's surrounding area and nearest big settlement. Also keep in mind that borders changed over the years. If you're looking for a Galician town, check both Poland (for western Galicia) and Ukraine (for eastern Galicia) as towns are indexed by their current affiliation.

Shtetlinks can even help you create your own town page if one doesn't already exist.

Shetlinks currently hosts pages for the following locations:

Belarus

Andryshevtsy, Azarichi, Bakshty, Balichi, Bartoshi, Belevtsy, Belitsa, Belogruda, Belyuntsy, Beneyki, Bereza, Bobruisk (Bobroisk), Bolshiye Pugachi, Bol'shiye Berezovtsy, Bol'shiye Knyazikovtsy, Bol'shoye Osovo, Bolshoye Selo, Bolsi, Borisov, Boyary, Butily, Byenyakoni, Byten (Butern), Bzhozuvka, Chaplichi, Damutsevtsy, Dembrovo, Dogi, Dokshitz, Dokudovo, Dolgoye, Drogicin (Drohitchin), Dubrovno, Dubrovo, Dvorets (Dvoretz), Dyatlovo, Dzekhtsyary, Farnyy Konets, Filevichi, Gav'ya, Germanishki, Goldovo, Gomel, Gonchary, Gornety, Gromki, Ignatkovtsy, Indura (Amdur), Ishchelnyany, Ivye, Kalechytse, Kamenets (Kamenetz Litovsk), Kholmich, Kleshnyaki, Konyukhi, Korelichi (Korelitz), Koshelevo, Kovali, Krasne, Kronki, Krupichovshchyzna, Krupovo, Kuken, Kulevtse, Kurenets (Kurnitz), Lechowitz, Lepel, Levashi, Leyki , Lida, Lipicanka, Lipkuntsy, Lopaty, Lyadsk, Lychkovtse, Maguny, Makhovichi, Malevichi, Mariampol', Meretz, Meyry, Minoyty, Mir, Mogilev, Motol, Motyli, Myta, Nacha, Naroshi, Neman, Nesvizh, Netsech', Nogorodovichi, Novy Dvor, Ogrodniki, Ol'khovka, Orlya, Ostrina, Papernya, Paracany, Pelevtse, Pelyasa, Permovomayskaya, Poletskishki, Potoka, Pyaskovtsy, Radin, Radzivonishki, Rakovichi, Repniki, Romanovichki, Rozanka, Ruda, Rudnya, Ruzhany (Rozinoi), Rulevichi, Rylovtsy, Savovshchina, Scadryn, Sedlisski, Selets, Shchenets, Shchuchyn, Sheybakpol, Shinkovtsy, Shnipkil, Skidel, Skorzhiki, Slonim, Slutsk, Smorgon, Soltanishki, Sopockin(Sopotskin),

Starodvortsy, Stary Yevasilshki, Stolbsty (Steibst), Strel'tsy, Subbotniki, Sukhval'nia, Tanevichy, Traby, Trokeli, Urechye, Ushachi (Ushatz), Vasilevichi, Vasilishki, Vaverka, Vaverka, Vekantsy, Verbilka, Vidzy, Vitebsk. Voronovo, Voronovo, Yelna, Yevlashi, Yuratsishki, Zabolot', Zachepichi, Zapolye, Zelva, Zheludok, Zhemloslav, Zhirmuny.

Latvia

Bausk, Courland Research Group, Dagda, Daugavpils (Dvinsk), Gostini, Liepaja (Libau), Ludza (Lutzin), Rezekne, Riga, Subate (Shubitz), Talsi (Talsen), Valdemarpils (Shasmaken), Varaklani (Varklian).

Lithuania

Akmene, Alytus, Ariogala (Rogala), Baisagola, Bazilionai (Bazelon), Birzai (Birz), Butrimantsy, Dieveniskes (Divinishuk), Dieviniskes, Eisiskes, Gargzdai (Gorsd), Joniskelis (Jonishkel), Jonava (Yaneve), Josvainiai (Yosven), Kalvarija, Kaniava, Kapciamiestis, Kaunas (Kovno), Keidainiai (Keidan), Kelme (Kelem), Klaipeda (Memel), Krakes (Krok), Kraziai (Kruzh), Krottingen, Kupiskis (Kupishok), Kudirkos Naumiestis, Kvedarna (Chweidan), Kybartai (Kibart), Lazdijai (Lazdei), Lida, Linkuva (Linkove), Mariampol, Merkine, Pakroujis (Pokroi), Panevezys (Ponavesh), Pikeliai, Pilviskiai, Plunge (Plungian), Pobrade (Podbrzezie), Polangen, Prienai, Raseiniai District, Reziai, Rietava, Rokiskis (Rokishok), Rozalimas (Rozalia), Salociai (Salaty), Seirijai, Seta (Shat), Shaki, Siauliai (Shavel), Simnas (Simno), Skapiskis (Skopishok), Skaudvile (Shkudvil), Sudargas (Sudarg), Svencionys (Shvintzion), Tauragnai (Toriguin), Trakai, Ukmerge (Vilkomir), Uzpaliai (Ushpol), Utena, Veisiejai, Veksnia, Vilkaviskis, Vilkija (Vilki), Vilnius (Vilna), Virbalis, Vistytus (Vishtinetz), Yurbarkas (Yurburg), Zeimelis (Zeimys), Zelva (Pazelva), Zemaiciu Naumiestis (Neishtot-Tavrig)

Poland

Augustow (Yagastova), Belchatow, Beuthen (Bytom), Biala Podlaska, Bialobrzegi (Bialobrzeg), Bialystok, Bircza, Brzeznica, Chmielnik, Ciechanow, Czemierniki (Cheminik), Czestochowa, Czyzewo, Debica, Drobin, Dukla, Gombin, Gorlice, Gostynin, Grodzisk Mazowiecki, Hrubieszow (Rubieshow), Janow Sokolski, Jozefow nad Wisla, Kalisz, Kanczuga, Kielce, Kleczew (Kletchoi), Knyszyn, Koden, Kolbuszowa Area (Kolbushiv), Kolno, Krakow (Kroke), Krosno, Kutno (Kutna), Łódż, Łomża, Lancut, Lezajsk (Lizhensk), Lubaczow, Lublin, Makow (Mazoweicki), Miedzyrzec Podlaski (Mezritch), Mielec, Minsk-Mazowiecki, Mlawa, Myslowice, Nowy Dwor, Nur, Opoczno, Opole-Lubelski, Orla, Ostroleka (Ostrolenka), Ostrow Mazowiecka, Ostrowiec, Pilzno (Pilsno), Plock, Przemysl (Pshemishyl), Radomsko, Radzilow, Rozwadow, Rzeszow (Reisha), Sompolno, Sanniki, Slupia Nowa, Suwalki (Suvalki), Tarnobrzeg, Tomaszow Mazowiecki, Tykocin (Tyktin), Ulanow, Wadowice, Wizna, Wyszkow, Wyszogrod, Yagelnitsa, Zabludow, Zambrow, Zdunska Wola, Zychlin, Zmigrod Nowy, Zolynia

Romania

Bihor County—Abram, Abramut, Alesd, Alsotopa, Astileu, Auseu, Baile Felix, Balc, Batar, Beius, Belenyes, Bihardioszeg, Biharia, Boianu Mare, Borod, Bors, Bratca, Brusturi, Budesti Ghica, Budureasa, Bulz, Cabesti, Cadea, Capilna, Cefa, Ceica, Ceisora, Cetariu, Cherechiu, Chiscau, Chislaz, Ciganest, Ciuhei, Ciumeghiu, Cociuba Mare, Copacel, Copaceni, Corbesti, Cotiglet, Curatele, Curtuiseni, Derna, Diosig, Dobresti, Doctor Petru Groza, Draganesti, Dragesti, Ghilaesti, Girda de Sus, Girisu de Cris, Hidis, Hidiselu de Sus, Holod, Husasau de Tinca, Iermata Neagra, Ineu, Latareni, Lazuri de Beius, Lelesti, Luncsoara, Madaras, Marghita, Meziad, Nimaesti, Nojorid, Nucet, Olcea, Oradea, Padurea Neagra, Pietroasa, Pocola, Pomezeu, Remetea, Rieni, Ropesti, Rosia, Sacadat, Salacea, Salard, Salonta, Sarvazel,

Sebes, Secueni, Seleus, Simbata, Simian, Sintandrei, Sinteu, Sirbi, Spinus, Suplacu de Barcau, Tauteu, Tileagd, Tilecus, Tinca, Tria, Tulca, Uileacu de Beius, Valea lui Mihai, Varaseni, Varzari, Vascau/Vaskoh, Viisoara, Virciorog, Voivozi, Zece Hotare.

Briceni County—Aleksandrovka, Brichany, Bulboaka, Kotyuzhany, Lipkany

Bucharest/Ilfov County—Afumati, Bucuresti, Balotesti-Ilfov, Berceni, Branesti, Buftea, Chitila, Ciorogirla, Clinceni, Crea Lesile, Fierbinti de Jos, Magurele, Miroslovesti, Moara Vlasie, Nuci, Peris, Snagov, Tunari, Voluntar

Dolj County—Afumati, Almaj, Apele Vii, Bailesti, Bechet, Birca, Bistret, Botosesti-Paia, Brabova, Bradesti, Bulzesti, Calafat, Castranova, Celaru, Cernatesti, Cetate, Cioroiasi, Ciuperceni-Noi, Cosoveni, Craiova, Dabuleni, Damian, Daneti, Desa, Diosti, Dragotesti, Dranic, Farcas, Filiasi, Ghercesti de Sus, Ghercestii Noi, Gighera, Gingiova, Giurgita, Gogosu, Goicea, Grecesti, Isalnita, Macesu de Jos, Macesu de Sus, Melinesti, Mischii, Mosna, Motatei, Motatei, Negoi, Orodel, Ostroveni, Perisor, Radovan, Rast, Sadova, Segarcea, Sopot, Terpizita, Terpizita, Unirea, Urzicuta, Valea Stanciului, Vela, Verbita, Virtop, Virvoru de Jos.

Galati County—Balenj, Balintesti, Baneasa, Bercea, Beresti-Tirg, Bojur, Brahasesti de Jos, Brahasesti de Sus, Buciumeni, Cavadinesti, Certesti, Chetrni, Corni, Corod, Costache Negrea, Costache Negri, Craesti Cuca, Cudalbj, Draganesti, Draguseni, Fartanesti, Firtanesti, Foltesti, Frumusita, Galati, Ganesti, Gohor, Grivita, Ivesti, Jorasti, Liesti, Movileni, Munteni, Namoloasa, Nicoresti, Oancea, Pechea, Piscu, Rogojeni, Scantiesti, Slobozia Conachi, Smirdan, Smulti, Tecuci, Tepu, Tirgu Bojur, Tudor Vladimirescu, Tulucesti, Umbraresti, Valea Marului, Vinatori, Virlezi, Vladesti.

Iasi County—Andrieseni, Belcesti, Birnova, Bivolari, Borosesti, Bosia, Breazu, Ciurea, Comarna, Costuleni, Cotnari, Curatura, Deleni, Dobrov, Dolhesti, Focuri, Golaesti, Grajduri, Halaucesti, Hirlau, Holboca, Horlesti,

Iasi, Tirgu-Yasski, Ilasi, Ipatele, Lespezi, Letcani, Madrijac, Miroslava, Miroslavesti, Moreni, Mosna, Motca, Movileni, Nagy Monujfalu, Oteleni, Paltinis, Pascani, Podu Iloaie, Popesti, Popricani, Prisacani, Probata, Raducaneni, Saveni, Scheia, Schitu Duca, Stolniceni-Praiescu, Strunga, Tibana, Tirgu Frumos, Todiresti, Tomesti, Trestiana, Trifesti, Tutora, Valea Seaca, Vama, Victoria, Vinatori, Vladeni, Voinesti.

Kishinev County—Baneshty, Chisinau, Durleshty, Talaeshty, Ganaseny de Pedure, Synzhera, Oneshty.

Maramures County—Arinis, Asuaju de Sus, Baia Mare, Baia Sprie, Baile Borsa, Baiut, Berbesti, Bicaz, Birsana, Bogdan Voda, Borsa, Botiza, Breb, Brodina, Budesti, Buzesti, Carnatin, Cavnic, Cimpulung Tisa, Copalnic-Manastur, Cornesti, Coroieni, Costiui, Culcea, Cupseni, Desesti, Dragomiresti, Feresti, Firiza, Giulesti, Grosi, Harnicesti, Hoteni, Ieud, Izvoarele, Lapus, Leordina, Lucacesti, Macirlau, Manastirea Giulesti, Marmatiel, Miresu Mare, Moiseiu, Nistru, Ocna Sugatag, Poienile Izei, Recea, Remeti, Repedea, Rona de Sus, Rozavlea, Ruscova, Sacalaseni, Sacel, Salistea de Sus, Salsig, Sapinta, Satu Satulung, Seini, Sighet, Somcuta Mare, Strimtura, Suciu de Sus, Sugatag, Szinervaralja, Tachevo, Tirgu-Lapus, Laposului, Tisa, Vima Mica, Viseu de Jos, Wisho.

Neamt County—Agapia, Ardeluta, Bahna, Baltatesti, Bargaoani, Bicaz, Bicaz-Chei, Bicazu-Ardelean, Borca, Borlesti, Bozienii de Sus, Ceahlau, Ciurea, Cordun, Cracaoani, Dagita, Damuc, Dobreni, Dulcesti, Dumbrava-Rosie, Dumesti, Durau, Farcasa, Faurei, Ghelaesti, Gheraesti, Hangu, Humulesti, Icusesti, Ion Creanga, Izvorul Muntelui-Bicaz, Margineni, Minasteria Neamt, Moldoveni, Oglinzi, Oniceni, Pastraveni, Piatra Neamt, Pipirig, Poiana Teiului, Prasin, Rediu, Roman, Romani, Ruginoasa, Sabaoani, Sagna, Savinesti, Stanita, Stefan cel Mare, Tarcau, Tazlau, Timisesti, Tirgu Neamt, Trifesti, Valea Ursului, Varatec, Vilsoara.

Oknitsa County—Byrladynany, Byrnovo, Dinzhany, Grinautsy-Raya, Khodoroutsy, Klokushna, Lipnik, Oknitsa, Verezheny.

Prahova County—Adunati, Azuga, Baba Ana, Baicoi, Balta Doamnei, Boldesti-Scaeni, Brazi, Breaza, Brebu, Busteni, Cheia, Caresu, Cheia, Cimpina, Comarnic, Cosminele, Dirvari, Draganesti, Dumbrava, Gherghita, Golgata, Gura Valdului, Intre Bisci, Izvoarele, Jugureni, Magurele, Maneciu, Manesti, Mizil, Ploesti, Plopeni, Plopu, Sinaia, Singeru, Slanic, Soimari, Starchiojd, Surani, Teisani, Urlati, Valea Calugareasca, Valea Doftanei.

Satu Mare County—Acis, Andrid, Apa, Ardud, Babesti, Beltiug, Bercu, Berveni, Bixad, Bocicoiu Mare, Bogdand, Botiz, Calinesti Oas, Camarzana, Capieni, Carei, Cauas, Cehal, Certeze, Cetate, Chisau, Cidreag, Coltirea, Craciunesti, Craiodolt, Doba, Dobolt, Dorolt, Eriu-Sincrai, Foeini, Gelu, Gherta Mica, Halmeu, Homoroade, Livada, Micula, Mihaileni, Negresti-Oas, Odoreu, Orasu Nou, Petea, Petresti, Pir, Piscolt, Plopis, Pomi, Porumbesti, Rona de Jos, Sacaseni, Sanislau, Santau, Satu Mare, Szatmar Nemeti, Slatina, Socond, Supuru de Jos, Surdesti, Szatmar, Tarna Mare, Tasnad, Tasnadu Nou, Terebes, Terebesti, Tirsolt, Turt, Urziceni, Valea Viseului, Vama, Vascauti, Viile Satu-Mare.

Suceava County—Adincata, Arbore, Baia, Baicauti, Breaza, Brodina, Brosteni, Buciumeni, Bunesti, Burdujeni, Cajvana, Calafindesti, Cimpulung-Moldovenesc, Cirlibaba, Comanesti, Cornu Luncii, Cozanesti, Crucea, Dolhasca, Dolhesti, Dornesti, Dornisoara, Dornu Candrenilor, Dumbraveni, Falticeni, Forasu, Frasin, Fratautii Vechi, Fratuitii Noi, Frumosu, Fundu Moldovei, Ganesti, Granicesti, Gura Haiti, Gura Humorului, Iacobeni, Ilisesti, Itcani, Izvoarele Sucevei, Lesu Ursului, Liteni, Lucacesti, Malini, Manasteria-Humorului, Marginea, Moldova-Sulita, Moldovita, Neagra Sarului, Oberpertestie, Ostra, Panaci. Pirtestii de Jos, Pirtestii de Sus, Podu Cosnii, Poiana Stampei, Pojorita, Preutesti, Putna, Raddauti (Radautz), Risca, Serbauti, Siminicea, Siret, Slatiaora, Slatina, Solca, St.Onufry, Straja, Stroiesti, Stulpicani, Suceava, Sucevita, Todiresti, Uidesti, Ulma, Vadu Moldovei, Vama, Vatra

Dornei, Vatra Moldovitei, Vicovu de Sus, Viseu de Mijloc, Voivodeasa, Volovat, Zamestea, Zvoristea.

Ukraine

Berdichev, Bibrka (Boiberke), Bogorodchany, Boguslav (Boslov), Bolekhov (Bolekhev), Borislav (Boryslaw), Borschev, Borzna, Brody, Berezhany, Buchach, Budanov, Burakuvla, Busk, Chmil'nyk (Chmelnik), Chortkov, Czernowitz (Chernovitsy), Debno, Delyatin (including Dora and Lanchin), Dolina (west of Ivano Frankivsk), Dolina, Drogobych (Drohobitch), Drohobycz (Drubich), Gorodenka, Gorodnitsa, Gorodok, Grimaylov, Gusyatin, Gvardeyskoye, Hotin, Ivano Frankivsk (Stanisle), Jagielnica, Kalush, Kamenka, Kaminetz-Podolsky, Khorostkov, Kibliltch, Klyuvintsy, Kolomya, Kopychintsy, Kopychintsy, Kosov, Kovel, Krivoluka, Kuty, Lanovtse, Luboml, Lukov (Maciejow), Lviv, Lvovo, Lyubar, Mikulintsy, Mukacsevo (Munkacs), Nadvirna (Nadvorna), Nezhin, Nizhnev, Ottynia, Odessa, Ostropol (Osterpolye), Ozeryany, Palashevka, Pavoloch (Pavolitch), Podkamen, Polonnoye, Pomortsy, Priluki, Probuzhna, Radomyshl, Rafalovka, Rohatyn, Romanovka, Romanowe Siolo, Rovno, Rozdol, Rozhnyatov, Sadgura, Sambir (Sambor), Satanov, Shargorod, Skala, Skalat, Sniatyn, Sosnovoye (Selisht), Staryy Sambir (Sambor), Strusov, Stryy (Stryj), Suchostav, Sudilkov, Svezhkovtse, Svidova, Tarnoruda, Terebovlya, Tlumach, Tributkhovtsy, Trochinbrod, Tolstoye, Tuchin, Tudorov, Tysmenitsa (Tismenitsie), Ulashkovtse, Vignanka, Vinnitsa, Vishnevets, Volhynia (Wolin) Gubernia, Volochisk, Voynilov, Yablanov, Zabolotov, Zhabokrich (Kryzhopol), Zalosce.

Other Localities

Alsace, Birobidzhan (Far Eastern Russia), Bukhara (Central Asia), Cazorla (Spain), Dettensee (Germany), Floss (Germany), Fulda (Germany), Giraltovce (Slovakia), Grimsby (England), Gyor (Hungary), Humenne (Slovakia), India, Italy, Jamaica, Jicin (Czech

SEE ALSO

See Chapter 13 for more detailed information about searching and entering data into the JewishGen FamilyFinder.

Republic), Kastoria (Greece), Melbourne (Australia), Libya, London (England), Lugo (Italy), Mikulov (Czech Republic), Monastir (Macedonia), Myjava (Miava, Slovakia), Ouderkerk aan de Amstel (Holland), Presov (Slovakia), Rhodes (Greece), Safov (Schaffa, Czech Republic), Stropkov (Sztropko, Slovakia), Teheran (Iran), Tunisia, Turkey, Valasske Mezirici (Czech Republic), Ujfeherto (Hungary).

Some groups also exist for certain localities in the United States, such as Brockton, Massachusetts and New York's Lower East Side.

JewishGen Family Finder

<www.jewishgen.org/jgff>

It's always a good idea to check the Family Finder to find others who are researching the same locality as you. Also make sure you are listed. Time and time again long-lost (and I mean really long-lost, fourth and fifth cousins) have found me through the Family Finder. When two people are researching a name like Przestrzeleniec from the town of Brok in Poland, you can be pretty sure you've got a common ancestor somewhere. Contact the people you find, share some of your family's history, and see what you may have in common. And, that may lead you to the next activity—coming together as a research group.

Shtetl Co-ops

Shtetl co-ops first formed as a way to bring people together with common interests in a town for fundraising and data entry purposes. Nearly 100 "shtetl co-ops" now exist to index their town's vital records for the Jewish Records Indexing – Poland project. At the same time, though, there's more to these co-ops than meets the eye and they aren't restricted to Poland. The coordinators—volunteers—lead the groups to determine the information they collectively hold about the town—photos, letters, memorial books, anniversary books, maps, *landsmanshaftn* records, census lists, business directory listings, and more. Members with special skills, such as knowledge of Hebrew, Yiddish, Russian, and Polish, are encouraged to come forward to help with indexing. Computer mavens are encouraged to help with data entry and web sites.

The data entry for the Borisov Revision Lists was completed by three members. The task at hand was to bring these three files together. It was more than I could handle. So I asked fellow member, Mike Levine, if he could help out. It took him no time at all and what a boon for the rest of the group!

If you join an existing co-op or research family, or want to start your own, remember the following: manage expectations, leverage the unique capabilities of each individual member, set priorities, understand not everyone is able or willing to make a financial commitment, and understand that not everyone is able to make a large time commitment. As anyone who has networked his or her way through genealogy knows, there is great satisfaction in "giving back."

CASE STUDY: THE OSTRÓW MAZOWIECKA RESEARCH FAMILY (OMRF)

As I sat among members of the Ostrów Mazowiecka Research Family around a long, wooden conference table, I got an eerie feeling.

Perhaps a century ago, our ancestors may have sat at a similar table discussing the affairs of the day. The town's Jewish community, through events they could not have foreseen, dispersed, and, of course, today no longer exists.

But here in this room, we sat reunited. Our grandparents knew each other. Their families married each other. How did it happen that the Jewish community of Ostrów Mazowiecka came together again in the diaspora?

It began in 1993 when a Family Finder listing in the Suwalki-Łomża Special Interest Group's publication, *Landsmen*, brought together two individuals whose past and future would be inextricably linked. Through the listing, Stanley Diamond of Montreal and Michael Richman of Maryland learned they both had ancestors from the town of Ostrów Mazowiecka (or "Ostrova" in Yiddish) in Poland's Łomża Gubernia. They founded the Ostrów Mazowiecka Research Family, a forerunner of shtetl-based research groups to come.

Through the use of technology, Diamond and Richman reached out to those who also had roots in the town (another reason to make sure you're listed in the Family Finder!), including me.

As a team, the accomplishments have been many, far exceeding what individuals could have done. The group:

Indexed all Jewish birth, marriage, and death records for the town from the LDS microfilms (1808-1865) and index pages provided by the Polish State Archives for Stanley Diamond's Beta-Thalassemia genetic research project (see Chapter 18) (1866-1897).

Members of the Ostrów Mazowiecka Research Family meet at the 19th International Conference on Jewish Genealogy in New York City, August 1999. Courtesy of Stanley Diamond.

Indexed 1826-65 Jewish vital records for neighboring Brok.

Indexed more than 1,000 entries in the 1928 Polish business directory for Ostrów Mazowiecka.

Indexed all 3,000 individuals memorialized in the town's yizkor book.

Indexed all burials in all Ostrover sections from New York area cemeteries.

Submitted hundreds of Pages to Testimony to Yad Vashem.

Translated portions of the yizkor book (for which OMRF member Judie Ostroff-Goldstein deserves special mention).

Created a web site that lists our collective resources.

Now, each year on the day before the opening of the Summer Seminar on Jewish Genealogy, we meet face-to-face. The group has grown to more than 40 members. At each meeting, Diamond and others share additional information that's useful to us: pages from books, maps, photos, videotapes, and recollections.

Members of the research group have found connections to each other. We share family trees as we find we have ancestors in common. By using our collective power, we share research costs to keep expenses down, especially when individual ancestors and their families are common to several members.

15 Jewish Genealogical Societies and Special Interest Groups

When my father and I walked into a 1990 meeting of the Jewish Genealogical Society of North Jersey, a member was giving a talk on how to construct a family tree using oversized graph paper. (Clearly this was before the proliferation of genealogical software programs and the Internet.) I found myself spellbound and finally among people who didn't think I was nuts because I was interested in finding information about dead relatives.

Eager and enthusiastic members showed me the society's resource library—drawers in a file cabinet, a few shelves of books, a collection of microfiche, and a huge, bound computer printout that contained the Family Finder.

What a treasure trove! Each month I anxiously arrived, desperate to get my hands on some of these popular resources, especially the Family Finder. I also found a place where I could get up-to-date news on resources, conferences, and great practical tips. This group introduced me to the Northeast Region of the National Archives. My entrée into the realm of Jewish genealogy was so much easier when surrounded by people I knew and people I could go to with my naïve questions.

Local Jewish genealogical societies have grown so much over the last ten years. They've been joined by a growing number of Special Interest Groups—a collection of individuals bound together by common interest in geographic areas or sources, a sort of present-day *landsmanshaft*.

If you're just starting to trace your family tree, you will reach your goals much faster when you join these groups. No matter how long you've been at it, you'll also find encouragement, enthusiasm, friendship, and collaboration from these groups. Become active in their organizations, or just be a member.

Meetings are usually held monthly and feature special programs like how to preserve photographs, a trip to the local LDS Family History Center, debriefing from the annual Summer Seminar on Jewish Genealogy, researching Russian and Polish records, and much, much more. Guest speakers are often engaged to bring members the best in subject matter expertise. Most local societies publish newsletters and journals, like the award-winning *Generations* from the JGS of Michigan and *Mass-pocha* of Massachusetts.

QUICK TIP
The annual summer seminars can help you learn from the experts, share with other researchers, and give you an opportunity to focus on your family's history. Locations have ranged from Israel and Paris to Washington, DC, Los Angeles, and New York. Check <www.jewishgen.org> for the latest information on upcoming seminars.

The Jewish Genealogical Societies (JGSs)

<www.jewishgen.org/iajgs/ajgs-jgss.html>

Below is a current listing of societies. Check the web site for the most up-to-date contact information. *Avotaynu* also publishes the listing in its Spring issue each year.

Local societies are members of the International Association of Jewish Genealogical Societies (IAJGS), a non-profit organization dedicated to coordinating the activities of local member groups around the world. Its goals are "to promote Jewish genealogy as a legitimate field of research within the academic community, to encourage Jews in the study of Jewish family history as a means of becoming acquainted with our rich heritage, and to develop, preserve, and distribute historical and genealogical records."

If a society does not exist in your area, you can contact the IAJGS to start one.

UNITED STATES

Arizona, Phoenix

Greater Phoenix Jewish Genealogical Society
Sam Arutt
P.O. Box 4063
Scottsdale, AZ 85261-4063
e-mail: sarutt@mindspring.com

Arizona, Tucson
Jewish Historical Society of
Southern Arizona, Genealogy Group
Alfred E. Lipsey,
Society President and Chair of the
Genealogy Group
4181 E Pontatoc Canyon Dr.
Tucson, AZ 85718-5227
telephone: (520) 299-4486
e-mail: lipseya@prodigy.net

California, Los Angeles
Jewish Genealogical Society of
Los Angeles
Scott Groll
P.O. Box 55443
Sherman Oaks, CA 91413-5443
telephone: (818) 771-5554
e-mail: sgroll@ix.netcom.com
web: <www.jgsla.org>

California, Orange County
Jewish Genealogical Society of
Orange County
Shmuel Fisher, President
8599 Amazon River Circle
Fountain Valley, CA 92708-5510
telephone: (714) 968-0395
e-mail: Shmuel@deltanet.com

California, Palm Springs
Jewish Genealogical Society of
Palm Springs
Gay Lynne Kegan
40111 Portulaca Court
Palm Desert, CA 92260-2332
telephone: (760) 340-6554
e-mail: Glynne@aol.com

California, Sacramento
Jewish Genealogical Society of
Sacramento
Art Yates, President
2351 Wyda Way
Sacramento, CA 95825-1160
telephone: (916) 486-0906 x361
e-mail: jgs_sacramento@
hotmail.com
web: <www.jewishgen.org/
ajgs/jgs-sacramento/>

California, San Diego
Jewish Genealogical Society of San
Diego
Roberta Berman, President
P.O. Box 927089
San Diego, CA 92192-7089
telephone: (858) 459-2074
e-mail: danber@cts.com
web: <www.homestead.com/sdjgs>

California, San Francisco
San Francisco Bay Area Jewish
Genealogical Society
Rodger Rosenberg, President
P.O. Box 471616
San Francisco, CA 94147-1616
telephone (415) 666-0188
e-mail: eandr@ix.netcom.com
web: <www.jewishgen.org/sfbajgs/>

Colorado
Jewish Genealogical Society of
Colorado
Myndel Cohen, President
6965 East Girard Ave.
Denver, CO 80224-2901
telephone: (303) 756-6028
e-mail: Hermyn@aol.com
web: <www.jewishgen.org/ajgs/jgs-
colorado>

Connecticut
Jewish Genealogical Society of
Connecticut
Jonathan Smith
394 Sport Hill Road
Easton, CT 06612-1714
telephone: (203) 268-2923
e-mail:
DeborahRachel@hotmail.com
web: <www.geocities.com/jgsct/>

District Of Columbia
Jewish Genealogy Society of
Greater Washington
Ellen Shindelman, President

P.O. Box 31122
Bethesda, MD 20824-1122
telephone: (202) 546-5239
e-mail: grapevyn@erols.com
web: <www.jewishgen.org/jgsgw/>

Florida, Fort Lauderdale
Jewish Genealogical Society of Broward County
Bernard I. Kouchel
P.O. Box 17251
Ft. Lauderdale, FL 33318-7251
telephone: (954) 472-5455
e-mail: koosh@worldnet.att.net
web: <www.seflin.org/jgsbc/jgsbc.mnu.html>

Florida, Miami
Jewish Genealogical Society of Greater Miami
Ron Ravikoff, President
P.O. Box 560432
Miami, FL 33156-0432
telephone: (305) 358-5000
fax: (305) 579-9749
e-mail: JGSMiami@aol.com

Florida, Orlando
Jewish Genealogical Society of Greater Orlando
Sim Seckbach, President
P.O. Box 941332
Maitland, FL 32794-1332
telephone: (407) 644-3566
e-mail: sseckbach@aol.com
web: <members.aol.com/JGSGO/>

Florida, Palm Beach County
Jewish Genealogical Society of Palm Beach County, Inc.
Sylvia Furshman Nusinov, President
P.O. Box 7796
Delray Beach, FL 33482-7796
telephone: (561) 483-1060
e-mail: curiousyl@aol.com

Florida, Sarasota
Jewish Genealogical Society of Southwest Florida
Lorraine Greyson, President
5221 Far Oak Circle
Sarasota, FL 34238-3306
telephone: (941) 924-6468
e-mail: Lgreys@aol.com or Lgreys@juno.com

Florida, Tampa Bay
Jewish Genealogical Society of Tampa Bay
Mark Baron, President
4270 Rudder Way
New Port Richey, FL 34652-4466
telephone: (727) 539-4521 (day) or (727) 842-5789 (evening)
e-mail: mark_baron@yahoo.com

Georgia
Jewish Genealogical Society of Georgia
Markam B. Hersh, President
P.O. Box 681022
Marietta, GA 30068-0018
telephone: (770) 977-9778
e-mail: jewishgenofga@ixpres.com
web: <ww.jewishgen.org/ajgs/jgsg/>

Hawaii, Honolulu
Jewish Genealogical Society of Hawaii
Marlene Hertz, President
237 Kuumele Pl.
Kailua, HI 96734-2958
telephone: (808) 262-0030
e-mail: marhertz@hgea.org

Illinois, Champaign-Urbana
Champaign-Urbana Jewish Genealogy Society
Dr. Sheila Goldberg
808 La Sell Drive
Champaign, IL 61820-6820
telephone: (217) 359-3102
e-mail: sheila@prairienet.org

Illinois, Chicago
Jewish Genealogical Society of Illinois
Judith R. Frazin, President

P.O. Box 515
Northbrook, IL 60065-0515
telephone: (847) 509-0201
e-mail: jrfraz@Megsinet.net
web: <www.jewishgen.org/jgsi/>

Illinois / Indiana

Illiana Jewish Genealogical Society
Trudy Barch, President
P.O. Box 384
Flossmoor, IL 60422-0384
telephone: (708) 957-9457
e-mail: ijgs@lincolnnet.net
web: <www.lincolnnet.net/ijgs>

Indiana, Indianapolis

Jewish Genealogy Society of Indiana
Barry Levitt, President
PO Box 68280
Indianapolis, IN 46268-0280
telephone: (317) 388-0632
e-mail: balcpa@iquest.net

Louisiana, New Orleans

Jewish Genealogical Society of New Orleans
Jacob and Vicki Karno
25 Waverly Place
Metarie, LA 70003-2553
telephone: (504) 888-3817
r-mail: jkarno@karnovsky.com

Maryland

Jewish Genealogical Society of Maryland
c/o Jewish Community Center
3506 Gwynbrook Ave.
Owings Mills, MD 21117-1498
telephone: (443) 255-8228
e-mail: JGSMaryland@AOL.com

Maryland

See also Jewish Genealogical Society of Greater Washington

Massachusetts

Jewish Genealogical Society of Greater Boston
Jay Sage and Daphnah Sage, Co-Presidents
P.O. Box 610366
Newton Highlands, MA 02461-0366
telephone: (617) 796-8522
e-mail: Jay_Sage@post.harvard.edu
dsage@juno.com
and Info@JGSGB.org
web: <www.jgsgb.org>

Michigan

Jewish Genealogical Society of Michigan
Marc D. Manson, President
30141 High Valley Road
Farmington Hills, MI 48331-2169
telephone: (248) 661-8515 (day) or (248) 661-0688 (evening)
fax (248) 661-2306
e-mail: MDMCOUSA@aol.com
web: <www.jgsmi.org>

Missouri, St. Louis

Jewish Genealogical Society of St. Louis
Affiliated with United Hebrew Congregation
Jerry Goldberg, President
13039 Musket Court
St. Louis, MO. 63146-4371
telephone: (314) 434-2566
e-mail: Jerfransl@cs.com
web: <www.stlcyberjew.com/jgs-stl>

Nevada, Las Vegas

Jewish Genealogy Society of Southern Nevada-West
Carole Montello, President
P.O. Box 29342
Las Vegas, NV 89126-3342
telephone: (702) 871-9773
e-mail: carmont7@juno.com

New Jersey, Bergen County

Jewish Genealogical Society of Bergen County
Edward Rosenbaum, President
135 Chestnut Ridge Road
Montvale, NJ 07645
telephone: (201) 384-8851

e-mail: erosenbaum@mail.com
web: <www.crosswinds.net/
~erosenbaum/jgsbc>

New Jersey, Central
Jewish Historical Society of Central Jersey
Nathan M. Reiss, President
228 Livingston Ave.
New Brunswick, NJ 08901-3061
telephone: (732) 249-4894
e-mail: reiss@rci.rutgers.edu
web: <www.jewishgen.org/jhscj>

New Jersey, Morris Area
Morris Area (NJ) Jewish Genealogical Society
Gary R. Platt, President
21 Rolling Hill Drive
Morristown, NJ 07960
telephone: (973) 993-1744 (day) or (973) 829-0242 (evening)
e-mail: grplatt@idt.net

New Jersey, Northern
Jewish Genealogical Society of North Jersey
Evan Stolbach
YM-YWHA of North Jersey
Charles & Bessie Goldman Library
1 Pike Drive
Wayne, NJ 07470-2494
telephone: (973) 595-0100 x36
e-mail: EStolb7395@aol.com

New York, Albany
JGS of the Capital District
Norman Tillman, President
P.O. Box 5002
Albany, NY 12205-0002
telephone: (518) 462-4815
e-mail: NTill10123@aol.com

New York, Buffalo
Jewish Genealogy Society of Buffalo
Dr. Renata Lefcourt
3700 Main Street
Amherst, NY 14226-3233
telephone: (716) 833-0743
e-mail: lefcourt@localnet.com

New York, Long Island
Jewish Genealogy Society of Long Island
Jackie Wasserstein, President
37 Westcliff Drive
Dix Hills, NY 11746-5627
telephone: (631) 549-9532
e-mail: jwasserst@aol.com
web: <www.jewishgen.org/jgsli>

New York, New York
Jewish Genealogical Society, Inc.
Estelle Guzik
P.O. Box 6398
New York, NY 10128-0004
telephone: (212) 330-8257
e-mail: JGSNY@aol.com
web: <www.jgsny.org>

New York, Rochester
Jewish Genealogical Society of Rochester
Bruce Kahn
265 Viennawood Drive
Rochester, NY 14618-4465
telephone: (716) 271-2118
e-mail: bkahn@servtech.com
web:< jgsr.hq.net/>

Ohio, Cincinnati
Jewish Genealogical Society of Greater Cincinnati
Jacob Rader Marcus Center
Nancy Felson Brant, President
3101 Clifton Ave
Cincinnati, OH 45220-2488
telephone: (513) 631-0233
e-mail: nfbrant@aol.com

Ohio, Cleveland
Jewish Genealogy Society of Cleveland
Arlene Blank Rich
996 Eastlawn Drive
Highland Heights, OH 44143-3126
telephone: (440) 449-2326
e-mail: BR1595@aol.com

Ohio, Columbus
Jewish Genealogical Group
Peggy H. Kaplan, Executive Director
Columbus Jewish Historical Society
1175 College Ave, Columbus OH
43209-2890
telephone (614) 237-7686
e-mail: cjhs@beol.net
web: <www.gcis.net/cjhs>
Joe Cohen, Chair
2673 Florabunda, Columbus
OH 43209-3117
telephone: (614) 231-7006
e-mail: joeacohen@aol.com

Ohio, Dayton
Jewish Genealogical Society of
Dayton
Dr. Leonard Spialter, President
P.O. Box 60338
Dayton, OH 45406-0338
telephone: (937) 277-3995
e-mail: spialterr@about.com

Oregon, Eugene
Eugene, Oregon Jewish Genealogy
Study Group
Reeva Kimble
2352 Van Ness
Eugene, OR 97403-1862
telephone: 541-345-8129
e-mail:
rKimble@oregon.uoregon.edu
web: <www.users.uswest.net/
~cfleishman/eugenegen.html>

Oregon, Portland
Jewish Genealogical Society of
Oregon
MJCC
Ronald D. Doctor, President
6651 S.W. Capitol Highway
Portland, OR 97219-1992
telephone: (503) 244-0111
e-mail: rondoctor@uswest.net
web: <www.rootsweb.com/~orjgs/>

Pennsylvania, Philadelphia
Jewish Genealogical Society of
Philadelphia
Joel L. Spector
109 Society Hill
Cherry Hill, NJ 08003-2402
telephone: (856) 424-6860
e-mail: jlspector@aol.com
web: <www.jewishgen.org/jgsp>

Pennsylvania, Pittsburgh
Jewish Genealogical Society of
Pittsburgh
Julian Falk
2131 Fifth Avenue
Pittsburgh, PA 15219-5505
telephone: (412) 471-0772
e-mail: JulFalk@aol.com

Texas, Dallas
Dallas Jewish Historical Society,
Genealogy Division
George L. Smith
7900 Northaven Road
Dallas, TX 75230-3392
telephone: (214) 739-2737, x261
e-mail: geode16@aol.com
web: <www.dvjc.org/history/
genealogy.shtml>

Texas, Houston
Greater Houston Jewish
Genealogical Society
Jeff Olderman, President
7115 Belle Park Drive
Houston, TX 77072-2417
telephone: (281) 495-9211
e-mail: jeffel55@aol.com

Virginia
See also Jewish Genealogy Society of
Greater Washington

Virginia, Norfolk
Jewish Genealogical Society of
Tidewater
Kenneth R. Cohen, President
7300 Newport Avenue
Norfolk, VA 23505

telephone: (757) 351-2190
e-mail: kcohen4@juno.com

Washington State
JGS of Washington State
Sheryl Stern, President
3633-86th St. SE
Mercer Island, WA 98040-3612
telephone: (206) 232-2666
e-mail: jgsws@hotmail.com
web: <members.tripod.com/~JGSWS>

Wisconsin, Milwaukee
Wisconsin Jewish Genealogical Society
Penny Deshur
9280 N. Fairway Drive
Milwaukee, WI 53217-1317
telephone: (414) 351-2190
e-mail: pdeshur@wi.rr.com

ACROSS THE WORLD

Argentina, Buenos Aires
Sociedad Argentina de Genealogia Judia
Paul Armony
Juana Azurduy 2223, P. 8
(1429) Buenos Aires, Argentina
e-mail: genarg@infovia.com.ar
web: <www.agja.org.ar/>

Australia, Adelaide
Australian Jewish Genealogical Society, Adelaide
Hilde Hines, Chair
c/o Adelaide Hebrew Congregation
P.O. Box 320
Glenside, Adelaide
South Australia, 5065 Australia
telephone: 61-8-79-6030
e-mail: kaiserr@senet.com.au
web: <www.zeta.org.au/~feraltek/genealogy/ajgs>

Australia, Brisbane
Australian Jewish Genealogical Society, Brisbane
Morris S. Ochert OAM
3/23 Lucinda St
Taringa, Brisbane
Queensland, 4068, Australia
web: <www.zeta.org.au/~feraltek/genealogy/ajgs>

Australia, Canberra
Australian Jewish Genealogical Society, Canberra
Sylvia Deutsch, Chair
C/O ACT Jewish Community Inc.
P.O. Box 3105
Manuka, Australian Capital Territory
2603, Australia
e-mail: deutand@ozemail.com.au
web: <www.zeta.org.au/~feraltek/genealogy/ajgs>

Australia, Melbourne
Australian Jewish Genealogical Society (Victoria)
Melbourne
Leslie Oberman, President
P.O. Box 189
Glenhuntly, Melbourne
Victoria 3163, Australia
telephone: 61-3-9571-8251
e-mail: sharpe@labyrinth.net.au
web: <www.melbourne.net/csaky/AJGSmainpage.htm>

Australia, Perth
Australian Jewish Genealogical Society, Perth
Michelle Urban, Chair
21 Broomhall Way
Noranda, Perth
Western Australia, 6062 Australia
e-mail: urban@wantree.com.au
web: <www.zeta.org.au/~feraltek/genealogy/ajgs>

Australia, Sydney
Australian Jewish Genealogical Society, Sydney
Sophie Caplan, Chair
P.O. Box 154
Northbridge, Sydney
New South Wales 1560, Australia
telephone: 61-2-9958-6317
fax: 61-2-9967-2834
e-mail: ajgsnsw@idx.com.au
web: <www.zeta.org.au/~feraltek/genealogy/ajgs>

Belgium
Jewish Genealogical Society of Belgium
Daniel Dratwa, President
74 Avenue Stalingrad
B-1000 Bruxelles, Belgique
telephone: 32-2-512.19.63
fax: 32-2-513-48-59
e-mail: d.dratwa@mjb-jmb.org
web: <www.mjb-jmb.org>

Brazil
Sociedade Genealogica Judaica do Brasil
Dr. Guilherme Faiguenboim
Caixa Postal 1025
13001-970 Campinas SP, Brazil
telephone: (5511) 881-9365 (Ms. Anna Rosa)
e-mail: faiguen@attglobal.net

Canada, Alberta
Jewish Genealogical Society of Alberta
Florence Elman, President
1607 - 90 Avenue SW
Calgary, Alberta T2V 4V7, Canada
e-mail: haflo@cadvision.com
web: <www.geocities.com/Heartland/Village/9200>

Canada, Montreal
Jewish Genealogical Society of Montreal
Stanley M. Diamond, President
5599 Edgemore Ave.
Montreal, Quebec H4W 1V4, Canada
telephone: (514) 484-0100
fax: (514) 484-7306
e-mail: SMSDiamond@aol.com
web: <www.gtrdata.com/jgs-montreal/>

Canada, Ottawa
Jewish Genealogy Society of Ottawa
Charles B. Lapkoff, President
c/o Donna Dinberg
Greenberg Families Library
Soloway JCC
1780 Kerr Ave.
Ottawa, Ontario K2A 1R9 Canada
telephone: (613) 995-9227(day) or (613) 731-0876 (evening)
e-mail: lapkoff@netrover.com or donna.dinberg@nlc-bnc.ca

Canada, Toronto
Jewish Genealogical Society of Canada (Toronto)
Gert Rogers
P.O. Box 446, Station "A"
Willowdale, Toronto
Ontario M2N 5T1, Canada
telephone: (416) 638-3280
e-mail: kelwel@iname.com

Canada, Vancouver
Jewish Genealogical Institute of British Columbia
Cissie Eppel
950 West 41st Ave.
Vancouver
BC V5Z 2N7, Canada
telephone: (604) 321-9870
e-mail: hgoldman@interchange.ubc.ca
web: <www.geocities.com/Heartland/Hills/4441>

Canada, Winnipeg
Jewish Heritage Centre of Western Canada Genealogical Institute
Bev Rayburn, President
C116 - 123 Doncaster St.
Winnipeg, Manitoba R3N 2B2, Canada
telephone: (204) 477-7460
fax: (204) 477-7465
e-mail: bjrayburn@aol.com
web: <www.jhcwc.mb.ca/geninst/shtml>

France, Paris
Cercle de Généalogie Juive
Claudie Blamont, President
14, rue Saint-Lazare
75009 Paris, France
telephone and fax: 33 1 40 23 04 90; Minitel: 3615 GENEALOJ
e-mail: cgjgenefr@aol.com
web: <www.genealoj.org>

France, Paris
GenAmi
Association de Généalogie Juive Internationale
Micheline Gutmann
76 rue de Passy
F-75016 Paris, France
telephone: 33 1 45 24 35 40
e-mail: michelinegutmann@compuserve.com
web: <www.chez.com/genami/>

Israel, Jerusalem
Israel Genealogical Society
Jean-Pierre Stroweis, President
POB 4270
91041 Jerusalem, Israel
telephone: 972-2-651-4996
fax: 972-2-671-0260
e-mail: igs@lexicom.co.il
web: <www.isragen.org.il>
Jerusalem branch
Rose Lerer Cohen, President
e-mail: roseron@shani.net

Israel, Mizra
Galilee Genealogical Society
Louis Zetler, President/Chair
Hoshaya M. P. O. Hamovil
17915, Israel
telephone: 972 (0)6 646-8180 Fax: 972 (0)6 646-8180
e-mail: zetler@kinneret.co.il
web: <www.geocities.com/Heartland/Hills/9698/>

Israel, Negev
Israel Genealogical Society of the Negev, Branch of Israel Genealogical Society
Martha Lev-Zion, President
e-mail: martha@bgumail.bgu.ac.il

Israel, Tel Aviv
Israel Genealogical Society, Tel Aviv Branch of Israel Genealogical Society, Eytan Shilo, President
e-mail: eitanshilo@ibm.net

Israel, Tel Aviv
Jewish Family Research Association (JFRA)
An Independent Jewish Genealogical Association
Aviva Neeman, President
POB 10099
61100 Tel Aviv, Israel
Telephone: 972-3-699-2813
fax: 972-3-699-3852
e-mail: aneeman@netvision.net.il

Netherlands
Nederlandse Kring voor Joodse Genealogie (Netherlands Society for Jewish Genealogy)
Erna Houtkooper, Secretary
Abbingstraat #1
1447 P.A. Purmerend, Netherlands
telephone: 31 299-644498
fax: 31 299-647661
e-mail: info@nljewgen.org
web: <www.nljewgen.org>

Russia, Moscow
Jewish Genealogical Society of the Former Soviet Union in Moscow
9, Mokhovaya Street #329 c/o Jewish University in Moscow
Moscow, Russia
telephone: 7-095-203-3441
e-mail: paley@mail.ru
web: <www.geocities.com/Heartland/Estates/6121>
Vladimir J. Paley, President
16-25, Klinskaya Street
Moscow 125475, Russia
telephone: 7-095-451-3382
e mail: paley@mail.ru

South Africa, Capetown
Jewish Family History Society of Cape Town
Paul Cheifitz, President
P. O. Box 51985, Waterfront, 8002
South Africa
telephone: 21-4344825
21-4230223
e-mail: jewfamct@global.co.za

South Africa, Johannesburg
Jewish Genealogy Society of Johannesburg
Colin Plen, President/Chairman,
Box 1388 Parklands 2121
South Africa
e-mail: evancol@iafrica.com

Sweden
Jewish Genealogical Society of Sweden
Carl H. Carlsson, President
c/o Gerber
Box 7427, 103 91
Stockholm, Sweden
telephone: 46-8-679 29 17
e-mail: Carl-Henrik.Carlsson@hist.uu.se
or maynard.gerber@mbox200.swipnet.se
web: <www.ijk-s.se/genealogi>

Switzerland
Schweizerische Vereinigung für Jüdische Genealogie
Raymond M. Jung, President
Scheuchzerstrasse 154
8006 Zürich, Switzerland
telephone: 41 1 361 71 54
web: <www.eye.ch/swissgen/ver/jeinfo-d.htm>

United Kingdom
Jewish Genealogical Society of Great Britain
George Anticoni, Chairman
P.O. Box 13288
London N3 3WD, England
telephone: 44-1923-825-197
fax: 44-1923-820-323
e-mail: jgsgb@ort.org
web: <www.jgsgb.ort.org/index.htm>

Special Interest Groups (SIGs)

Gesher Galicia Special Interest Group coordinator Shelley Kellerman Pollero addresses the annual meeting. Courtesy of Roni Seibel Liebowitz.

The structure of the local societies provides a solid foundation upon which to build a new set of groups dedicated to research in shared geographical areas. For example, the Suwalki-Łomża SIG formed among people whose families came from that area of Poland and Lithuania. This group banded together to publish extracts of LDS records and lists from other sources in a publication called *Landsmen*. A Galician group followed with its publication, *The Galitzianer*, and spawned many shtetl-based research groups. Some publish a journal; some publish an "e-zine" (online newsletter). Some charge membership fees, some do not. Several have hundreds of members, all there to learn and share.

SEE ALSO
As you read earlier in Chapter 13, SIGs like Belarus and Lithuania are totally web-based and offer valuable databases accessible through JewishGen.

Like the local JGSs, you'll find others who share your interests and perhaps those who have information that will be pertinent to your family's research. For instance, information published in *The Galitzianer* led me to write to Warsaw for my family's vital records, to contact specific private researchers in Poland and Ukraine, and researchers interested in the Zuckerkandel family.

Yet there are other SIGs, like the Yizkor book SIG mentioned in Chapter 11, dedicated to publishing necrologies and translated book portions on JewishGen so the information is widely available.

There are also many geography-based groups you can join. As you'll see from the list below, there's probably a SIG that will interest you.

Belarus SIG—focuses on the former Russian Empire gubernias of Grodno, Minsk, Mogilev, and Vitebsk.

Bohemia-Moravia—covers Bohemia and Moravia (now the Czech Republic), plus parts of Austria, especially Vienna.

Denmark—covers Denmark, the Danish West Indies, and other Scandinavian countries.

Early American SIG—a forum for those researching Jewish immigrants to the United States prior to 1880.

German-Jewish—covers Germany and other German-speaking areas such as Austria, parts of Switzerland, Alsace, Lorraine, Bohemia, and Moravia.

Gesher Galicia ("Bridge to Galicia")—focuses on Austrian Poland, a province of the Austro-Hungarian Empire from 1772 until 1917, now in southern Poland and western Ukraine.

Hungary—includes areas considered as "Greater Hungary," comprising parts of today's Slovakia, Poland, Ukraine, Czech Republic, Hungary, Austria, and Romania.

Kielce-Radom (southern Russian Poland)—specifically designed to address two gubernias of the Kingdom of Poland (Russian Poland), now in south-central Poland, covering much of the area between Warsaw and Kraków.

Suwalki-Łomża—specifically designed to cover two northeastern gubernias of Russian Poland, now in northeast Poland and southwest Lithuania.

Latin America—focuses on all Spanish and Portuguese-speaking countries in the area, including Mexico and South America.

Latvia—provides a forum for researchers of Jewish families of Latvian descent.

Lithuania (Litvak)—addresses records from Kovno and Vilna gubernias, covering much of the area that is now Lithuania.

Romania—covers Romanian territory including Moldova, Bessarabia, and Bukovina.

Sephardic—ETSI, the Sephardic Genealogical and Historical Society.

Ukraine—covers the former Russian Empire gubernias now in Ukraine: Podolia, Volhynia, Kiev, Poltava, Chernigov, Kharkov, Kherson, Taurida and Ekaterinoslav.

Southern Africa—includes South Africa, Lesotho (Basutoland), Botswana (Bechuanaland), Zimbabwe (S. Rhodesia), Zambia (N. Rhodesia), Swaziland, Mozambique, and the former Belgian Congo.

Many of these groups have web pages and discussion groups hosted by JewishGen, and many are dedicated to Jewish records access, publishing records databases online.

There is great power in networking. Town-based groups have been able to pursue European record extraction projects, town information collections, and more—all due to the power of shared interests.

PART V

Researching Your Medical History

16 Jewish Genetic Disease

In November 1999, researcher Roni Seibel Liebowitz of Scarsdale, New York, posted this to the Jewish Records Indexing – Poland project online discussion group:

"The next time someone asks us, why are we wasting our time looking for dead people, we can tell them about our efforts to save the lives of the living. The international cooperation of genealogists searching for descendants of Jeff Bornstein's ancestors is remarkable . . . genealogists were contacted in the hopes of locating the best donors for a potential bone marrow transplant for this 29-year-old doctor recently diagnosed with leukemia.

"Within days, genealogists in Canada, the U.S., Poland, Israel, and Australia, to name a few, sprang into action. Synagogues, newspapers, Jewish organizations, *landsmanshaftn* [town-based societies], radio and TV stations were contacted. In the process of searching the family for a potential bone marrow match, an impressive tree of Jeff's ancestors has been compiled. Through vital records and family reports, the Bornstein tree is growing. Living, breathing descendants are being contacted and made aware of the need for a genetically linked donor for Jeffrey. Both guest books linked from the web page have messages from other Bornsteins, and a few people have made genealogical connections.

"As genealogists, I think we can all feel very proud of the work that continues to be done not only for Jeffrey but for all those waiting for bone marrow transplants. Please encourage others to take this simple blood test and enter the bone marrow registry. Even if you can't attend a bone marrow drive, the simple blood test can be done at your local bone marrow facility or ask your physician . . . What better use of genealogical research than this!"

What better use indeed! Using genealogical research to uncover family medical history and potentially save lives is one of the best applications of our work. Yet, we often wait to collect and share this information until we are confronted with health challenges.

"Genetically speaking, Jewish people are one big family. We share a common ancestry and therefore, common genes and blocks of genetic material," says Dr. Robert Burk, professor of epidemiology at the Albert Einstein College of Medicine at Yeshiva University and principal investigator of the Cancer Longevity, Ancestry and Lifestyle (CLAL) study in the Jewish population currently focusing on prostate cancer.

The Importance of Researching Your Health History

Researching your medical history can help you and medical professionals preserve your family's health for generations to come. As much as one-half of all health conditions may have a genetic component, passed down within families from generation to generation. A recent issue of the *Mayo Clinic Health Letter* points out that it's important to remember that many significant medical problems have familial tendencies, including heart disease, high blood pressure, diabetes, some cancers, and certain psychiatric disorders.

The Seven Most Common Jewish Genetic Diseases

Many think of Tay-Sachs when they hear the words "Jewish genetic disease," but seven genetic diseases most commonly afflict the Jewish population.

Tay-Sachs Disease—a fatal disorder of infancy that progressively destroys the central nervous system. It can be traced to the lack of a single enzyme. Approximately one in every 25 Ashkenazic Jews carries the gene versus one in every 250 in the general population.

Canavan Disease—a progressive disease of the central nervous system for which there is no treatment and is typically fatal in childhood. About one in every 40 Ashkenazic Jews carries the gene.

Niemann-Pick Disease—about one in every 70 Ashkenazic Jews carries the gene of this disease, an infantile neurodegenerative condition that includes loss of brain function and liver enlargement. No treatment is available.

Gaucher Disease (Type 1)—the most common genetic disorder among the Ashkenazic population with a carrier frequency of about one in 18, this disease causes spleen and liver enlargement, blood abnormalities, and orthopedic problems. Enzyme replacement therapy has shown to be useful in treating Gaucher disease.

Cystic Fibrosis—no cure is available for this progressive, lifelong condition in which the glands that produce mucus, sweat, and intestinal secretions malfunction. It is not restricted to any ethnic group. It is, though, most common among Caucasians, with a carrier frequency of about one in 25.

Bloom Syndrome—about one in every 100 Ashkenazic Jews carries the gene for this condition in which children are small, grow poorly, have frequent infections, and may have learning disabilities. Children and young adults with the condition can also develop breast cancer, colon cancer, and leukemia.

Fanconi Anemia (Type C)—a chronic disease associated with small stature, bone marrow failure, congenital malformations, and a predisposition to leukemia. The condition may also involve learning disabilities or mental retardation. About one in every 90 Ashkenazic Jews carries it.

Genetic Testing

When meeting with medical practitioners, you'll often be asked to provide your family's medical history. Says Virginia Tech genetic technologies expert Doris Teichler Zallen, "Accurate knowledge of one's family history is an important prerequisite for susceptibility gene testing. The health problems experienced by

ON THE BOOKSHELF
Zallen's *Does It Run in the Family: A Consumer's Guide to DNA Testing for Genetic Disorders* can give you an excellent overview of testing.

older family members may herald the kinds of health problems that younger members of the family may face. Layers of confusion may need to be penetrated before the real family medical history becomes clear and a pattern emerges that points to the possible involvement of a susceptibility gene."

No one has a perfect collection of genes. We all have some mutations in our DNA—our deoxyribonucleic acid—that stores all of our genetic information. Experts estimate that each of us has about eight genes where changes have occurred that could severely impair our health. But a change in DNA does not necessarily translate into a genetic disorder. It depends on where the gene is located, what type of task it directs, and how well surrounding genes function.

In general, there are four different types of genetic testing:

- Direct testing can find specific mutations or alterations in the gene's DNA.
- Linkage testing assesses the likelihood that a form of the gene has been inherited along with the marker—a reference point that distinguishes one DNA pattern from another.
- Susceptibility testing looks for a gene whose presence can increase the chances of developing a health problem later in life.
- Carrier testing determines if a healthy individual has a flawed gene that, if discovered in his or her children, could lead to a genetic disorder. This very difficult process is currently available for Tay-Sachs, Thalassemia, sickle cell disease, and hemophilia.

The results? According to Dr. Robert Desnick, director of the Mt. Sinai Center for Jewish Genetic Diseases and chair of the Department of Human Genetics at Mt. Sinai Hospital, the ability to predict a genetic disorder may translate into the ability to prevent it.

Still got Grandma's lock of hair or Grandpa's pipe? Being able to give samples of stored tissue (or even tumors!) to your medical professional can help explore the presence of a susceptibility gene with today's DNA tests. Stored tissue is critical if linkage testing is being considered in families where affected members have died.

Genetic testing is done at three stages: prenatal, presymptomatic, and premarital. Pre-natal testing helps to bypass diseases that affect children like Tay-Sachs. Presymptomatic testing is conducted for conditions we have in our genes that predispose us to a disease, such as prostate or breast cancer, because these diseases run in families. For instance, 5-10% of all breast cancer is inherited, meaning that one in every 200 women is at risk for an inherited form. Testing is done for two different genes that account for 70-80% of these cases. Premarital testing is perhaps the most controversial but can help avoid potential problems and harmful family legacies.

At the 1999 Summer Seminar on Jewish Genealogy in New York City, Desnick said, "No other group in the world can be tested for so many diseases. There must be a reason why we carry these lethal recessive genes." He also noted that Mt. Sinai tests for the seven most common diseases found among Ashkenazic Jewry.

Meeting the Challenge Through Networking and Support

"Knowledge is power," says Phyllis Goldberg of Rockville, Maryland. When her grandson was born with Fanconi Anemia, she made a promise that she would leave no stone unturned until she found every member of her family who was at risk. The eastern European Jewish variety of the disease makes up about 15 percent of the total cases. Goldberg believes she has traced the disease to her paternal great-grandparents from Galicia and is now hoping to work within the Fanconi Anemia community to find the mutant gene's geographic roots.

Reaching out to others who share an affliction can give you support, comfort, and information. More than one hundred volunteer health organizations have been formed to raise awareness among researchers and to raise funds for research, ranging from the Alzheimer's Association to the United Parkinson's Foundation.

Another useful activity is to enroll in a registry so genetic researchers can find you and your family. The registry collects information on a number of families bearing a certain medical

SEE ALSO
Read more about Stanley Diamond's search for his Beta-Thalassemia roots in Chapter 18.

condition or genetic disorder. It keeps track of affected family members and those who are at risk.

Dr. Simon Kreindler, a psychiatrist in Toronto and the father of Jeffrey Bornstein's friend, turned to Montreal Jewish Genealogical Society president Stanley Diamond, who has developed a reputation as a lay expert on genealogical research for medical purposes, specifically the Beta-Thalassemia trait.

When Diamond learned Bornstein's roots were in Poland, the Jewish Records Indexing – Poland project (see *Heritage Quest* 81, May/June 1999) sprang into action, and got results with the help of Shirley Rotbein Flaum, ShtetLinks web master and archives coordinator for Łódż, an ancestral home to Bornstein, Flaum, and Diamond. Flaum told Diamond, "I am a breast cancer survivor . . . I understand what is involved, and I will do everything I can to help Jeff." Through the efforts of Flaum, Liebowitz, and Kreindler, more than 12,000 people turned up at donor drives in Toronto, Montreal, and Israel to help Bornstein and others.

Says Desnick, "We are in a great period of gene discovery, and the study of rare and common diseases in Ashkenazic Jewish families can enhance the identification of the causative genes or predisposing genes for many diseases. If larger families in which certain rare or common diseases are identified, these families may be of great value to certain gene discovery projects."

As long as we are gathering family information, we would be extremely well served to delve more into our medical history, applying genealogy to the best of purposes—our family's health and ongoing medical research.

DISCUSSION GROUPS AND WEB RESOURCES

GenDisease-J

GenDisease-J is a discussion list for those individuals concerned with the various genetically-transmitted diseases affecting Jewish populations, though discussions are not limited to Jews. Subscribers include professionals, patients, researchers, students, parents, and other interested parties. To subscribe to the mailing list, send the following e-mail request:

To: listserv@maelstrom.stjohns.edu
Subject: [blank] or some character if your mail program requires an entry
Message: sub GenDisease-J <firstname> <lastname>

Online Mendelian Inheritance in Man

<www.ncbi.nlm.nih.gov/Omim>

This database catalogs all known human genes and genetic disorders, providing links to relevant literature. You may need a medical dictionary.

National Genealogy Society Family Health and Heredity Committee

<www.ngsgenealogy.org/comfamhealth.htm>

17 Developing Your Family's Medical Pedigree

According to Dr. Doris Zallen, oral histories alone may distort the real truth. She says, "For any genetic assessment to be carried out, it is necessary to find out who the members are in the nuclear family and in the extended family and exactly how they are related. Further, it is important to know what health problems they have, or, if they have died, what health problems they had. The genetic specialists use the family history, which they organize into a diagram, as the basis for identifying what the genetic problems may be and for providing estimates of risk."

So the next time the family gathers for a reunion or a holiday celebration, you've got a mission to record as much information as you can about everyone's health history.

Interviewing

Start with your parents, siblings, and children. Then add data from and about grandparents, aunts and uncles, cousins, nieces and nephews. The more information you can gather, the better. Be sympathetic and honor the need for privacy. Requesting medical information requires diplomacy and sensitivity. Some relatives will probably be reluctant to admit there are certain familial traits and tendencies.

Here are some rules of thumb:

1. Develop a list of questions and a list of medical conditions you're researching.

2. Focus on those branches and individuals who may be able to provide the key leads for expanding the search.

3. Never assume anything. People often don't know or can't remember their exact medical history. Check and double-check. Ask for permission to talk to family doctors or anyone who has been involved with the family's health. This is particularly relevant when tracking genetic traits that can be a potential disaster for future generations, as not everyone will recognize the implications of the trait they carry.

4. Enlist others in the family, particularly doctors and other medical professionals who understand and support the aims of the research.

Information on any medical ailment may prove useful. Pay special attention to serious conditions such as cancer, high blood pressure, heart disease, diabetes, depression, and alcoholism. Be sure to also jot down your relative's age when an illness was diagnosed.

Interviews are just the beginning. Oral history is great but may be distorted. To fill in the gaps and verify oral testimony, here's a list of other information sources that can give you critical medical information.

Death certificates. There's usually more to the story than a death certificate's "cause of death" entry. For instance, my father's death certificate gives heart failure as the cause of death, but he suffered from diabetes-related kidney failure and was on dialysis for quite some time. Ask questions about medical conditions, when family members first got sick, how long the illness lasted, how long the hospital stay was, etc.

Obituaries. Reading an obituary carefully can help identify useful medical facts. Look for where to send donations, such as a foundation or memorial fund.

Cemetery and funeral records. Using a map of Chicago's Waldheim Cemetery, Stanley Diamond was able to locate the gravestones of two immigrant ancestors, first cousins, who married. With the help of a supportive cemetery staff member, Diamond contacted the man responsible for the graves' perpetual care. This is how he met his cousin, Alex, also diagnosed as a Beta-Tha-

NEW JERSEY STATE DEPARTMENT OF HEALTH
CERTIFICATE OF DEATH

LOCAL FILE NUMBER — STATE FILE NUMBER

SPACES BELOW FOR STATE USE ONLY

1. NAME OF DECEASED (Type or Print) (First) Max (Middle) (Last) Krasner
2. Sex: Male
3. DATE OF DEATH: Nov. 6, 1969
4. Color or Race: White
5. Age (in yrs. last birthday): 93 — If under 1 Yr. Months Days — If under 24 Hrs. Hours Min.
6. Date of Birth: May 1, 1876
7. Was deceased ever in U.S. Armed Forces? (Yes, no, or unknown) (If yes, give war or dates of serv.): No
8. Birthplace (State or foreign country): Russia
9. Citizen of what country? USA
10. Married ☐ Never Married ☐ Widowed ☒ Divorced ☐
11. Social Security No.: 150-26-5473 A

RESIDENCE

12. PLACE OF DEATH a. County: Hudson
b. City ☐ Boro ☐ Twp. ☐ (Check box and give name): Kearny
c. Name of Hospital or Institution (If not in hospital or institution give street address): West Hudson Hospital
13. USUAL RESIDENCE (If institution: residence before admission) a. State: N J b. County: Hudson
c. City ☐ Boro ☐ Twp. ☐ (Check box and give name): Kearny
d. Street Address (If rural, P.O. Address): 1 Elizabeth Avenue
14. a. Usual Occupation (Give kind of work done during most of working life, even if retired): Checker
14. b. Kind of Business or Industry: Shop-Rite Food Market
15. Father's Name: Unknown
16. Mother's Maiden Name: Breina Dobra
17. Informant's Name and Address: Milton Krasner, 36 Clinton Ave. Kearny NJ

CAUSE

18. PART I DEATH WAS CAUSED BY — Enter only one cause per line for (a), (b) and (c) — Approximate interval between onset and death
Immediate Cause (a) 1) Arteriosclerotic Heart Disease
Conditions, if any, which gave rise to above cause "(a)", stating the underlying cause last — Due to (b) 2) Complete Heart Block
Due to (c)

Conditions contributing to death but not related to the immediate cause.

PART II OTHER SIGNIFICANT CONDITIONS
19a. Was autopsy performed? Yes ☐ No ☒
19b. If yes, were findings considered in determining cause of death? Yes ☐ No ☐
20a. Accident ☐ Suicide ☐ Homicide ☐ to the best of my knowledge.
20b. Date and Hour of Injury M.
20c. How Injury Occurred (Enter nature of injury in Part I or II of Item 18).
20d. Injury Occurred While at Work ☐ Not While at Work ☐
20e. Place of Injury (e.g. in or about home, farm, factory, street, office bldg., etc.)
20f. City, Town or Location — County — State

CROSS CLASS.

21. I (attended, examined) the deceased (from, on) 11/4/69 to 11/6/69 and last saw (him, her) alive on 11/6/69
Death occurred at 2 A.m. on the date stated above; and to the best of my knowledge, from the causes stated.

CENSUS TRACT

22a. Attending Phys. ☒ Med. Exam. ☐ County Phys. ☐
Signature: [illegible], M.D.
22b. Address: 107 Grand Place, Arlington, N.J.
22c. Date Signed: 11/6/69
23a. Burial, Cremation, Removal (Specify): Burial
23b. Cemetery or Crematory Name: Oheb Shalom Cemetery
23c. Location City: Hillside State: N J
23d. Burial Date Mo. Day Yr.: Nov. 9, 1969
24a. Funeral Home Name: Goldsticker Memorial Home
24b. Funeral Home Address: 228 Chancellor ave. Newark N J
24c. Funeral Director Signature: [illegible] N. J. License No. 1650
25a. Registrar Issuing Permit – Signature: [illegible]
25b. Date Rec'd. by Local Registrar: 11-7-69

REG. 18 JAN. 68

Kearny Board of Health
THIS IS A TRUE COPY
NOV 12 1969
Rose L. Gibb Registrar.
Walter J. Nic[illegible] Health Officer

Max Krasner's death certificate identifies cause of death.

13558

Certificate of Death

Certificate No. 13558

FILED

JUN PM 2 : 16

1. NAME OF DECEASED (Print or typewrite) ESTHER (First Name) TOBY (Middle Name) ANTEL (Last Name) None (Social Security Number)

PERSONAL PARTICULARS (To be filled in by Medical Examiner)

2. USUAL RESIDENCE: (a) State New York (b) Co. Kings (c) City, Town or Village Brooklyn (d) No. 1854 - 68th Street (If in rural area, give location) (e) Length of residence or stay in City of New York immediately prior to death 80 years

3. SINGLE, MARRIED, WIDOWED, OR DIVORCED (write the word) Widowed

4. WIFE / HUSBAND of Hyman

5. DATE OF BIRTH OF DECEDENT (Month) (Day) (Year)

6. AGE 82 yrs. mos. days. If LESS than 1 day, hrs. or min.

7. Occupation: A Trade, profession, or particular kind of work done, as spinner, sawyer, bookkeeper, etc. Housewife. B Industry or business in which work was done, as silk mill, sawmill, bank, own business, etc.

8. BIRTHPLACE OF DECEDENT: (a) State or Country Poland (b) County (c) City, Town or Village

9. OF WHAT COUNTRY WAS DECEDENT A CITIZEN AT TIME OF DEATH? Poland

10. WAS DECEASED WAR VETERAN? IF SO, NAME WAR No

PARENTS OF DECEASED

11. NAME OF FATHER OF DECEDENT Zelik Drevener

12. BIRTHPLACE OF FATHER (State or Country) Poland

13. MAIDEN NAME OF MOTHER OF DECEDENT Rose (Unknown)

14. BIRTHPLACE OF MOTHER (State or Country) Poland

MEDICAL CERTIFICATE OF DEATH (To be filled in by Medical Examiner. See over.)

16. PLACE OF DEATH: (a) NEW YORK CITY: (b) Borough Brooklyn (c) Name of Hospital or Institution Bklyn. State Hosp. (If not in hospital or institution, give street and number) (d) If elsewhere than in hospital or own residence, specify character of place of death, as hotel, office, store, street, taxicab, etc.

17. DATE AND HOUR OF DEATH (Month) June (Day) 29th, (Year) 1944 (Hour) P. M.

18. SEX Female 19. COLOR OR RACE White 20. Approximate Age 80

21. I hereby certify (a) that in accordance with Sections 878-2.0 and 878-3.0 of the Administrative Code for the City of New York, I went to, and took charge of the dead body at Kings County Morgue this 30th day of June 19 44

(b) that I examined the body and investigated the circumstances of this death, and *(Cross out terms that do not apply.)

I further certify from the investigation, (complete autopsy)* (partial autopsy)* (incision)* and examination (c) that, in my opinion, death occurred on the date and at the hour stated above and resulted from (natural causes)* (accident)* (suicide)* (homicide)* (undetermined circumstances pending further investigation)*, and (d) that the causes of death were:

Arteriosclerotic Heart Disease: Fractured Right Femur:- From accidental fall on ward while a patient in the hospital:

M. E. Case No. 3142

Signed [signature] Assistant Medical Examiner

Approved [signature] Chief Medical Examiner

Date 6/30/44

15. SIGNATURE OF INFORMANT Abraham Antel RELATIONSHIP TO DECEASED Son ADDRESS 1019 Ward Av Bronx

22. PLACE OF BURIAL OR CREMATION United Hebrew Cem DATE OF BURIAL OR CREMATION June 30, 1944

23. FUNERAL DIRECTOR Schwartz Bros ADDRESS 33-2 Av PERMIT NUMBER 3382

BUREAU OF VITAL RECORDS AND STATISTICS—DEPARTMENT OF HEALTH—CITY OF NEW YORK

This is to certify that the foregoing is a true copy of a record on file in the Department of Health. The Department of Health does not certify to the truth of the statements made thereon, as no inquiry as to the facts has been provided by law.

IRENE A SCANLON
CITY REGISTRAR

Do Not accept this transcript unless it bears the raised seal of the Department of Health. The reproduction or alteration of this transcript is prohibited by Section 3.21 of the New York City Health Code.

BUREAU OF VITAL RECORDS — DEPARTMENT OF HEALTH — THE CITY OF NEW YORK

DEPARTMENT OF HEALTH · THE CITY OF NEW YORK

DATE ISSUED MAY 16 1990

DOCUMENT NO. B 898751

VR134-50M-9PC2255

Esther Entel's death certificate could not explain that her condition would have been called Alzheimer's Disease today.

lassemia carrier, and how he was able to move the genesis of the trait back one more generation in Poland.

Mortality schedules. These lists will probably only be helpful if your family came to America before the massive wave of immigration. The Federal Government kept these lists between 1850 and 1885 and included information on cause of death for twelve month periods before the census (1 June through 31 May 1849, 1859, 1869, 1879, 1884), organized by state. Not all deaths are represented, but the schedules should be consulted, especially if you have no other vital records. You can find them in state archives and at the National Archives. They are also available on loan or by purchase through Heritage Quest.

Insurance records. As you interview relatives and rummage through family papers, carefully consider any information you may find about insurance policies and the insurance company. The company may have detailed medical information, though it may be difficult to obtain.

Service and pension records. Why was a family member rated "4F" in World War II? Did a veteran receive any special compensation as a result of injury? Checking service and pension records can be illuminating.

SIDEBAR: SOME FAMILY HEALTH QUESTIONS

Are there any unusual traits in our family?

Were there any miscarriages or stillbirths?

Was anyone extremely obese or thin?

Who suffered from major diseases?

Did anyone have any reconstructive surgery?

Who was hospitalized, for what, and for how long?

Did any cousins marry cousins in our family?

Did anyone abuse alcohol or drugs?

Did anyone suffer from recurring maladies, such as allergies (and to what), headaches, and others?

Organizing and Documenting Medical Information

Once you've collected your family's medical facts, you may wonder about the best way to organize and document them. Even if you've already put together your family's genealogical pedigree, you'll want to be able to present a "medical pedigree" to your health professional.

A medical pedigree uses standardized symbols to indicate gender and relationships (e.g., biological and non-biological). Names are not necessary, and you generally don't have to include more than three or four generations. It is important, however, to show brothers and sisters, who typically don't show up on a standard genealogical pedigree. Charting your family's medical conditions can also help you and your doctor visualize the patterns that can sometimes get lost in lists of names, dates, and places.

One pedigree format is the genogram, a popular clinical tool for assessing connections between family members and illness. Says Dr. Monica McGoldrick, co-author of *Genograms: Assessment and Intervention, Second Edition,* "When there is a genogram in the medical record, the clinician can glance at it and get an immediate picture of the family and medical situation without wading through a stack of notes. Indication on the genogram of previous illnesses or symptom patterns may lead to early detection of a problem and preventive treatment of family members at risk."

Several genealogical software programs contain fields where you can input medical information. Family Tree Maker®, for instance, allows you to document any individual's medical information. Lifelinks is another genealogical program that features a Family Medical History section and can print out a Family History Report that protects individual privacy. Another program, Cyrillic 3, specializes in charting for medical purposes—it even calculates breast cancer risks.

MEDICAL PEDIGREE SOFTWARE

Genogram Programs

Relativity (TM) from WonderWare, Inc., 2706 Randolph Road, Silver Spring, MD 20902. E-mail: wonderware@idealink.washington.dc.us. Phone: (301) 942-3254. PC software that generates genograms from text input. GEDCOM supported.

Humanware from The Computerized Genogram Company, 780 Baconsfield Drive, Building 3, Suite 34, Macon, GA 31211.

E-mail: genogram@mindspring.com.

Macintosh—MacGenogram

IBM—Genogram-Maker®

Graphics utilities that create genograms

AutoGenogram®—intended for computer novices, asks users a series of questions about their families. It then compiles and creates a genogram that can be read and modified by other Humanware genogram programs.

Family Pattern Analyzer®—by completing a computerized interview of more than 600 questions, the user can pinpoint the major issues and patterns of the family. The program generates a Family Pattern Report that describes family pattern hypotheses.

Other Programs and Web Resources

Family Tree Maker
<www.familytreemaker.com>

Lifelinks
<www.lifelinks.mb.ca>

Cyrillic 3
<www.cyrillicsoftware.com/products/cyril3.htm>

GenerationalHealth.com
<www.generationalhealth.com>
Just fill in the blanks to create an online family medical history tree.

SAMPLE MEDICAL PEDIGREE

Medical practitioners and counselors often ask for a medical pedigree or family tree to capture medical information. They will use a visual layout of information about you, your parents, siblings, aunts and uncles, grandparents, and others. Seeing a pattern helps early detection and can suggest preventive treatments.

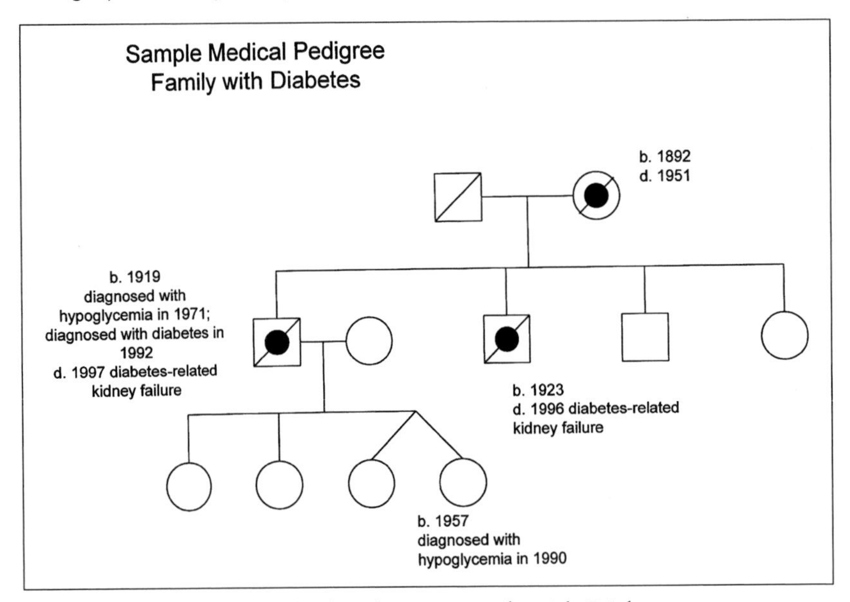

Sample Medical Pedigree—Family with Diabetes.

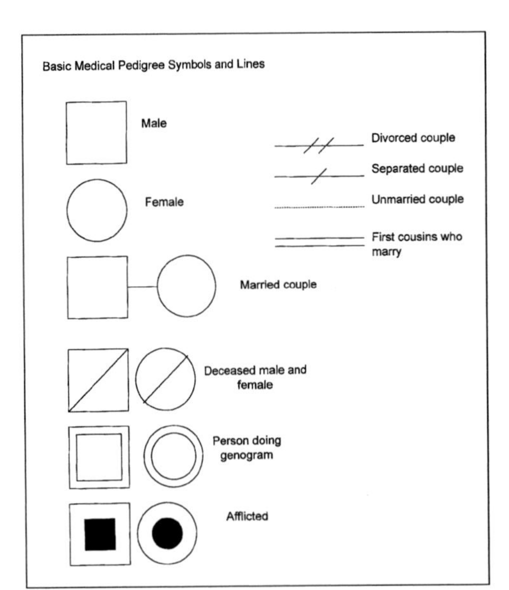

Basic Medical Pedigree Symbols and Lines.

18 Case Study: Stanley Diamond and Beta-Thalassemia

"Genealogy with a Special Reason," reads retired Montreal businessman Stanley Diamond's calling card. He is a carrier of a newly identified mutation of the Beta-Thalassemia trait—a discovery that drives him to identify his trait-carrying ancestors. He is also concerned that carriers like him are unaware that they can pass the characteristic on to their children in a deadly form.

Diamond learned he was a carrier of the trait when he submitted to a blood test to help diagnose a nephew's illness. With the help of Montreal Children's Hospital Research Institute's Dr. Charles Scriver, he learned he carried an uncommon mutation of the gene. Independently, Dr. Ariella Oppenheim at Jerusalem's Hebrew University - Hadassah Hospital made a similar discovery with a woman from Bobruisk, Rita Pharan, who had recently emigrated. Diamond's and Pharan's families had originated about 300 miles from each other in the Pale of Settlement, the name given to an eastern European geographic area in which Jews were allowed to settle.

SEE ALSO
See Chapter 2 for more information on the Pale of Settlement.

Even though he is a carrier, Diamond is in no immediate danger. However, left unchecked, or misdiagnosed with mild chronic anemia, other Beta-Thalassemia carriers may pass the trait on to their descendants, unaware that there is a 25% chance that children of two carriers will inherit a deadly form of Thalassemia and not live past early adulthood. While Beta-Thalassemia, which affects two million Americans, is well known to people of Mediterranean, Middle and Far Eastern descent, and

Stanley Diamond holding up the 1865 Ostrów Mazowiecka, Poland birth register that contains the birth record of his great-grandmother, Pułtusk Branch of the Polish State Archives.
Courtesy of Stanley Diamond.

Diamond and fellow Ostrów Mazowiecka Research Family member, Michael Richman, explore original records during one of their research trips to Poland.
Courtesy of Stanley Diamond.

With the help of Dr. Charles Scriver (left), Diamond (right) learned he carried the Beta-Thalassemia Trait.
Courtesy of Stanley Diamond.

to a lesser extent Sephardic Jews, it had never before affected Ashkenazic Jews.

The Search

"Genes and genealogy are two sides of the same personal history coin," says Dr. Scriver. This was certainly proven as an unexpected familial relationship between Diamond and Pharan surfaced. Through his careful genealogical research, Diamond identified their common ancestors living in 1825. It may be impossible to exactly identify their common progenitor due to unavailability and incompleteness of Jewish records, made worse by the fact that Jews in these areas were not required to have surnames until the early nineteenth century.

SEE ALSO
Refer to Chapter 3 for more on surname adoption among eastern European Jews.

Diamond traced his roots to Ostrów Mazowiecka, Poland, called "Ostrova" by its Jewish inhabitants. He formed a town-based research group to pool efforts and share the costs of onsite research in archives in Poland. Using these records, he successfully traced his family to his great-grandfather, Jankiel Widelec, and his wife, Sara Nowes. Jankiel was the son of Hersz Widelec. But, Diamond was unable to find carriers among the descendants of Jankiel's or Sara's siblings. It appeared that he had hit a wall, though he knew he had not yet found descendants of all the siblings.

A breakthrough came in February 1998 when he located descendants of Hersz's daughters, Fejga and Chaia, whose children married each other. The key to the breakthrough was a map.

Early in 1998, a California member of the Ostrów Mazowiecka Research Family gave Diamond a partial map of Waldheim's "Ostrover Verein" plot—the map she was handed by the Forest Park, Illinois, cemetery's office to find the interment locations of her Dunn family relatives among members of this town-based society. Diamond, also interested in the Dunn family, examined the map and spotted the names of David and Fannie Lustig. He quickly surmised that these names were the American equivalents assumed by Dawid Lustig and his wife, Frajda Bengelsdorf. David and Fannie were the children of sisters Fejga and Chaja Widelec and the nephew and niece of Diamond's great-grandfather, Jankiel Widelec. Knowing that both may have inherited the Beta-Thalassemia trait, a potential catastrophe for

The graves of David and Fannie Lustig at Chicago's Waldheim Cemetery provided the key to Diamond's genealogical breakthrough. Courtesy of Judie Ostroff-Goldstein.

their children, Diamond had been searching for their descendants for three years. Finding their gravestones was an enormous breakthrough.

Diamond verified the couple's identity with Waldheim's Family Services and Preplanning manager and shared details of his research. Understanding the importance of the request, the manager noted the fathers' given names on the stones and gave the names to him. Diamond learned that Alex Lustig—David and Fannie's 80-year-old grandson in Wilmette, Illinois—was listed as the person responsible for the two graves' perpetual care.

The Family Condition

Says Diamond, "Fortunately, I was able to quickly locate the telephone number for the only Alex Lustig in the Chicago area. I immediately called and followed up with documentation about the family history and my genetic research." Lustig says very modestly, unaware of the contribution he has made to genetic research, "I gave Stan as much information as I knew." Lustig, it turns out, was diagnosed as a Beta-Thalassemia carrier by his personal doctor, a hematologist, some fifteen years earlier.

Lustig, upon finding out that Diamond was going to be in Phoenix the following week, urged his newfound cousin to call his son, Steven, a resident of the area. Diamond called him on his first day in town and was glad he did. Steven told Diamond that for years he carried a card that said: "Beta-Thalassemia, elevated A2 Hemoglobin; do not take iron." Diamond says at that point, "I started to shake."

A few days later, Diamond contacted Steven's second cousin, Jim, a physician in Toledo, Ohio. Jim told him that Alex's first cousins, Lou and George, had been carriers of the trait and that Lou's son and grandson are also carriers. "That means that it is virtually certain," says Diamond, "that the trait had to have been passed on to Alex, Lou, and George through their fathers, Hyman and Abraham—the sons of a marriage between first cousins. And these first cousins were the son of Feiga and the daughter of Chaia."

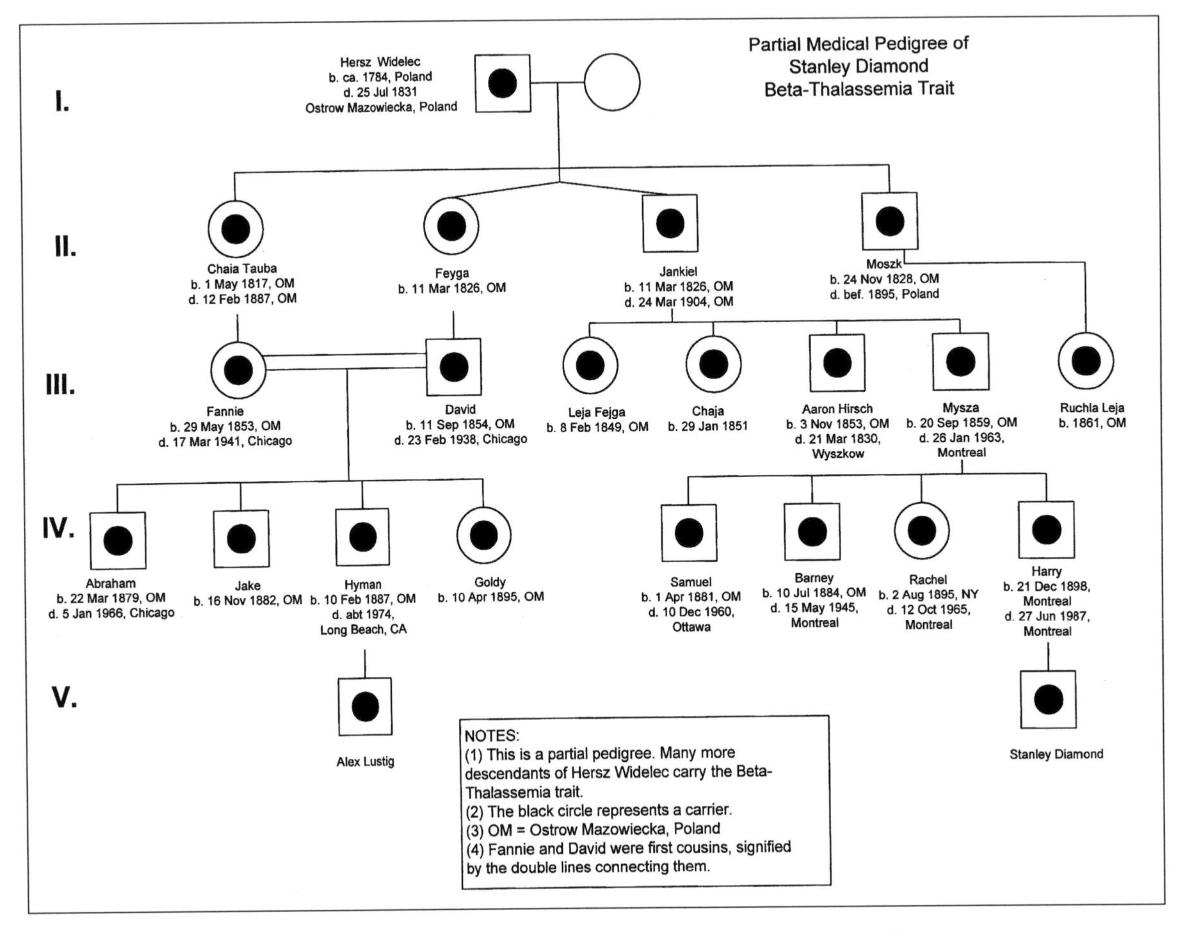

Partial medical pedigree of Stanley Diamond and his family's Beta-Thalassemia trait.

Luckily, Jim has been tracking and warning that part of the family. He is actively involved in locating and warning other distant branches of the Lustig family.

Impact on Genetic Research

Upon finding these Lustig cousins, Diamond dashed off an excited e-mail message in December 1998 to Dr. Scriver and Dr. Oppenheim, both of whom have been following the trait among eastern European Jews. "I am quite certain I have made the long awaited breakthrough to take the source of the Beta-Thalassemia trait in my family back one generation. As you know, until now I have been stuck in 1826, the birth year for my great-grandfather, Jankiel Widelec, and his wife, Sara Nowes . . . Last week I finally found living descendants of Jankiel's sisters, Fejga and Chaia. These were the last two families for which I had not been able to make a connection . . . This breakthrough will make it possible to refocus my efforts on certain branches that have not been exhaustively researched and, at the same time, drop a long list of surnames which are no longer relevant."

The discovery that David and Fanny's descendants were carriers of the Beta-Thalassemia trait convinced Diamond and these two geneticists that Hersz Widelec, born in 1785, must be the source of the family's novel mutation. (Earlier, Diamond eliminated Hersz's wife Gutka as the source, since no carriers were found among the known descendants of Gutka's four sisters.) Diamond now provided the scientists with the greatest number of generations ever reconstructed in the study of the Beta-Thalassemia trait in a clean gene pool.

This groundbreaking work helps geneticists all over the world understand the trait and its effects on one family. Says Dr. Oppenheim, "A most important contribution of Stanley Diamond's work is increasing the awareness among his relatives and others to the possibility that they carry a genetic trait which, with proper measures, can be prevented in future generations. In addition, the work has demonstrated the power of modern genetics in identifying distant relatives and helps to clarify how genetic diseases are being spread throughout the world."

Several renowned medical institutions—including Yeshiva University's Cancer Research Center at the Albert Einstein College of Medicine, Yale University's Cancer Genetics Program, the Epidemiology-Genetics Program at the Johns Hopkins School of Medicine, and Mount Sinai Hospital's School of Medicine—have recognized Diamond's pioneering work.

Identifying Families at Risk

Says Diamond, "Genealogists have the obligation to reach out and caution family members. In my case, finding family members that were either unaware they carried the Beta-Thalassemia trait or had only learned the news late in life—usually when undergoing exhaustive tests for pre-surgery or other medical problems—has been the norm rather than the exception. Recognizing the potential existence of hundreds of unsuspecting carriers in distant branches and that this trait is virtually unknown in Ashkenazim is what drives my genealogical/genetic research purpose."

Diamond has now documented more than 50 additional branches of his own family who may be at risk. His strong outreach efforts have turned up other families carrying the trait. Some have already launched programs to alert their extended families to the potential danger to future generations. He says, "Directing family members to medical professionals who are trained to communicate the appropriate information is the responsibility of every genealogist charting his or her family's medical history."

Without Diamond's comprehensive family history, based on archival records, the familial relationship between him and the Bobruisk family could not have been identified.

Inspiration to Others

Diamond has set the *de facto* standard for genealogy applied to genetic research. Many seek his guidance when they want to research their family's medical history. His passionate lectures about his search for the roots of his family's Beta-Thalassemia trait are deeply moving.

Networking among genealogists has proven to be supportive, insightful, and satisfying. Reba Solomon of Plainview, New

York, for instance, was the first to contact Diamond and follow his lead. In her letter to family members, she wrote, "We have just learned that a rare blood trait is carried genetically within our family, inherited either through Ephraim Presant or Faiga Gensil. Many of their children, grandchildren, and great-grandchildren carry the trait of Beta-Thalassemia. This blood mutation is so rare, we are only the thirteenth European-Jewish family in the world to be identified with the trait." She goes on to urge them to check previous blood tests to determine likely carrier status.

Now that he has been able to trace the trait to a single ancestor, Diamond sums up his search, "Every member of the family now knows if they do or do not carry the trait and the importance of alerting their offspring. Simply stated, they now know, their doctors know, and the information is likely to be passed on."

QUICK HIT

For more information about Diamond's research, access his web site at <www.geocities.com/Heartland/Pointe/1439>.

PART VI

Tying It All Together

19 Archives and Repositories Preserve Your History For Future Generations

It was late Thursday night, 12 November 1998, when Gesher Galicia Coordinator Shelley Pollero called to tell me her dear friend and Gesher Galicia treasurer, Sheiala Moskow, had died. I didn't know Sheiala very well—I had just met her a few months before at the annual Summer Seminar on Jewish Genealogy in Los Angeles. During that week, I sensed she had a wonderful *joie de vivre*. The state of her health declined very rapidly. Suddenly, she was gone.

In thinking about her and her dedication to Jewish genealogy, I wondered: what will happen to all her research on her Gelernter and Ratner families? More broadly, what will happen to all of our work when we're gone?

Here are seven steps you can proactively take today:

1. **Plan Ahead**—Line up family members now who will care for your files, documents, photographs, and other genealogical information. Make sure you have up-to-date printouts of your family information that can be accessed without going onto your computer. Let family members know where your primary and backup data files are. If you have a PC password, let them know that, too.
2. **Document**—Think about the facts that only you may know, such as burial plot locations, especially if

the cemetery is not well kept or does not have a good recordkeeping system. For example, my Krasner great-grandparents are buried in the Ain Yankiff section of the vandalized, desecrated Grove Street Hebrew Cemeteries in Newark, New Jersey. I am the only living descendant who knows to enter the gate from Grove Street after you pass the mausoleum for Rabbi Cohen and go up ten rows, turn right. I am the only member of my immediate family, now that my father is gone, who knows where his parents are buried in a small Hillside, New Jersey cemetery that is invisible to drivers on the main road. Fortunately, when my father and I visited the cemetery in the fall of 1997 just two weeks before his death, I wrote down the directions and made careful note of how and where to enter the cemetery.

3. **Compile**—Compile research results into books or reports. Many software programs today, including Family Tree Maker, make it very easy to incorporate photos into charts for a more meaningful report without the overwhelming task of having to write a complete family history.

4. **Share**—Share your research results freely with members of your family, even your local Jewish Genealogical Society, regional Special Interest Groups, and members of your Shtetl Co-op, if appropriate. Create your own family history web site so others can find you.

5. **Donate**—Arrange for your files to be donated to one of the Jewish Genealogical Societies and/or a regional Special Interest Group. Or better yet, donate copies of your files yourself—now. In addition, consider submitting your materials to one or more of the central repositories listed in the sidebar.

6. **Contribute to a Database**—Contribute your family trees to centralized databases such as the "Family

The Family of

Milton Krasner
and
Lillian (Pryzant) Perlman

A Photo Retrospective
Commemorating Their 50th Wedding Anniversary
March 24, 1996

by Barbara Krasner-Khait

Preserve your history by compiling, documenting, and sharing your research.

A Quiet Strength:
A Photo Retrospective of
Milton Krasner
(1919-1997)

Written by
Barbara Krasner-Khait
August 1998

SEE ALSO
Refer back to Chapter 13 to learn how to access the Family Tree of the Jewish People database.

Tree of the Jewish People," which has a goal of preserving family history for future generations.

7. **Preserve and Label**—Preserve and label photos with as much detail as you can. Take photos of mementos and memorabilia and share them widely.

I have now resolved to pass everything I have on to my son who shows some interest in genealogy. He has accompanied me to many a reunion and many a cemetery. I have also resolved to will copies of my files and documents to an array of interested cousins and the Jewish Genealogical Society of North Jersey. I will pass my compendium of more than 1,000 Galician Zuckerkandels to my network of Zuckerkandel researchers.

After Sheiala's memorial service, Shelley Pollero went back to the Moskow family residence for a while. A couple of Sheiala's cousins began to ask questions about their shared heritage. Shelley sat at Sheiala's computer, accessed the genealogy files, and not only verified data with the cousins but was able to input new data. These cousins eventually received electronic versions of the data, and they vowed to get some genealogical software.

Take the time now to carefully consider your options and take the necessary steps to preserve your family's history.

WHERE TO DONATE YOUR MATERIALS

United States

Center for Jewish History
15 West 16th Street
New York, NY 10011
(212) 294-8301
<www.cjh.org>

New York's Center for Jewish History is the largest repository outside of Israel documenting the Jewish experience. The Center's five partners, well known for their contributions to the study of Jews—American Jewish Historical Society, American Sephardi Federation, Leo Baeck Institute, Yeshiva University Museum, and YIVO Institute for Jewish Research—have combined holdings of about 100 million archival documents, a half million books, and thousands of photographs and other visual materials. The Center also has a Genealogy Institute, which is now home to New York's Jewish Genealogical Society.

Rachel Fisher, director of the Genealogy Institute, recommends that you donate self-published family histories to one of the Center partners. If you'd like to donate reference materials, though, like guides to record types and repositories, etc., contact her at (212) 294-8324 or gi@cjh.org.

American Jewish Historical Society
15 West 16th Street
New York, NY 10011
Lyn Slome, Interim Director of Library and Archives
lslome@ajhs.org
(212) 294-6167

Donations can be made to the society at two levels: collection and book. For collections, donations must be approved by the Library and Archives Committee, following the acquisitions policy of the society to determine the areas in which they seek information. Materials include personal papers, written manuscripts, and correspondence. If you have such a collection, you will need to prepare a description of the contents. If the collection is large, an archivist may need to come to your home to accession it and prepare it to be transported. Once received, it can take quite a while to process the materials, possibly up to two years. The archivist processes the collection, determines what is useful to researchers, and puts the materials in "intellectual order," develops a finding aid, and includes the materials at the collection level in the card catalog.

According to Lyn Slome, the society will accept scanned images on CD and computer diskettes.

At the book level, the society will, in most cases, readily accept family genealogies and histories. This does not need to go through a committee decision-making process. Just send the book, even if unpublished, to the society—they will send an acknowledgment letter and include the book in their card catalog. Please note that the card catalog can only be searched at the society.

Leo Baeck Institute
Frank Mecklenburg, Director of Research and Chief Archivist
(212) 744-6400
fmecklenberg@lbi.cjh.org

If your family members were German-speaking Jews, consider donations to the Leo Baeck Institute's Archives as well as to the Family Research Department. The Archives houses family papers, community histories, and business and public records donated by individuals, families, and organizations. The Family Research Division has thousands of family trees. You can submit family trees, histories, and research documents. The materials will be analyzed, organized, and catalogued.

New York City's Center for Jewish History houses the American Jewish Historical Society, American Sephardi Federation, Leo Baeck Institute, Yeshiva University Museum, and YIVO Institute for Jewish Research.

Electronic files are not accepted. All cataloguing is online, and the potential for cross-referencing is optional.

YIVO Institute for Jewish Research
Marek Web, Chief Archivist
(212) 246-6080
mweb@yivo.cjh.org

YIVO accepts materials whenever they fit fields of interest, and Jewish genealogy is certainly one of those fields. Materials would be archived in YIVO's special collection of Genealogy and Family History. Today, this collection consists of family research and a modest number of documents. A specially designated archivist, Leo Greenbaum, works with donors. Marek Web's advice is to "select the most essential documents for donation—those of real essence to the subject matter. People who create the documents are in the best position to determine this." To donate your materials, you will need to keep them well organized and submit a description or summary. Your materials will be catalogued under your name or your family name, whichever is appropriate.

American Jewish Archives
Hebrew Union College
3101 Clifton Ave.
Cincinnati, OH 45220
Kathy Spray, Genealogical Reference Archivist
(513) 221-1875

The Archives prefers to have condensed family histories on any American Jewish family for its collection. Donors are urged not to send letters, notes, papers, or other extraneous information. It accepts only paper (not electronic versions) right now.

Send your history to the Archives with a cover letter stating you'd like to enter it into the Archives' "small collection." The Archives has an electronic card catalog that researchers can query on several fields, including surname, donor name, and major place. Note that it may take up to six months to catalog the information. Eventually, the Archives plans to have the catalog searchable on the Internet.

Archivist Dorothy Smith advises, "Be concise. Give a lot of good information that you think will help other people."

Library of Congress
Local History and Genealogy
Collection Development
101 Independence Avenue, SE
Washington, DC 20540-4660
(202) 707-5537
<http://lcweb.loc.gov/rr/genealogy/>

Anglo-American Acquisitions Division-USA Gifts
101 Independence Avenue, SE
Washington, DC 20540-4174
(202) 707-9503

If you published a family history or local history, seriously consider sending a copy of the work to the Library of Congress. The Library of Congress Local History and Genealogy Collection Department has an extensive collection of U.S. and foreign genealogical and historical publications. The collection began in 1815 when it purchased the Thomas Jefferson library, and it now boasts more than 40,000 compiled family histories and 100,000 U.S. local histories. Donated publications may be brought to the Library's Local History and Genealogy Reading Room or to the Anglo-American Acquisitions Division, or you may choose to simply mail your work to them.

Since 1988, Marcia Meyers of Connecticut has been sending her biannual family newsletter to the Library of Congress. She says, "The reason I send all my newsletters—they contain the research I've done on my father's family—I felt I wanted to share my research so I wouldn't be the only one to have all the data."

The New York Public Library
<www.nypl.org>

U.S. History, Local History & Genealogy Division
Room 315S
The New York Public Library
Fifth Avenue & 42nd Street
New York, NY 10018-0828
(212) 930-0828

The library's U.S. History, Local History and Genealogy Division collects materials documenting American history on the national, state, and local level as well as genealogies and other materials relating to heraldry. Other researchers can learn of your work through an online catalog at its web site. The division accepts published and unpublished genealogies.

Western Jewish History Center
Judah L. Magnes Museum
2911 Russell Street
Berkeley, CA 94705
Laura O'Hara, Archivist
(510) 549-6932
<www.magnesmuseum.org>

The Western Jewish History Center is interested in materials that pertains to the 13 Western states (Alaska, Arizona, California, Colorado, Hawaii, Idaho, Montana, Nevada, New Mexico, Oregon, Utah, Washington, and Wyoming) and is considered both Jewish and historical. It accepts family trees and personal and organizational papers. It does accept electronic disks. "Think about your goals," says Laura O'Hara, the Center's archivist. "Think about whether you want to have your material accessible to everyone or to keep it in the family." The Center advises potential donors to think about multiple repositories for their materials such as regional, multi-regional, and national; archivists can help you determine which ones would be best suited for your materials. A card catalog will guide researchers to your materials.

Israel

Douglas E. Goldman Genealogy Center
Beth Hatefusoth
P.O. Box 39359
Tel Aviv 61392, Israel
Diana Sommer, Director
<www.bh.org.il/Geneology/index.htm>

The Goldman Center collects primarily digitized material, family trees, and research material such as cemetery lists, civil records, census records, and Jewish community records.

While the Goldman Center has a reference library, it is not an archive, and therefore needs to make decisions about paper-based donations on a case-by-case basis. The center is also concerned about its limited physical space and staff as well as continued public accessibility. You will need to bear this in mind if you want to donate family books, genealogy reference books, or community records.

Canada

The policy of the National Archives of Canada is to not accept personal genealogical records collections from individuals. But Lawrence Tapper, library archivist and former JGS-Ottawa President, advises individuals to donate a copy of your family histories to local Jewish community libraries such as the Jewish Public Library in Montreal. There are also Jewish libraries in Winnipeg, Toronto, Ottawa, and Vancouver. You should also deposit two copies with the National Library of Canada in Ottawa.

It was only after I began researching my family's history that I saw a picture of the woman I was named for, my great-grandmother Breina.

Breina's husband, Mordechai Krasner.

20 Case Study: The Dvorkin Family

The somewhat common name of Dvorkin was the maiden name of my great-grandmother, Breina, after whom I was named. She was born about 1842 somewhere in Belarus and died in 1937 in Newark, New Jersey.

When I first began to research my family in late 1989, I knew nothing about her or her Dvorkin family. The narrative that follows explains the steps I took to find out who they were and how they fit into my family tree.

Interviewing Relatives

I started asking one of my father's cousins, Adele, questions about Breina. Adele, who had lived with her, was extremely knowledgeable. She told me the Krasner family lived in Newark, New Jersey. The first to come over from Minsk was Hillel Meyer, the first son of Mordechai and Breina. She then proceeded to tell me about the other Krasner children: Chaike or Ida, my grandfather, Mendel, and Adele's mother, Hesia or Bessie. Two children had not come to America: Doba and Malka, though their children did. She made special mention of Malka's daughter, Minnie Goldberg, who came at the age of 10 and stayed with Mordechai and Breina before moving to Baltimore.

Adele also told me about Breina's brother, Chaim Ber, and his wife, Leah, who also lived in Newark and had preceded the Krasner family's migration. She spoke of related families who

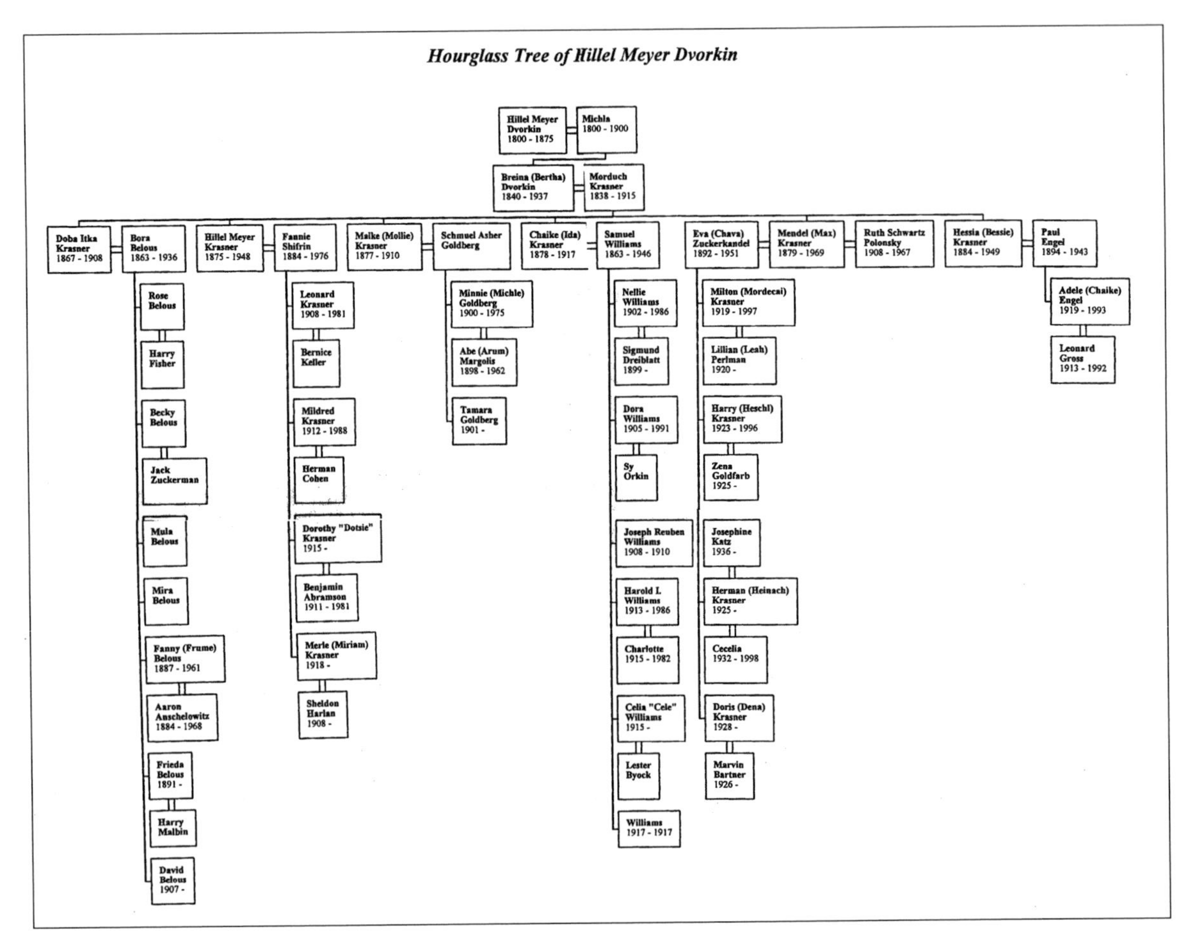

Breina Dvorkin Krasner's Family Tree.

would often visit and attend family functions: Fine from Dover, New Jersey; Wisch from Brooklyn; Sklut and Shavelson from Delaware; and Kean from Maplewood, New Jersey.

I began to chart out the information and called other cousins, some of whom my family had no contact with for years. Cousin Dotsie, one of Hillel Meyer's daughters, sent me a photo of Breina. I had never seen a picture of her.

I continued to call relatives, many of whom I had never known or even heard of, and asked questions about the family. I found that two of Chaim Ber's children headed west to Butte, Montana, to homestead there. William was the first to go there and became a successful plumber. He then persuaded his sister Fanny to follow.

Census Records

Armed with the Newark address of 65 Boston Street, I headed off to the Newark Public Library's New Jersey Room to check out the state census records and found the family's listings for 1905 and 1915. I also checked out the federal census records for 1900, 1910, and 1920.

According to the 1900 U.S. federal census, there was a Meyer Kastner residing with Simon Devorkin, who could have been Meyer Krasner, cousin of Simon.

Using LDS Family History Center microfilms of the enumeration districts for the 1910 census, which was not indexed for New Jersey, I became acquainted with the geography of Newark and located Boston Street, and then the Krasner family entry. I repeated this for Chaim Ber and his family.

The 1900 U.S. federal census indicated that Leah was the mother of five children, and all are accounted for. However, a 1970s family tree presented at the 50th wedding anniversary of Harry and Mae Dvorken indicates Leah was the mother of twelve children. It was rumored that the other seven died in Russia during pogroms. That same census indicated that Breina was mother to seven, with only six living children.

The 1920 U.S. federal census showed a dispersed family. And another interesting fact: Breina was getting younger and younger as the years went by.

New Jersey
Essex

[...]ER DIVISION OF COUNTY

[...]E OF INSTITUTION

DEPARTMENT OF COMMERCE AND LABOR—BUREAU OF THE CENSUS

THIRTEENTH CENSUS OF THE UNITED STATES: 1910—POPULATION

123

SUPERVISOR'S DISTRICT NO.

ENUMERATION DISTRICT NO. 56

SHEET NO.

NAME OF INCORPORATED PLACE Newark City part of

WARD OF CITY

ENUMERATED BY ME ON THE Twenty second DAY OF April 1910.

ENUMERATOR

NAME	RELATION.	PERSONAL DESCRIPTION.	NATIVITY.	CITIZENSHIP.		OCCUPATION.		EDUCATION.	OWNERSHIP OF HOME.
of each person whose place of abode on April 15, 1910, was in this family.	Relationship of this person to the head of the family.		Place of birth of each person and parents of each person enumerated.		Whether able to speak English; or, if not, give language spoken.	Trade or profession of, or particular kind of work done by this person	General nature of industry, business, or establishment in which this person works		

The 1910 U.S. federal census indicated that Breina was the mother of seven children, six of whom were living.

Extracting census records became one of the "must-do's" of my research methodology. I collected census data on Max and Isadore Kean, trying to somehow pinpoint the connection to my family.

Vital Records

On a trip to the New Jersey State Archives in Trenton, I found birth, marriage, and death records for the Krasner and Dvorkin families, including:

Death records—Mordechai Krasner, Breina Krasner, Chaim Ber Dvorkin (listed as Joachim), and Lizzie Dvorkin. I had also received some death certificates by mail and was able to locate cemetery locations.

Marriage records—Ida Krasner, Meyer Krasner, Max Krasner, Bessie Krasner, Anna Shavelson, and Sam Dvorkin, among others. Anna's marriage record listed her parents as Sam and Bessie "Solomonoff" Shavelson. Morton Sklut had told me his grandmother was Shendl Basha Fine.

Records from New York City's Health Department gave me Nathan Fine's 1937 death certificate. His parents were Joseph Fine and Chana Horowitz. Also from New York I received death certificates of Benjamin Wisch and Isadore Kean.

Raising More Questions

Breina's 1937 death record identified her father as Hillel Meyer Dvorkin and her mother as Michla. Chaim Ber's 1915 death record identified his father as Elias Meyer and his mother as Chaya. I have no way of knowing if Michla and Chaya were the same person or if Michla's mother was Chaya Sora, a common naming combination, which might mean Chaim Ber was Breina's uncle instead of brother. I have often found in my family's records that names do not always match the generation.

Cemetery Research

I have been searching for Chaim Ber's gravesite at the Grove Street cemeteries in Newark for more than a decade, and even

Chaim Ber Dvorkin. *Chaim Ber's wife, Leah.*

STATE OF NEW JERSEY. BUREAU OF VITAL STATISTICS. 47

CERTIFICATE AND RECORD OF MARRIAGE.

Full name of husband.. Samuel Dworkin

Maiden name of wife..... Gladys Clafter

Place of marriage....... Elizabeth N.J. [City, township and county.]

Date of marriage.. March 30th 1909

Groom's	Residence. [If in a city, give name, street and number; if in township, give name and county.]	134 Court st. Newark N.J.		Bride's	Residence.	315 Bond st. City
	Age.	36 years	Number of marriage. 1st		Age.	24 years, Number of marriage. 1st
	Color.	White			Color.	White
	Occupation.	Clothier			Name if a widow.	
	Birthplace.	Russia			Birthplace.	Austria
	Father's name.	Hyman			Father's name.	Herkel Clafter
	Mother's maiden name.	Leah Sadelson			Mother's maiden name.	Frume C. Steinlov

Witnesses: Samuel L. Biow; Lena Sturm

Signature of person officiating and P. O. address: S. Schoenkopf, Rabbi Cong. B'nai Isr. 321 South st.

No incomplete or mutilated certificate will be received.

A trip to the New Jersey state archives in Trenton provided me with many vital records, like this marriage record for Chaim Ber's son, Samuel.

1 PLACE OF DEATH
STATE DEPARTMENT OF HEALTH—BUREAU OF VITAL STATISTICS
County Essex State NEW JERSEY Registered No. 8025
Township or Borough
City Newark No. 204 Fairmount Ave St. Ward
(If death occurred in a hospital or institution give its NAME instead of street and number.)
2 FULL NAME (Surname last) (First name here) Breina Krasner
If a veteran what war?
3 Residence. No. 204 Fairmount Ave St. Ward
(Usual place of abode; in institutions, homes, etc., former residence should be stated.) (If non-resident give city, town and State.)
Length of residence in city or town where death occurred 35 yrs. mos. days. How long in U. S., if of foreign birth? 35 yrs. mos. days.

PERSONAL AND STATISTICAL PARTICULARS
4 SEX Female
5 COLOR OR RACE White
6 Single, Married, Widowed or Divorced (write the word) Widow
7 If married, widowed or divorced HUSBAND OF (or) WIFE OF (Give full maiden name) Mordecai
8 DATE OF BIRTH (Month, day and year) Unknown 1848
9 AGE Years 89 Months Days If Less Than One Day Hrs. Min.
OCCUPATION
Trade, profession, or particular kind of work done, as spinner, sawyer, bookkeeper, etc. none
Industry or business in which work was done, as silk mill, saw mill, bank, etc.
Date deceased last worked at this occupation (month and year)
Total time (years) spent in this occupation
11 BIRTHPLACE (City or town) (State or country) Russia
FATHER
12 NAME Hillel —
13 BIRTHPLACE (City or town) (State or country) Russia
MOTHER
14 MAIDEN NAME Michla —
14a BIRTHPLACE (City or town) (State or country) Russia
15 SIGNATURE OF INFORMANT Meyer Krasner
(Address) 53 Cleveland St. [illegible]
20 PLACE OF BURIAL Cremation or Removal [illegible]
DATE 5-24-1937
21 FUNERAL DIRECTOR Philip Apter [illegible] N. J. License No. 759
(Address) Newark
16 RECEIVED 5-24-37 1937 [illegible] Local Registrar.

Plain terms, so that it may be properly classified. Exact statement of occupation is very important.

MEDICAL CERTIFICATE OF DEATH
17 DATE OF DEATH May 23 1937
18 I HEREBY CERTIFY, That I attended deceased from May 15 1937 to May 23 1937
I last saw her alive on May 23 1937, death is said to have occurred on the date stated above, at 11 a.m.
The principal cause of death and related causes of importance in order of onset were as follows: Hypostatic pneumonia
Date of onset 5-16-37
Contributory causes of importance not related to principal cause: Senility
Name of operation — Date of
What test confirmed diagnosis? —
Was there an autopsy? —
If death was due to external causes (violence) fill in also the following
Accident, suicide, or homicide? — Date of injury 19
Where did injury occur? — (Specify city or town, county, and State)
Specify whether injury occurred in industry, in home, or in public place
Manner of injury —
Nature of injury —
Was disease or injury in any way related to occupation of deceased? —
If so, specify
(Signed) Arthur A. [illegible] M. D.
[illegible] Ave

Breina's 1937 death certificate said her father was Hillel Meyer and her mother was Michla.

1 PLACE OF DEATH
State of New Jersey—Bureau of Vital Statistics.
CERTIFICATE AND RECORD OF DEATH.
County Essex
Township or Village or City Newark
(No. 56 Sterling St. Ward)
(If death occurred in a hospital or institution give its NAME instead of street and number.)
Registered No. 4124
2 FULL NAME OF DECEASED [illegible] Dvorkin

PERSONAL AND STATISTICAL PARTICULARS
3 SEX Male
4 COLOR OR RACE White
5 SINGLE, MARRIED, WIDOWED OR DIVORCED (Write the word) Married
6 DATE OF BIRTH Unknown (Month) (Day) 1851 (Year)
7 AGE 64 yrs. mos. ds. If LESS than 1 day, hrs. or min.?
8 OCCUPATION (a) Trade, Profession, or particular kind of work Retired
(b) General nature of Industry, business, or establishment in which employed (or employer)
9 BIRTHPLACE (State or country) Russia
PARENTS
10 NAME OF FATHER Elias Meyer
11 BIRTHPLACE OF FATHER (State or country) Russia
12 MAIDEN NAME OF MOTHER Chaya
13 BIRTHPLACE OF MOTHER (State or country) Russia
14 THE ABOVE IS TRUE TO THE BEST OF MY KNOWLEDGE
(Informant) Samuel Dvorkin
(Address) 56 Sterling St.
15 Filed 191 REGISTRAR.

MEDICAL CERTIFICATE OF DEATH
16 DATE OF DEATH Dec 24th (Month) (Day) 1915 (Year)
17 I HEREBY CERTIFY, That I attended deceased from Dec 10, 1915, to Dec 29, 1915,
that I last saw him alive on Dec 23, 1915,
and that death occurred, on the date above stated, at 6 a.m.
The CAUSE OF DEATH* was as follows: [illegible]
(duration) yrs. mos. ds.
Contributory (SECONDARY) [illegible]
(Duration) yrs. mos. 4 ds.
(Signed) [illegible] M. D.
[illegible], 1915 (Address) [illegible]
*State the Disease Causing Death, or, in deaths from Violent Causes, state (1) Means of Injury; and (2) whether Accidental, Suicidal, or Homicidal.
18 LENGTH OF RESIDENCE (FOR HOSPITALS, INSTITUTIONS, TRANSIENTS, OR RECENT RESIDENTS)
At place of death yrs. mos. ds. In the State 20 yrs. mos. ds.
Where was disease contracted, if not at place of death?
Former or usual residence 56 Sterling St.
19 PLACE OF BURIAL OR REMOVAL DATE OF BURIAL [illegible] Dec 26th 1915
20 UNDERTAKER Philip Apter & Son ADDRESS Newark NJ

Chaim Ber Dvorkin's 1915 death certificate said his father was Elias Meyer and his mother was Chaya.

working closely with the cemetery office, have not been able to find the site. I thought, perhaps, that his stone might reinforce that his father's name was Hillel Meyer. In the spring of 2001, a telephone conversation with International Cemetery Project coordinator, Alice Gould, identified the site.

City Directories

I followed the Dvorkin family throughout the Newark city directories, keeping track of their business and residence addresses and trade. Simon Devorkin was in the clothing business with his brother, Samuel. It appears they worked with Meyer Krasner at Union Clothing Co. on Market Street in Newark in 1904. The Dvorken Brothers had two stores, one at 30½ Belleville Avenue and one at 13 Ferry Street.

I also checked the entry for Max Kean and found that he was in the dry-cleaning business. Could there be a link between tailoring and dry-cleaning?

Telephone Directories

While on business trips, I looked up phone numbers for the Sklut family in Delaware and the Szerlip and Tabb families in Baltimore, the latter two Adele mentioned as related to us.

Morton Sklut and his wife, Ruthie, met me in downtown Washington, DC, and showed me photos over a lovely dinner. I also corresponded with Martha Szerlip, daughter of Eva Dvorken, daughter of Simon. Martha shared family photos with me, including showing me large portraits of Chaim Ber and Leah. Phyllis Tabb was the daughter of Minnie Goldberg Margolis, daughter of Malka Krasner.

Surnames

A few years ago, I was frustrated because I couldn't identify Max Kean's relationship to my Krasner/Dvorkin line. I had been looking for this connection for six years—without results. Sitting around with fellow genealogists at the 1996 Jewish Genealogy annual conference, I mapped out what I knew. I then jokingly

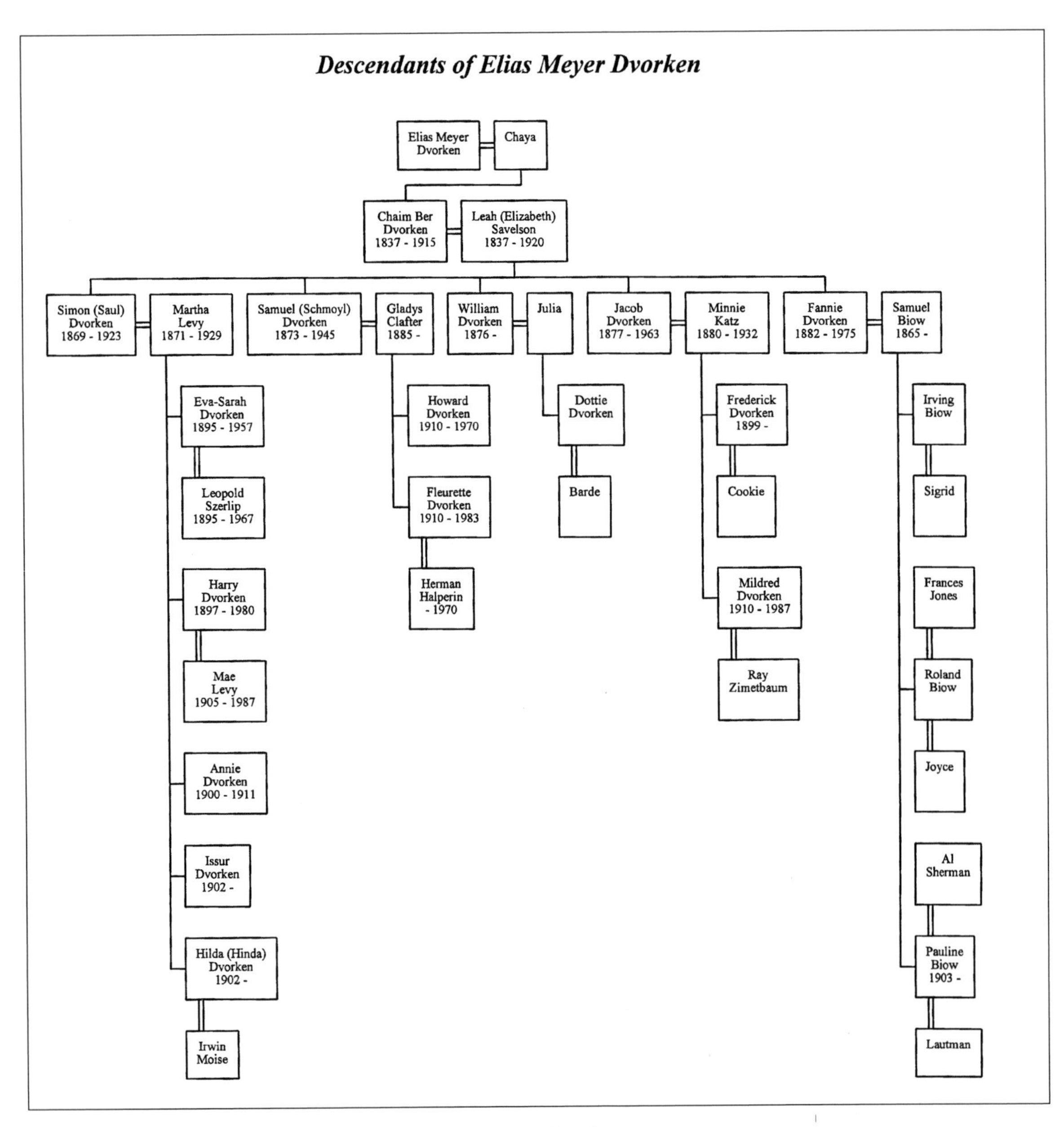

Chaim Ber's family tree.

said that since Kean is pronounced "Keen" and Dvorkin is pronounced in Russian with a "keen" ending, perhaps Kean was originally Dvorkin and the "Dvor" was dropped. After the conference, I asked Max's daughter-in-law (it took me six years to piece together the information to find her) about the original family name. She confirmed the name had been Dvorkin. Apparently, Max Dvorkin left Russia and stopped in England, working there for a while. His boss told him he needed a name the customers could pronounce. Max saw the name Edmund Kean on a Piccadilly Circus marquee (so the story goes) and he adopted the name.

All the clues were there. His name was pencilled in at the bottom of the Dvorkin family tree. Harry Dvorkin's signature appeared on his naturalization papers. But, it took a clear head and creative "what if" scenarios to create working hypotheses and to achieve a breakthrough.

The name Wisch that Adele had told me about was also not an original name. She said it had been something like Wischerevin.

Social Security Applications

I sent for Benjamin Wisch's and Isadore Kean's Social Security applications and found that Benjamin was the son of Meyer and Rifka Feinberg [Wisch] and that Isadore was the son of William [Wolf] and Sara Lefkowitz [Kean].

Passenger Records

My father's cousin, Merle, daughter of Hillel Meyer, told me about her father's journey to Hamburg to avoid conscription in the Russian Army. I found a listing of Hillel Krasner in the Hamburg direct indices. It took me by surprise, because we had known him only as Meyer. Now I knew he was named for his grandfather, Hillel Meyer Dvorkin, so Breina's father must have died about or before 1875 when Breina's son was born.

Breina's son came to America in July 1896 on the ship *Palatia*. He was going to join his Dvorkin cousins. My grandfather's passenger record stated that he was going to his brother's home at

UNITED AMERICA

PETITION FOR NATURALIZATION

To the Honorable the Common Pleas Court of Essex County, New Jersey:

The petition of Max Kean hereby filed, respectfully sh[ows]:

First. My place of residence is 166 Maplewood ave Maplewood, New [Jersey].

Second. My occupation is Tailor

Third. I was born on the 15 day of July anno Domini 1885 at Minsk, Russia

Fourth. I emigrated to the United States from Southampton on or about the 25 day of Aug. anno Domini 1902 and arrived in the United States, at the port of New York on the 10 day of Sept. anno Domini 1902 on the vessel unknown

Fifth. I declared my intention to become a citizen of the United States on the 10 day of 1921 anno Domini 1 at Newark in the Com. Pleas Court of Essex Co. N. J.

Sixth. I am married. My wife's name is Fannie She w[as born] in Russia and now resides with me

I have 2 children, and the name, date and place of birth, and place of residence of each of said children is as follows:
Leo born Feb 16 1913 Newark
William " May 22 1921 Maplewood Both resdg with me

Seventh. I am not a disbeliever in or opposed to organized government or a member of or affiliated with any organization or body of persons teaching disbelief in organized government. I am not a polygamist nor a believer in the practice of polygamy. I am attached to the principles of the Constitution of the United States, a[nd it is my] intention to become a citizen of the United States and to renounce absolutely and forever all allegiance and fidelity to any foreign prince, potentate, state, or sove[reignty, and] particularly to The State of Russia, of whom at this time I am a subject, and it is [my intention] to reside permanently in the United States.

Eighth. I am able to speak the English language.

Ninth. I have resided continuously in the United States of America for the term of five years at least immediately preceding the date of this petition, to wit, since the 10 day of Sept, anno Domini 1902, and in the State of New Jersey, continuously next preceding the date of this petition, since the 15 day of Oct, anno Domini 1912, being a residence within this State of at least one year next preceding the date of this petiti[on].

Tenth. I have not heretofore made petition for citizenship to any court. (I made petition for citizenship to the ... at ... on the ... day of ... anno Domini 1... and the said petition was denied by the said Court for the following reasons and causes, to wit, ... and the cause of such denial has since been cured or [removed].)

Attached hereto and made a part of this petition are my declaration of intention to become a citizen of the United States and the certificate from the Department [of Labor] together with my affidavit and the affidavits of the two verifying witnesses thereto, required by law. Wherefore your petitioner prays that he may be admitted a citi[zen of the] United States of America.

Max Kean
(Complete and true signature of petitioner.)

Declaration of Intention No. 27681 and Certificate of Arrival from Department of Labor filed this 22 day of Sept.
Note to Clerk of Court.—If petitioner arrived in the United States on or before June 29, 1906, strike out the words reading "and Certificate of Arrival from Department of Labor."

AFFIDAVITS OF PETITIONER AND WITNESSES

STATE OF NEW JERSEY, Essex County, } ss:

The aforesaid petitioner being duly sworn, deposes and says that he is the petitioner in the above-entitled proceedings; that he has read the foregoing petition and [knows the] contents thereof; that the said petition is signed with his full, true name; that the same is true of his own knowledge except as to matters therein stated to be al[leged upon] information and belief, and that as to those matters he believes it to be true.

Max Kean
(Complete and true signature of petitioner.)

Harry Dooken occupation Sawyer residing at Roselle, N. J.
and Walter Farber occupation Mfgr residing at Newark, N. J.
each being severally, duly, and respectively sworn, deposes and says that he is a citizen of the United States of America; that he has personally known Max Kean the petitioner above mentioned, to have resided in the United States con[tinuously] immediately preceding the date of filing his petition, since the 1 day of Sept, anno Domini 1922, and in the State in which [the above] entitled petition is made continuously since the 1 day of ... anno Domini 1922, and that he has personal know[ledge that] the said petitioner is a person of good moral character, attached to the principles of the Constitution of the United States, and that the petitioner is in every way qualif[ied, in his] opinion, to be admitted a citizen of the United States.

Walter Farber

Harry Dvorken
(Signature of witness.)

Subscribed and sworn to before me by the above-named petitioner and witnesses in the office of the Clerk of said Court at Newark, N. J., this 22 day of Sept. anno Domini 1927

Deputy Clerk.

[OVER.]

Harry Dvorken was a witness to Max Kean's (a.k.a. Dvorkin) 1927 Petition for Naturalization.

30½ Belleville Avenue in Newark—which is where the Dvorkin cousins were living.

Because the census records showed Chaim Ber arriving in the United States before 1897, I was not able to rely on the New York Passenger Index. I could have looked through actual manifests filmed by the National Archives, but instead turned to the Balch Institute's *Migrations from the Russian Empire*. There I found Chaim as a passenger aboard the *S.S. State of Georgia* from Glasgow. He had taken the indirect route from Hamburg, which arrived in New York harbor in 1886. His wife and several of his children arrived in 1888 on the *S.S. Circassia*, also from Glasgow. Their emigration had originated on the *S.S. Prague* from Hamburg.

I checked Hamburg indices for Dvorkin with any first name beginning with an "M" to find Max Kean. I still haven't found him.

I did findVecherevin/Wiczerewin in the New York Passenger Arrival Indices and found only an index card reference to Meyer and Rifka Wiczerewin (Polish spelling for the Russian Vecherevin), who came to America on the *S.S. Gneisenau* in 1907 from Bremen. Even the National Archives did not have the original page from the ship's manifest. Both Meyer and his wife returned to Europe. I found a record for their son who became Benjamin Wisch. I was not able to find a record for a son Adele called "Jama." From these records, I found reference to a married daughter in New York, Masha Rosenheim, and a daughter in Europe, Hana Schereschewski.

QUICK TIP

After a decade searching, I was finally able to find Max Kean's passenger record and that of his mother and two brothers by using the online Ellis Island records at <www.ellisislandrecords.com>. Moral of the story? Persistence will eventually pay off.

Naturalizations

Through the Essex County courthouse in Newark, New Jersey, I first found mention of the ancestral homestead: the district of Borisov in Minsk Gubernia. Samuel Dvorkin's 1911 Declaration of Intention revealed this. I also found petitions for his brothers Simon and William. My grandfather's declaration also showed Borisov as his birthplace.

European Records

I put an ad in *Avotaynu*'s Family Finder section in the summer of 1991—this was before the Internet was available—and it provided one of the only means to let people know what surnames and towns you were researching. I got a response from a paid researcher in Minsk. Over the next year, he and his daughter helped me find mention of the Krasner and Dvorkin families among documents in the Minsk Archives. He sent me some results from the 1874 Russian Revision Lists. My great-grandparents were enumerated in Minsk Gubernia, Borisov district, town of Logoisk, or Lahoysk in Yiddish. I did find it odd though, that no children were enumerated as well, since Doba had surely been born by then.

The Family History Library eventually filmed these revision lists, including those for Borisov in 1834. While reading the film, I came across "Shevelson" in Cyrillic. I knew we had some sort of connection to that name through oral tradition. I took a closer look and felt very grateful for my six years of Russian study. It turned out that the surname was not Shevelson—it was Gurevich, and the entry said Shevel, son (of head of household.) On the female side of the entry, I saw a daughter, Michla, born in 1814 to Meyer Simonovich Gurevich and his wife, Sora. My head began to swirl. Breina's mother was Michla, born about 1814. Since there was no mandate yet to adopt surnames among Jews in Russia, I wondered if Shevel's family adopted the name Shavelson. I recalled that Nathan Fine's mother was a Horowitz, the transliteration of Gurevich. Fine was connected to Horowitz, who was connected to Shavelson.

Minsk Vital Records

Relying on my ability to read Cyrillic and surname lists published by the Belarus SIG, I attacked the LDS Family History Library films of Minsk vital records. I found the name Vecherevin, the original name of the Wisch family on this list and rented the film through my local Family History Center. These vital records had Russian entries on one side of the ledger and Hebrew on the other. I used the Hebrew to verify the Russian. I found the Vecherevin entries and found the birth of Berko in the 1852 records, born to Sora and Iosel. Sora, according to the Hebrew, was the daughter of Hillel. Could it be then, that Sora was Breina's sister? That would explain what Adele had told me—that Benjamin and Jama Wisch had referred to Breina as *mooma* in Yiddish or "aunt." (And that alone was a shock to me since I had only known the word *tanta* for aunt.)

From the SIG list I also saw the name Novoselsky, which sparked a memory—Morton Sklut had told me that there was a Novoselsky family in Washington, DC, who were related. The 1866 Minsk birth records included a record for Vulf Novoselsky, born to Pesia, daughter of Hillel, and her husband, Schmuel. Again, could Pesia be another sister of Breina and explain the relationship to Novoselsky?

Mogilev Vital Records

Schelley Dardashti and Bella Nayyer had created an index of male births in Mogilev, compiled from the LDS Family History Library's filmed records. They first made it available at the 1996 Summer Seminar on Jewish Genealogy. The list was teeming with Dvorkin entries. I combed through the films myself and extracted information, even though I could not make any direct connections. There was a Hillel Meyer Dvorkin death record in 1875. The record contained very little information, and with the name Dvorkin being somewhat common in Belarus, I don't know if this was Breina's father.

JewishGen—Belarus SIG, All Belarus Database

The Minsk Homeowners list, included in the Belarus SIG's All Belarus Database on JewishGen, identified Yosel Vicherevin and his son, Hillel Meyer, supporting the hypothesis that Sora was Breina's sister. Then I linked that to the 1907 passenger record of Meyer Wiczerewin.

Networking

From the beginning, I made sure the surnames and towns I was researching were included in the Family Finder. Often overlooked, this database—now online—has proved time and again to connect me not only to other researchers, but indeed, long-lost family. For instance, in 1999 I received an inquiry from Michael Kean in California. It turns out he's descended from Abraham Dvorkin, a brother of Max. I only know they're related to Chaim Ber Dvorkin, though I can't say for sure what the relationship is. I also received inquiries from members of the Shavelson family, who are directly related to the branch I'm researching.

In 1991, we held a Krasner-Dvorkin family reunion at Mt. Holly, New Jersey. It was the first time Morton Sklut and his siblings had seen Adele and Merle in fifty years. There were tears in their eyes. We held a follow-up meeting in Delaware the next year. But soon afterward, several family members became too fragile to travel long distances. Sadly, they have since passed away.

I can't say I will ever be finished with my family's history. Some things I'll never know, simply because there are no vital records that survived the Holocaust for my family's ancestral area. But I do know that I've documented the family's history for all who succeed me.

The pursuit is more than collecting names and dates. It's the journey that makes all the difference—the people you meet along the way, friends, *landslayt*, family. There's a certain feeling of *beshert*, a feeling of predestination, to the activity. A now-retired volunteer at my local LDS Family History Center once told me that our ancestors want us to find them. I don't doubt that for a minute.

I hope you have the same wonderful experiences discovering your Jewish ancestors!

Bibliography

Chapter One

DeBartolo Carmack, Sharon. *Organizing Your Family History Search.* Cincinnati, O.H.: Betterway Books, 1999.

Rose, Christine and Kay Germain Ingalls. *The Complete Idiot's Guide to Genealogy.* New York: Alpha Books, 1997.

Wolfman, Ira. *Do People Grow on Family Trees: Genealogy for Kids and Other Beginners.* New York: Workman Publishing Company, 1991.

Zimmerman, Bill. *How to Tape Instant Oral Biographies.* Cincinnati, O.H.: Betterway Books, 1999.

Chapter Two

Abrahams, Israel. *Jewish Life in the Middle Ages.* New York: Atheneum, 1969.

Barnavi, Eli, ed. *A Historical Atlas of the Jewish People: From the Time of the Patriarchs to the Present.* New York: Schocken Books, 1994.

Ben Sasson, Hayim Hillel, ed. *A History of the Jewish People.* Cambridge, M.A.: Harvard University Press, 1976.

Chorzempa, Rosemary A. *Polish Roots.* Baltimore: Genealogical Publishing Company, 1993.

Dubnow, Simon M. *History of the Jews in Poland and Russia.* Teaneck, N.J.: Avotaynu, 2000. (Reformatted and republished from the 1915 edition.)

Encyclopaedia Judaica. Jerusalem: Keter Publishing, 1971.

Gerber, Jane S. *The Jews of Spain: A History of the Sephardic Experience.* New York: The Free Press, 1992.

Roth, Cecil. *A History of the Jews.* New York: Schocken Books, 1961. Paperback edition of *A Bird's Eye View of Jewish History.*

Sachar, Abram Leon. *A History of the Jews.* New York: Alfred A. Knopf, 1964.

Chapter Three

Beider, Alexander. *Ancient Ashkenazic Surnames:Jewish Surnames from Prague (15th-18th Centuries).* Teaneck, N.J.: Avotaynu, Inc. 1994.

Beider, Alexander. *Dictionary of Ashkenazic Given Names: Their Origins, Structure, Pronunciation, and Migrations.* Teaneck, N.J.: Avotaynu, Inc. 2001.

———*A Dictionary of Jewish Surnames from the Kingdom of Poland.* Teaneck, N.J.: Avotaynu, Inc., 1996.

———*A Dictionary of Jewish Surnames from the Russian Empire.* Teaneck, N.J.: Avotaynu, Inc., 1993.

Feldblyum, Boris. *Russian-Jewish Given Names.* Teaneck, N.J.: Avotaynu, Inc., 1998.

Gorr, Rabbi Shmuel Gorr. *Jewish Personal Names: Their Origin, Derivation and Diminutive Forms.* Teaneck, N.J.: Avotaynu, Inc., 1992.

Guggenheimer, Heinrich W. and Eva Guggenheimer. *Jewish Family Names and Their Origins: An Etymological Dictionary.* Hoboken, N.J.: Ktav, 1992.

Hoffman, William F. and George Wiesław Helon. *First Names of the Polish Commonwealth: Origins and Meanings.* Chicago: Polish Genealogical Society of America, 1998.

Kaganoff, Benzion C. *A Dictionary of Jewish Names and Their History.* New York: Schocken Books, 1977.

Kolatch, Alfred J. *The Complete Dictionary of English and Hebrew First Names.* Middle Village, N.Y.: Jonathan David, 1984.

Kurzweil, Arthur. *From Generation to Generation, rev. ed.* New York: Harper Collins Publishers, 1994.

Chapter Four

Cohen, Chester G. *Shtetl Finder Gazeteer.* Bowie, M.D.: Heritage Books, 1989.

Mohrer, Fruma and Marek Web, comp. and eds. *Guide to the YIVO Archives.* New York: YIVO Institute for Jewish Research, 1998.

Mokotoff, Gary and Sallyann Amdur Sack. *Where Once We Walked: A Guide to the Jewish Communities Destroyed in the Holocaust.* Teaneck, N.J.: Avotaynu, Inc. 1991.

Mokotoff, Gary. *WOWW Companion.* Teaneck, N.J.: Avotaynu, Inc., 1995.

Schwartz, Rosaline and Susan Milamed. *Guide to YIVO's Landsmanshaftn Archives.* New York: YIVO Institute for Jewish Research, 1986.

Chapter Five

Colletta, John P. *They Came in Ships.* Salt Lake City, U.T.: Ancestry, Inc., 1993.

Glazier, Ira, ed. *Migration from the Russian Empire.* 6 volumes. Baltimore: Genealogical Publishing Co., 1995 and later. Covers the period from 1875-1891.

Morton Allen Directory of European Passenger Steamship Arrivals. Baltimore: Genealogical Publishing Co., 1987.

National Archives. *Guide to Genealogical Research in the National Archives, rev. ed.* Washington, D.C.: National Archives Trust Fund Board, 1991.

Newman, John J. *American Naturalization Records 1790-1990: What They Are and How to Use Them.* Bountiful, U.T.: Heritage Quest, 1998.

Schaefer, Christina K. *Guide to Naturalization Records of the United States.* Baltimore: Genealogical Publishing Co., 1997.

Stolarik, M. Mark, ed. *Forgotten Doors: The Other Ports of Entry to the United States.* Philadelphia: The Balch Institute Press, 1988.

Szucs, Loretto Dennis. *They Became Americans: Finding Naturalization Records and Ethnic Origins.* Salt Lake City, U.T.: Ancestry, Inc., 1998.

Tepper, Michael. *American Passenger Arrival Records.* Baltimore: Genealogical Publishing Co., 1993.

Chapter Six

Bernard, Gildas. *Les familles Juives en France.* Paris: Archives Nationales, 1990.

Brandt, Edward R., et al. *Germanic Genealogy: A Guide to Worldwide Sources and Migrations.* St. Paul, M.N.: Germanic Genealogy Society, 1991. Includes a chapter on Jewish genealogy by George E. Arnstein.

Ellmann-Krüger, Angelika G. Edward David Luft. *Library Resources for German-Jewish Genealogy.* Teaneck, N.J.: Avotaynu, Inc., 1998.

Frazin, Judith. *A Translation Guide to 19th-Century Polish-Language Civil Registration Documents, 2nd ed.* Chicago: Jewish Genealogical Society of Illinois, 1989.

Katz, Pierre. *Recueil des déclarations de prise de nom patronymiques des Juifs du Bas-Rhin en 1808, 2nd ed.* Paris: Cercle de généalogie juive, 1995.

Katz, Pierre. *Recueil des déclarations de prise de nom patronymiques des Juifs du Haut-Rhin en 1808, 2nd ed.* Paris: Cercle de généalogie juive, 1999.

Kollárova, Zuzana and Jozef Hanus. *A Guide to the Slovak Archives.* Presov, Slovakia: Universum, 1999.

Rhode, Harold and Sallyann Amdur Sack. *Jewish Vital Records, Revision Lists and Other Jewish Holdings in the Lithuanian Archives.* Teaneck, N.J.: Avotaynu, Inc., 1996.

Shea, Jonathan D. *Russian Language Documents from Russian Poland: A Translation Manual for Genealogists* 2nd Edition. Buffalo Grove, I.L.: Genun Publishers, 1989.

Shea, Jonathan D. and William F. Hoffman. *Following the Paper Trail: A Multilingual Translation Guide.* Teaneck, N.J.: Avotaynu Inc., 1994.

———*In Their Words: A Genealogist's Translation Guide to Polish, German, Latin, and Russian Documents, Volume One: Polish.* New Britain, C.T.: Language & Lineage Press, 2000.

Weiner, Miriam. *Jewish Roots in Ukraine and Moldova: Pages from the Past and Archival Inventories.* Secaucus, N.J. and New York: Miriam Weiner Routes to Roots Foundation, Inc. and YIVO Institute for Jewish Research, 1999.

———*Jewish Roots in Poland: Pages from the Past and Archival Inventories.* Secaucus, N.J. and New York: Miriam Weiner Routes to Roots Foundation, Inc. and YIVO Institute for Jewish Research, 1997.

Wynne, Suzan F. *Finding Your Jewish Roots in Galicia: A Resource Guide.* Teaneck, N.J.: Avotaynu Inc., 1998.

Chapter Seven

Sack, Sallyann Amdur. *A Guide to Jewish Genealogical Research in Israel.* Teaneck, N.J.: Avotaynu, Inc., 1995.

Chapter Eight

Alfasi, Yitzhok. *Entsiklopedyah HaChasidut.* Jerusalem: Mosach ha-Rav Kuk, 1980.

Eisenstadt, Benzion. *Dor Rabanow we-sofrow.* New York, 1905.

———*Sefer Dorot Ha-Aharonim.* Brooklyn, 1936-1941.

Friedberg, Ch. B. *Bet Ekhed Sefardim he-hadash.* (Bibliographical Lexicon). Lists texts from 1474 to 1950. 1974-1976.

Freedman, Chaim. *Eliyahu's Branches: The Descendants of the Vilna Gaon and his Descendants.* Teaneck, N.J.: Avotaynu, Inc., 1997.

Friedmann, Rabbi Nathan Zvi. *Otsar Ha-Rabanim* (Rabbi's Encyclopedia). B'nei Brak: Agudar Otsar Ha-rabanim, 1975.

Gotlib, Scholom Noah. *Sefer Ohole-Shem.* Israel: Tefutsah, 1983.

Halperin, Raphael. *Atlas 'ets Hayim, Aharonim.* Israel: Hotsa'at Hekdesh Ruah Ya'akov, 1981.

———*Toldot 'am Yisrael.* 15 volumes. Israel: Hotsa'at Hekdesh Ruah Ya'akov, 1980-1987.

Rosenstein, Emanuel. *Latter Day Leaders, Sages and Scholars.* Elizabeth, N.J.: Computer Center for Jewish Genealogy, 1983.

Rosenstein, Neil, *Rabbi Elijah (1720-1797), the Gaon of Vilna and His Cousinhood.* Elizabeth, N.J.: Computer Center for Jewish Genealogy, 1997.

———*The Unbroken Chain, 2 vol.* Lakewood, N.J.: Computer Center for Jewish Genealogy, 1990.

Rand, Oscar, ed. *Toldot anshe shem.* New York: 1950.

Sherman, Moshe D. *Orthodox Judaism in America.* Westport, C.T.: Greenwood Press, 1996.

Wunder, Meir. *Meori Galicia. (Encyclopedia of Galician Rabbis and Scholars.)* Jerusalem: Makhon le-hantsahat Yahadut Galitsyah, 1978. (Note: You may find this listed under the author name of "Vunder.")

———*Elef Margaliyot : sefer `ezer le-heker yuhasin : toldot hayehem ve-shalshelet yihusam shel yoter me-elef avot mishpahtenu gedole Yi'sra'el, ge'onim ve-tsadikim, manhigim u-farnasim, me'so's dor va-dor mi-yeme kedem `ad avinu `ateret roshenu ...* Yi'sra'el Aryeh Margaliyot, ha-admur mi-Premishlan be-London / ne`erkhu ve-nisderu lefi mekorot rabim `al yede Me'ir Vunder. Yerushalayim : ha-Makhon le-hantsahat Yahadut Galitsyah, 1993.

Zubatsky, David S. and Irvin N. Berent, Irvin. *Jewish Genealogy: A Sourcebook of Family Histories and Genealogies.* New York: Garland, 1983.

Chapter Nine

Gerber, Jane S. *The Jews of Spain: A History of the Sephardic Experience.* New York, The Free Press, 1992.

Rottenberg, Dan. *Finding Our Fathers: A Guidebook to Jewish Genealogy.* Baltimore: Genealogical Publishing Co., 1998. (Reprint edition.)

Stern, Malcolm H. *Americans of Jewish Descent: A Compendium of Genealogy.* New York: Ktav Publishing House, Inc., 1971. (Reprinted from the 1960 American Jewish Archives, Hebrew Union College edition.)

———*First American Jewish Families: 600 Genealogies 1654-1988, 3rd ed.* Baltimore: Ottenheimer Publishers, Inc., 1991.

Chapter Ten

Faber, Eli. *The Jewish People in America: A Time for Planting, the First Migration 1654-1820.* Baltimore: The Johns Hopkins University Press, 1992.

Karp, Abraham J., ed. *The Jewish Experience in America: Selected Studies from the Publications of the American Jewish Historical Society, Volume 1: The Colonial Period.* Waltham, M.A. and New York: American Jewish Historical Society and Ktav Publishing House, Inc., 1969.

Stern, Malcolm H. *Americans of Jewish Descent: A Compendium of Genealogy.* New York: Ktav Publishing House, Inc., 1971. (Reprinted from the 1960 American Jewish Archives, Hebrew Union College edition.)

———*First American Jewish Families: 600 Genealogies 1654-1988, 3rd ed.* Baltimore: Ottenheimer Publishers, Inc., 1991.

Chapter Eleven

Guide to Unpublished Materials of the Holocaust Period. Jerusalem: Hebrew University of Jerusalem and Yad Vashem, 1975-1981.

Gutman, Israel. *Encyclopedia of the Holocaust.* New York: Macmillan, 1990.

Klarsfeld, Serge. *Memorial to the Jews Deported from France, 1942-1944.* New York: Beate Klarsfeld Foundation, 1983.

Mokotoff, Gary. *How to Document Victims and Locate Survivors of the Holocaust.* Teaneck, N.J.: Avotaynu, Inc., 1995.

Weiner, Miriam. *Jewish Roots in Poland: Pages from the Past and Archival Inventories.* Secaucus, NJ and New York: Miriam Weiner Routes to Roots Foundation, Inc. and YIVO Institute for Jewish Research, 1997.

Chapter Twelve

Firestein, Cecily Barth. *Making Paper and Fabric Rubbings: Capturing Designs from Brasses, Gravestones, Carved Doors, Coins and More.* Asheville, N.C.: Lark Books, 1999.

Goberman, David. *Carved Memories: Heritage in Stone from the Russian Jewish Pale.* New York: Rizzoli, 2000.

Gruber, Samuel and Phyllis Myers, eds. *Survey of Historic Jewish Monuments in Poland, Second Edition.* New York: Jewish Heritage Council, World Monuments Fund, 1996.

Guzik, Estelle, ed. *Genealogical Resources in the New York Metropolitan Area.* New York: Jewish Genealogical Society, Inc., 1989.

Inskeep, Carolee. *The Graveyard Shift: A Family Historian's Guide to New York City Cemeteries.* Orem, UT: Ancestry, Inc., 2000.

Postal, Bernard and Samuel H Abramson. *Traveler's Guide to Jewish Landmarks of Europe.* New York: Hill and Wang, 1971.

Weiner, Miriam. *Jewish Roots in Ukraine and Moldova: Pages from the Past and Archival Inventories.* Secaucus, N.J. and New York: Miriam Weiner Routes to Roots Foundation, Inc. and YIVO Institute for Jewish Research, 1999.

———*Jewish Roots in Poland: Pages from the Past and Archival Inventories.* Secaucus, N.J. and New York: Miriam Weiner Routes to Roots Foundation, Inc. and YIVO Institute for Jewish Research, 1997.

Chapter Sixteen

Bennett, Robin L. *The Practical Guide to the Genetic Family History.* New York: John Wiley & Sons, Inc., 1999.

Daus, Carol. *Past Imperfect: How Tracing Your Family Medical History Can Save Your Life.* Santa Monica, C.A.: Santa Monica Press, 1999.

Krause, Carol. *How Healthy Is Your Family Tree?* New York: Simon and Schuster, 1995.

Nelson-Anderson, Danette L., R.N., B.S.N., and Cynthia V Waters. *Genetic Connections.* Washington, M.O.: Sonters Publishing, 1995.

Willard, Jim, Terry Willard, and Jane Wilson. "Your Medical Heritage." Chapter Eight in *Ancestors: A Beginner's Guide to Family History and Genealogy,* 89-102. Boston and New York: Houghton Mifflin, 1997.

Chapter Seventeen

McGoldrick, Monica, Randy Gerson, and Sylvia Shellenberger. *Genograms: Assessment and Intervention.* New York: W. W. Norton & Company, 1999.

McGoldrick, Monica and Randy Gerson. *Genograms in Family Assessment.* New York: W.W. Norton & Company, 1985.

Marlin, Emily. *Genograms.* Chicago: Contemporary Books, 1989.

Other

Blatt, Warren. *Resources for Jewish Genealogy in the Boston Area.* Boston: Jewish Genealogical Society of Greater Boston, 1996.

Kurzweil, Arthur and Miriam Weiner. *Encyclopedia of Jewish Genealogy, Volume 1: Sources in the U.S. and Canada.* Northvale, N.J.: Jason Aronson, 1991.

Mokotoff, Gary and Warren Blatt. *Getting Started in Jewish Genealogy.* Teaneck, N.J.: Avotaynu, Inc., 1999.

Szucs, Loretto Dennis and Sandra Hargreaves Luebking, eds. *The Source: A Guidebook of American Genealogy, Revised Edition.* Salt Lake City, U.T.: Ancestry, Inc., 1997.

Index

E

F

G

H

I

J

K

L

M

N

O

P

R

S

T

U

V

W

Y

Z